TEACHING 3–8

SECOND EDITION

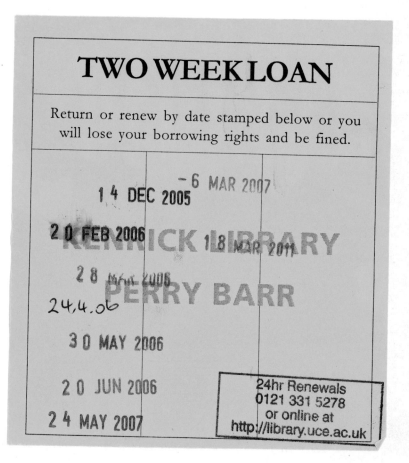

Reaching the Standard
Series Editor Mark O'Hara

Teaching 3–8

SECOND EDITION

Mark O'Hara

continuum
LONDON • NEW YORK

Continuum

The Tower Building   15 East 26th Street
11 York Road   New York, NY 10010
London
SE1 7NX

British Library Cataloguing-in-Publication Data
A catalogue record for this book is available from the British Library.

ISBN: 0 8264 7004 1 (hardback) 0 8264 7005 X (paperback)

Library of Congress Cataloging-in-Publication Data
A catalogue record for this book is available from the Library of Congress.

Designed and typeset by Ben Cracknell Studios
Printed and bound in Great Britain

Contents

Acknowledgements

I would like to thank colleagues at Sheffield Hallam University for their advice and suggestions in compiling this book. I would also like to thank friends, former colleagues and Debbie Curtis, for providing samples of work, documentation and planning sheets some of which illustrate the text.

Preface

This book is aimed at teacher training students on 3–8 courses, and newly qualified teachers (NQTs) working with the same age range. This age range is a crucial time in children's development, and effective teaching in nursery and lower primary education will help to lay the foundations for their future success both as learners and as citizens.

Good teaching is a complex, highly skilled activity requiring judgements on how to act. Becoming effective as a teacher will depend upon the acquisition of skills and knowledge through personal experience, the support and training received from other professionals, making reference to the literature on the subject and developing a good understanding of how young children learn. One of the devices by which initial teacher training (ITT) students are required to develop a positive and proactive approach to their own professional development is to demonstrate achievement against the Standards, or competences, set out in the Professional Standards for the Award of Qualified Teacher Status (TTA, 2002), and to use this process to compile a Career Entry Profile (CEP). Once in post, NQTs are also required to address a further set of competences in order to complete their induction year successfully. This book uses the Professional Standards for the Award of Qualified Teacher Status as the basis for discussing key aspects of 3–8 teaching and for directing trainee and newly qualified teachers towards further reading and sources of information.

Competences can
- provide clear goals and targets to aim for;
- engender greater confidence in trainees about the skills and knowledge that they have already acquired;
- help to establish exactly which areas should be covered by those training to become teachers; and
- give (future) employers some assurance about what an NQT can do.

However, competence approaches to teaching and teacher training are not without their shortcomings:

- It is possible for some competence statements to mean different things to different readers.
- Competence statements tend to emphasize outcomes – they are statements about what

teachers must achieve; they do not in themselves always provide any insights into the process or processes by which these achievements are to be attained, nor can they necessarily guarantee that a competence, once demonstrated, will be demonstrated again at other times and in other contexts.

- Teaching is not just about acquiring teaching skills and curriculum knowledge; it is also about the values and attitudes that impact upon a teacher's decision-making processes, values which are not always fully identified in a competency approach to training.

Teaching involves much more than the unthinking mastery of a set of competences. Teachers need to have lively intellects and be able to exercise understanding and judgement. They have to be adept at problem-solving and communication, and be able to make links and connections between theory and practice. Good teachers are thoughtful, creative, self-critical and believe that all children can make progress. Teachers need to be reflective in their practice and engage in self-appraisal, reading and research, rather than simply ticking off a list of competences.

One of the difficulties facing a writer of an introductory text on 3–8 teaching is the temptation to try to cover every aspect in depth. This is clearly impossible in the space available. Consequently, this book offers an introduction to some of the issues and ideas relating to the Professional Standards for the Award of Qualified Teacher Status (TTA, 2002), and directs the reader to further sources of information. It aims to provide a platform from which trainees and NQTs can launch themselves into the further research and investigation that will be necessary if they are either to achieve qualified teacher status (QTS), or to complete successfully their induction period in nurseries and schools.

How to Use the Book

The book follows broadly, but not precisely, the structure of the Standards document (TTA, 2002). Where particular aspects of practice and the role of the teacher appear in more than one location within the Teacher Training Agency (TTA) documentation some of the commentary on individual Standards has been combined in particular chapters to avoid duplication. In other instances the reader is directed to related sections elsewhere within the text.

For example, Standard 1.6 requires teachers to understand the contribution of support staff to teaching and learning (TTA, 2002, p. 12). Standard 3.1.4, however (TTA, 2002, p. 40), requires teachers to be able to work as part of a team and to be able to deploy non-teaching colleagues effectively during teaching and learning. In this case the reader will find that commentary relating to support staff is largely combined and located within Chapter 1.

Standard 1.1, meanwhile (TTA, 2002, p. 5), states that teachers should have high expectations of all their pupils irrespective of gender, class, race or ability. Standard 2.6 (TTA, 2002, p. 32) requires teachers to know about their duties under the SEN Code of Practice and Standard 3.3.4 (TTA, 2002, p. 59) concerns the need for teachers to differentiate their teaching in order to meet the needs of all pupils including those with special educational needs (SEN). In this instance the reader will find discussion relating to SEN in different chapters and is therefore directed to the related sections in other parts of the text.

Each of the chapters begins with a brief summary outlining those aspects of the Professional Standards for the Award of Qualified Teacher Status that are discussed.

SUMMARY

Chapter 2 dealt with the need for 3–8 teachers to have a good knowledge and understanding of the curriculum and children as learners. However, knowing what needs to be taught is insufficient on its own to make someone effective as a teacher. Teachers of 3–8 pupils must also be good planners, managers and communicators, and they must be able to deploy a range of effective strategies in the nursery/classroom that facilitate teaching and learning.

By the end of this chapter you should:

- know about planning and target setting with Foundation Stage and lower primary pupils;
- know about monitoring, assessing and reporting on pupils' learning;
- know about differentiating lessons and responding to the needs of individual children, including pupils with special educational needs (SEN);
- know about classroom organization and management; and
- know about effective teaching strategies.

Within each chapter each section begins with a brief audit statement linking the contents more closely to the Professional Standards for the Award of Qualified Teacher Status.

AUDIT

By the end of this section you should

- know about the teaching of Communication, language and literacy in the Curriculum Guidance for the Foundation Stage (QCA, 2000, pp. 44–67);
- know about the teaching of English in the National Curriculum (QCA, 1999, pp. 42–58);
- know about the National Literacy Strategy (NLS) and its relationship with English in the National Curriculum (QCA, 1998b).

At various points throughout the text, Example displays indicate the use of exemplar material linked to the topic under discussion. All the identities of pupils, teachers, nurseries and schools have been altered or deleted to ensure anonymity.

Eg | *Evolution of a child's idea*

During a nursery placement a student teacher was asked to work with children engaged in a construction activity using junk materials and paint. She asked one child about his model and he replied that it was a fire engine. Later in the session the student teacher praised the construction (a series of cardboard boxes, glued together and painted bright red). 'That's a fantastic fire engine you've made.' 'It's not a fire engine,' the child replied indignantly, 'it's a lighthouse.'

At other points there are questions, further exemplar materials and suggestions on how trainee and newly qualified teachers can begin to address the competences set out in the Professional Standards for the Award of Qualified Teacher Status and Induction Standards.

✔ | *Developing your presence as a teacher*

- Show consistency in your expectations and actions.
- Radiate a sense of confidence by not hesitating or rushing your speech, making eye contact and adopting appropriate body postures and tones of voice.
- Exhibit firm, though gentle, insistence when necessary.
- Avoid being overly and inappropriately friendly, especially in the early stages of the year or with older pupils.
- Establish a clear and simple set of rules or conventions within which the activities of the class will take place.

Each chapter also contains suggestions on further reading and sources of information that trainee and newly qualified teachers can use to enhance and extend their knowledge and understanding.

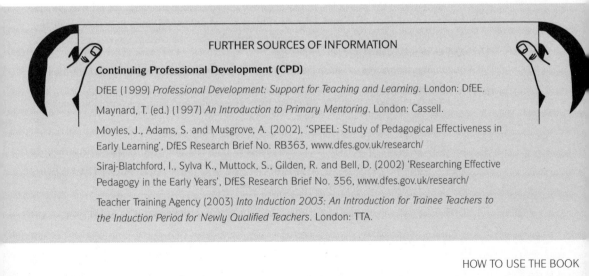

FURTHER SOURCES OF INFORMATION

Continuing Professional Development (CPD)

DfEE (1999) *Professional Development: Support for Teaching and Learning*. London: DfEE.

Maynard, T. (ed.) (1997) *An Introduction to Primary Mentoring*. London: Cassell.

Moyles, J., Adams, S. and Musgrove, A. (2002), 'SPEEL: Study of Pedagogical Effectiveness in Early Learning', DfES Research Brief No. RB363, www.dfes.gov.uk/research/

Siraj-Blatchford, I., Sylva K., Muttock, S., Gilden, R. and Bell, D. (2002) 'Researching Effective Pedagogy in the Early Years', DfES Research Brief No. 356, www.dfes.gov.uk/research/

Teacher Training Agency (2003) *Into Induction 2003: An Introduction for Trainee Teachers to the Induction Period for Newly Qualified Teachers*. London: TTA.

Introduction

Chapter 1 deals with additional professional requirements to which all teachers, including 3–8 teachers, are subject. Teachers have to conduct themselves within an environment governed by extensive regulation, laws and systems. Trainee and newly qualified members of the profession need to:

- have high expectations of all their pupils, irrespective of their social, cultural, ethnic backgrounds or their abilities;
- be effective at establishing partnerships with parents;
- engage in whole-school and team approaches to delivering the complete curriculum;
- have an understanding of how schools and nurseries are managed;
- be aware of their responsibility for their own Continuing Professional Development (CPD);
- have a working knowledge of the legislation relating to equality of opportunity, health and safety, and children's welfare; and
- fulfil their responsibility to maintain good order in the classroom, without which there can be no successful teaching.

Chapter 2 deals with knowledge and understanding of the 3–8 curricula. The chapter uses the broad areas of learning from the Curriculum Guidance for the Foundation Stage as a framework for the discussion. Student teachers and NQTs need to:

- be familiar with the principles and structure of the Curriculum Guidance for the Foundation Stage;
- be familiar with the principles and structure of the National Curriculum for primary pupils;
- know about the structure and delivery of literacy and numeracy hours in primary school;
- know about a range of special educational needs that may be encountered in 3–8 settings and be familiar with the Code of Practice;
- be familiar with ways in which children's development can affect teaching and learning in 3–8 settings; and
- know about the content of the different areas of learning and National Curriculum subjects to be taught.

Chapter 3 deals with teaching and learning in the classroom. Knowing *how* to teach something effectively to young children is every bit as important as knowing *what* to teach. Teachers of 3–8 pupils need to

- have a good grasp of the different aspects of their role during teaching and learning;

- be able to plan lessons and sequences of lessons that contain appropriate yet challenging learning objectives;
- be able to make accurate assessments of children's learning and to record the results;
- be able to give constructive feedback to pupils and make accurate reports to parents;
- be able to differentiate during teaching, taking into account the needs and abilities of pupils, including pupils with SEN; and
- be highly efficient organizers and managers of the learning environment.

1

Professional Values and Practice

SUMMARY

Teaching is about much more than a set of competences, such as the mechanics of planning a lesson or organizing a display board. Teaching is a profession, not just a job, and as such its members are subject to certain professional standards, expectations and codes of conduct outlined in the Professional Standards for the Award of Qualified Teacher Status (TTA, 2002). Teaching young children requires a degree of familiarity with the legislation and systems governing teachers' actions, as well as an ability to make use of inspection and research evidence to inform and improve good practice. Teachers need to be able to deal with some of the uncertainties of teaching and be ready, able and willing to continue to learn from experience, adapting and improving their practice to increase both their competence and their confidence. The chapter goes on to consider the responsibilities and legal liabilities of teachers including the maintenance of good order in the classroom.

By the end of this chapter you should

- know about the need to have high expectations of all your children;
- know about communicating and working with parents and other adults;
- know about playing a full part in the wider life of the nursery/school; and
- know about developing a commitment to Continuing Professional Development (CPD).

Having High Expectations of All Children

By the end of this section you should

• understand the impact that teacher attitudes can have on pupil attainment.

AUDIT

The ethos in nursery and primary settings is informed by legislation such as the Education Reform Act 1988 and the Education Act 1996. Under the legislation, all children have a right to expect that their teachers will provide them with every opportunity to achieve their full potential irrespective of their gender, race, ability or social class. They are entitled to an education that will enable them to participate fully in society, an education that prepares them for the opportunities, responsibilities, choices and experiences of adult life (QCA, 1999).

Adult conduct is central to the task of establishing a learning environment in which the ethos is encouraging and supportive of all pupils. The teacher is hugely influential in children's learning and development. Staff expectations can have a powerful influence on children's achievement and self-esteem. Trainee and newly qualified teachers need only to think back to their own school days to appreciate the important role that teacher expectations can play in a child's achievement and motivation. The more persistent low expectations are, the greater their impact on a child's self-esteem and the more deep rooted his/her low- or under-achievement is likely to become.

Eg

High expectations

Teachers expect all children to

• try their hardest;
• take pride in their work;
• concentrate;
• listen; and
• participate.

Educators of young children have to consider the ways in which learning takes place and is experienced by children as well as the content of the curriculum. How children are encouraged to learn is every bit as important as what they learn. The paradox at the heart of having high expectations of all is that this apparent equity may only be possible by treating children differently on occasion. In their desire not to be unfair to children, some teachers adopt the position of trying to *treat everyone the same*. This is sometimes the result of an understandable wish to avoid making mistakes that give offence and possibly cause conflict. However, treating all children in the same way may not be respectful of the children's varied backgrounds and capabilities nor does it ensure equality of opportunity, but has quite the reverse effect (Miller *et al.*, 2002). Such a policy ignores and fails to tackle the individual needs and differences of children. It is also a mistake to think that children themselves are ignorant of the differences between them. They can be very conscious of them and may have their attention drawn to these differences outside school/nursery. The education of 3–8 pupils should include the promotion of positive attitudes towards diversity, and those teaching Foundation Stage and primary children play a key role in modelling such positive attitudes for children when they are most receptive to new ideas.

Expectations relating to work

Teacher expectations ought be based on a professional appraisal of the needs and capabilities of the pupils and not on stereotypical assumptions about the children's intellectual, emotional, social and physical attributes (Adams, 1994).

Which children
- Are highly inquisitive and curious?
- Are self-confident, adventurous, and enjoy decision-making?
- Are in need of more support and encouragement to take risks and respond positively to new things and experiences?
- Thrive on practical problems?
- Prefer intellectual problems?
- Are quiet, steady, composed?
- Are gregarious?
- Enjoy the written word?
- Prefer the spoken word?
- Find visual information most instructive?

Engaging in conversation with children and listening to them, as well as monitoring and observing their work, will assist you in seeking out materials and experiences likely to be both challenging and appropriate for pupils from a wide range of backgrounds.

Communicating your expectations to children and others

- Group classes to ensure a balance in terms of gender, race, ability and class.
- Ensure that the principle of equality of opportunity permeates planning and teaching and that the curriculum is enriched and enhanced by positive reference to diversity.
- Include non-teaching staff (e.g. playtime and lunchtime supervisors) in discussions about the nursery/school equal opportunities policy and help to develop appropriate strategies to translate the principles into practice.
- Work to develop a shared understanding of the nursery/school policy and practices among parents, governors and other staff.
- Provide resources that actively and positively promote diversity in terms of culture, class, gender and ability.
- Make concerts and assemblies inclusive of all groups in the nursery/class, including good work assemblies.

- Deal promptly and efficiently with biased or discriminatory attitudes and actions. Discriminatory behaviour, including bullying, on the basis of gender, race, disability or class is unacceptable. Operate a policy of 'zero tolerance' and make sure that when such incidents occur pupils are encouraged to confront their assumptions, actions and the consequences of those actions.
- Help children to identify the similarities, as well as the differences, that exist between them and their classmates. Help them to understand the differences and to behave in a considerate manner.

4

Working with Parents and Other Adults

AUDIT

By the end of this section you should

- know about parental roles in children's learning;
- know about effective ways of liaising and communicating with parents;
- know about working as part of a team and managing the work of other adults in the nursery/classroom;
- know about some of the other professionals involved in the care and education of young children and about the contribution that non-teaching support staff can make to children's learning.

Partnership with Parents

Eg

An impossible request

Philip's father accompanied him to school on the day that he started in Year 2. He explained to Philip's teacher that Philip had not always been well behaved in his Year 1 class and that he wanted the school to know that he was in complete support of their efforts to get Philip to improve his behaviour. He told Philip's teacher that she had his permission to give Philip a 'good hiding' if he misbehaved. Philip's teacher explained that such an act would be illegal and would run counter to the school's policy of promoting responsibility and self-discipline among the children. 'I see,' replied Philip's father. 'Well, in that case, if he messes you about, tell me and *I'll* give him a good hiding.'

A successful partnership with parents is often cited as a prerequisite for the successful education of young children. The Curriculum Guidance for the Foundation Stage (QCA, 2000) makes clear the importance of partnership with parents of 3–5 year olds in its initial principles (pp. 6–25) and the arguments in favour of partnership are no less meaningful for children between 5 and 8. Educators of young children are continuing a learning process that has been initiated by parents; consequently, parents should be valued as active partners in their child's continuing learning.

Effective partnership between parents and teachers can help parents to exert a positive influence on their child's progress through their attitudes towards education and the support they give. The potential gains for children and their teachers include motivation, good behaviour and positive relations. These outcomes may help to avoid conflict between the home and the nursery/school and minimize confusion for the children that can result from differing expectations and norms. Effective liaison is also beneficial for parents and teachers in that parents can become much more knowledgeable about young children's learning, for example being persuaded of the value of play as a vehicle for learning, or undertaking activities with their children that will help to prepare them for entry into nursery/school.

Ways in which parents can help to support their children's education

- Spending time with and showing an interest in the child.
- Listening to the child.
- Talking with and asking questions of the child.
- Exploring feelings and ideas with the child.
- Reading to and with the child.
- Encouraging the child to try new things and solve simple problems.
- Playing with the child.

Although effective partnership between nurseries, schools and parents has much to recommend it, such relationships are by no means unproblematic either to initiate or to maintain. It is important for 3–8 teachers to keep the powerful arguments in favour of effective home–school links clearly in mind given some of the impediments to cooperation. In some cases the challenges to partnership may originate in schools. There may be a lack of will on the part of teachers, some of whom may feel threatened at having their work exposed to public scrutiny, while others may regard partnerships as a relatively minor part of their role. Lack of training for teachers in working and liaising with parents could be a contributory factor to attitudes such as these. Alternatively, schools may be very keen to develop partnerships but lack the staff and the time to plan and implement partnership activities.

Real partnership requires real dialogue

A newly qualified teacher (NQT), keen to encourage parents into the classroom, invited a parent to visit the class. When the parent arrived the NQT asked her to supervise a group of six reception children doing a baking activity in an adjacent utility room. The activity was intended to give the children experience of exploring and handling equipment and materials, and talking about how materials change when mixed and/or heated, but this was not communicated to the parent. When the NQT went into the utility room a little later to check on how the activity was proceeding she found that the children had had almost no hands-on experience with the tools and materials and all the discussion was purely procedural in nature. It became clear to the NQT that the parent was primarily concerned with the end-product and that she would have to make a point in future of explaining and communicating the purposes of tasks properly instead of using parents as little more than a spare pair of hands.

In other situations the challenges to partnership originate elsewhere. Parents are no more homogeneous than the diverse society from which they and their children's teachers come; what works well in one place, for one set of parents, may not be so effective in a different context. There may be a lack of will on the part of some parents to be involved in partnership with the nursery/school. Some parents may have had negative experiences in relation to their own schooling or may be anxious about their own skills and knowledge, for example a parent whose first language is not English or who feels their own knowledge and skills in particular curriculum areas are weak. In other cases parents would welcome the opportunity for greater involvement but find themselves unable to liaise closely with the nursery/school due to other commitments or problems, for example those in full-time employment; those caring for younger siblings or elderly relatives; those wishing to re-enter education themselves now that their children have started nursery/school; or those who are experiencing personal traumas of one kind or another such as marital breakdown, ill health or bereavement.

A further set of challenges to partnership can arise from clashes of culture between schools and parents. The overwhelming majority of parents desire to see their children happy and successful. However, while there is certainly much common ground between teachers and parents in this respect, there are also some key differences, not least the fact that while a parent's starting point is their own child, the teacher has to consider the happiness and success of all children. There can also be differences in terms of beliefs, with some activities valued by teachers but not valued or appreciated by some parents, for example promoting anti-racist policies in an area characterized by endemic racism, or defending parity of esteem for the wider curriculum in the face of preoccupations with Standard Attainment Tests (SATs) scores for English and mathematics.

Understandable but unhelpful parented input

How would you respond to these concerns?

• 'I've told our Barry that if anyone hits him, he's to hit them back harder!'

• 'That Wendy from Mrs Smith's class has been threatening our Claire and taking her sandwiches at dinnertime.'

A key concern for parents will be that their child will be safe and secure while in nursery/school. There is an apparent tension here between a school's desire to be open and welcoming to parents while at the same time ensuring a secure environment for the children using in some cases security fences, CCTV systems and combination locks. Parents may wish to know about:

- the timing of the school day, equipment and clothing expectations, and arrangements for the collection/non-collection of children;
- the physical arrangements to prevent intruders and 'escape attempts';
- the supervision arrangements while in the nursery/classroom;
- the supervision arrangements outside the classroom (e.g. during outdoor play, local walks, trips and visits);
- school policies including the behaviour policies and codes of conduct for staff, parents and children.

(Roffey and O'Reirdan, 2001)

Parents also want to know that their child is learning and making progress. Enquiries about the curriculum may constitute a further source of tension between nursery/school and home when some parents anticipate particular educational practices based on their own (possibly secondary) schooling. If they then perceive a mismatch between their ideas on education and existing practice in their child's class they may well raise this with the class teacher. Teachers may have to become advocates for developmentally appropriate teaching and learning on occasions and challenge preconceived ideas about educational practice. Similarly, some parents may feel they have little to offer their children in terms of support as a result of their own experiences of schooling, or worries about recent curriculum developments. Communicating the purpose of different activities, explaining the teaching and learning process and offering advice on how they can help their child may help to assuage some of these concerns. Parents may wish to know about

- teaching and learning methods (*'Why are they playing?' 'Why aren't they all sitting at desks?' 'Why aren't they all silent?'*);
- curriculum and assessment arrangements (*'Why teach a broad and balanced curriculum?'*);
- partnership arrangements (*'How can I get in touch with my child's teacher and when?' 'What can I do to help my child learn?' 'Is there a way in which I could help the nursery/school?'*).

(Roffey and O'Rierdan, 2001).

How would you respond to these concerns?

- 'I'm not happy about Chris's reading books that you're sending home. They're too easy for him.'

- 'I want you to give me some homework for Irfaan [aged 6] so that I can do lessons with him at home.'

- Daniel's parents asked to see the teacher in charge of nursery, Mrs Cooper. They explained that they were very worried about Daniel's preference for spending large amounts of time in the role-play area wearing dresses, high-heeled shoes and carrying a handbag. Daniel's father, in particular, wanted Mrs Cooper to take steps to steer Daniel into activities more 'normal' for a boy.

Home and school are the two most important factors in a young child's life. Families contain relationships that are not replicated anywhere else while nurseries and schools offer children an introduction to group life where they can acquire new social skills. Although the roles of nursery/school and home are somewhat different, their aspirations for the children are similar. This similarity in aspiration means that communication and sharing information are vital in promoting positive parental involvement and this can take place during events (some formal, others informal) at which both parents and staff are present, or in writing.

Communication with parents

• **Regular parent – teacher contact**
Everyday interactions between parents and practitioners can produce considerable insight into home circumstances, needs and problems. Parents can give teachers useful information when they arrive at the start or end of the day on topics ranging from local problems to children's learning. They need to be made to feel welcome. Parents who are knowledgeable and have a positive attitude towards the nursery/school can be highly effective in promoting that nursery/school in the rest of the community. It is important to deal promptly and effectively with everyday queries on such things as pupil progress, transition to new classes and teachers, seating arrangements or lunchtime problems.

• **Joint teaching/work in the classroom**
Inviting parents into nursery/school to work with the children offers opportunities for shared classroom experiences. Teachers need to be professional and to adopt a partnership approach which includes explaining to, taking advice from and working cooperatively with parents. They should be prepared to discuss current educational ideas and practices with parents; things may well have changed dramatically since the parents' own school days. Remember that you might feel you are approachable, but others may not share that view. Be open with parents, show them that you can be discreet and will refrain from gossiping. Parents need to be sure that they can talk to you in confidence. Show parents that you listen to their comments and take their concerns seriously by taking action where necessary. Offer parents opportunities to contribute to children's learning in a range of ways including working with groups, listening to readers or talking to larger groups and classes about their experiences or interests. Although this is a time-consuming approach, it is more likely to make parents feel valued than an approach where they are in the classroom but are engaged only superficially on the margins of teaching and learning.

• **Home visits**
These can be an effective, albeit resource intensive, approach to sharing information and establishing close links between parents and the nursery/school. Such visits can help to ensure that parents, carers and children are properly inducted into the life of the

nursery/school, for example in terms of understanding the ethos and approach to good behaviour and discipline. They also help teachers to acquire an understanding of the children's linguistic or cultural background. Home visits may provide a less threatening forum in which 3–8 teachers can discuss ways of preparing children for entry into nursery/school and ways of supporting their continued progress once they have made the transition.

• Nursery/school events

Less formal opportunities for parental involvement in the work of the nursery/school include fund-raising events such as jumble sales, sports days, summer fairs and invitations to assemblies and concerts. Formal events such as parents' evenings, open evenings, talks and curriculum events are also useful venues at which parents and staff can share information and concerns. They can enhance parents' perceptions of how and what their children learn in nursery/school. It is important to adopt a professional approach to these occasions. Teachers do need to remember that parents have many commitments, and should be sensitive to the dangers of overloading parents or overestimating the level of financial support available. The timing of events needs to take account of the constraints under which many parents find themselves, such as going out to work and caring for other children. Furthermore, during parents' evenings the numbers invited ought not to preclude meaningful dialogue with staff, and the atmosphere should be conducive to positive and productive communication. Providing refreshments and things for parents to look at or do while they are waiting helps to make parents feel less awkward.

• School handbooks

Documentation should be attractive to encourage parents to look at it; including examples of children's work is one way of doing this. At the same time, the content should be clear, brief, easy to find and the booklet should not be overly large as this can be off-putting, as indeed can inappropriate text that is too dense or badly spaced. When parents' first languages are not English, text in alternative languages should also be used. Such handbooks can provide valuable information for parents on the curriculum their child will experience, supervision arrangements in and out of the classroom, school policies and codes of conduct (e.g. dealing with incidents of bullying).

• Letters, notices and circulars

Much of the communication between nurseries/schools and parents is in written form including school handbooks, letters, notices and reports. Children should be encouraged to remember to give letters and notices to their parents. Putting their names on them helps, so too does following up and checking that delivery has actually taken place. This can be particularly important with the youngest children who may have more important things on their minds than letters. It is a good idea to include return slips at the bottom of letters where answers are needed, and to keep copies for future reference.

Managing Other Adults in the Nursery/Classroom: Working as Part of a Team

Having other adults in the nursery/classroom, in addition to the teacher, can significantly enhance children's learning. In some instances, the additional adult support available to 3–8 teachers is on a voluntary basis, for example parents. At other times, the support is professional in nature and may involve a wide variety of staff, both internal and external. In all cases, teachers should value adult support and treat those involved with respect. Teachers need to be able to make the most of this expertise and become effective both as leaders and as members of a team. In nurseries, especially, the teamwork required is particularly noticeable, including as it does both the core nursery team (nursery teachers, nursery nurses and child-care assistants (CCAs)) and the wider team (language support staff, special needs staff and parents). While not necessarily trained as teachers themselves, other adults can bring new and useful skills and experiences to the learning environment. In the case of planning, for example, a team approach enables staff to

- produce a more comprehensive set of learning opportunities;
- improve their individual capabilities by learning from one another;
- utilize particular strengths;
- promote continuity and progression; and
- ensure a unified and coherent philosophy and ethos.

It is the teacher's job to take responsibility for managing this valuable human resource. At one level this involves decisions on which activities and pupils adult support staff should be responsible for, and on discussing the purposes and processes of lessons or activities with them. However, teachers also need to think about the wider curriculum which includes the ethos and philosophy of the nursery/classroom. Non-teaching adult support can be effective in helping to inculcate certain values and attitudes in young children such as fairness, respect and honesty.

The job of managing, leading and taking responsibility for a team, some of whose members may be only occasional visitors, is a demanding task. It is a real test of teachers' interpersonal and communication skills as well as their professional expertise to do this successfully. It can be particularly challenging for trainee and newly qualified teachers whose experience is still limited in relation to many of the other adults they are being asked to manage. Some of the skills and qualities needed by teachers when leading or working in a team are listed in the example below.

- assertiveness;
- determination;
- consideration towards the feelings of others;
- energy;
- creativity;
- flexibility;
- ability to focus clearly on a task;
- good organizational skills;
- excellent communication skills;
- ability to delegate;
- knowledgeable about young children and the curriculum;
- good negotiating skills;
- being thoughtful and reflective;
- good problem-solving abilities; and
- ability to motivate and support others.

11

The list above makes clear the demanding nature of teamwork. Although there is no foolproof method for responding to this challenge, there are certain principles that teachers ought to keep in mind when considering the best ways to organize and manage the work of other adults in the nursery/classroom.

Improving your expertise in working with other adults

- **Thinking ahead**. Planning and preparation enhance your chances of success.
- **Participation**. The whole team should be involved (in appropriate ways) in planning, organizing and managing the learning environment.
- **Communication**. If you fail to discuss your intentions and ideas with non-teaching colleagues or fail to listen to their ideas and observations, there is a danger of inconsistency in approach and outcomes.
- **Leading by example**. This is something that you are already experienced in through your interactions with children. If you wish to foster a positive, supportive and calm manner in other adults it helps to exhibit those qualities and characteristics yourself.
- **Reviewing**. Being a reflective practitioner and reviewing the outcomes of using non-teaching support are essential if your skills and capabilities in this area are to improve.

Who Are the Other Adults?

Parents constitute one group of adults who may be working alongside teachers in the classroom and suggestions relating to work with parents have already been made. The following paragraphs deal briefly with some of the other adults who may be involved in 3–8 settings.

    Nursery nurses are trained in child development and health care, including early language development, numeracy, and personal and social development. They are also knowledgeable about the organization and management of early learning environments as well as being very well trained in a range of observation techniques useful in the monitoring and assessment of children's needs and attainment. They are an important part of the teaching team in a nursery/reception classroom. In terms of their interactions with the children, the responsibilities are very similar to those of teachers – preparing materials, setting out equipment and facilitating children's learning. It can sometimes be difficult at first glance in many nurseries to distinguish between the teachers and the nursery nurses. The teacher, however, is ultimately responsible for planning and organizing both the curriculum and the day-to-day running of the nursery/classroom, albeit in consultation and collaboration with the nursery nurse(s).

Child-care assistants (CCAs), **non-teaching assistants (NTAs)** and **specialist teaching assistants (STAs)** can take on some of the daily routines such as mounting pictures, freeing more teacher time for planning and teaching. Equally important, however, is their ability to work alongside the teacher. In so doing they can extend and enhance the quality of educational provision for the children by targeting those who need extra support, providing such pupils with access to valuable one-to-one attention, and encouraging children to talk, discuss and extend their speaking and listening skills (e.g. when reading stories and listening to readers). Very often, schools must share non-teaching support staff between classes, although the numbers of non-teaching practitioners seem set to rise and government initiatives (DfES, 2003b) envisage an increased role for such staff, including the supervision and teaching of whole classes.

Liaison also needs to take place between teaching staff and non-teaching colleagues not directly involved in classroom activities such as school secretaries, lunchtime supervisors and caretakers. Both groups may need to talk about problems that particular children have and need to discuss what may constitute appropriate action in particular circumstances. For example, new children can be supported in adapting to a new school/nursery environment by special and friendly attention during lunchtimes. Other pupils have medical conditions such as allergies which the teacher knows about but which also need to be communicated to other responsible adults.

At various times nurseries and schools will be visited by a wide variety of adults in both professional and volunteer capacities, all of whom may need to be included in a team approach, albeit on a temporary basis. These visitors include:

• nurses;
• speech therapists;
• health visitors;
• Educational Welfare Officers (EWOs);
• educational psychologists;
• special needs staff;
• language support staff;
• students; and
• occasional visitors (e.g. community police officers, local theatre groups).

Health visitors and nurses conduct medical examinations of children, for example when they start nursery/school. They also carry out screening for possible problems such as hearing loss or visual impairment at regular intervals. Although many children with these difficulties are identified prior to starting school, others are not, and teachers have an important part to play in helping health professionals to identify and assist pupils with difficulties.

Educational Welfare Officers (EWOs) are mainly concerned with the enforcement of compulsory school attendance. However, they can also be involved in wider aspects of child welfare such as neglect or illegal employment. In addition, EWOs may be involved in supplying adequate clothing, meals and transport for pupils from poor homes. EWOs are a useful link between teachers and the local social services.

Many schools and nurseries will draw on the expertise of individuals beyond the world of education in an effort to make the curriculum more relevant and exciting; some of these experts may be parents or relatives. A good visitor can do much to motivate and enthuse children but teachers must bear in mind that while a visitor may have considerable expertise in his/her particular field, it is the teacher who is the child specialist. There is an onus upon the teacher to liaise with outside experts beforehand to ensure that the content will be appropriate for the children and that it will be presented in a suitable manner.

Poor liaison, poor teaching

An education officer from one of the public utilities was asked to come and talk to a class of Year 1/2s about his industry as part of a project that the children had been doing. When the education officer arrived he set up his slide projector and overhead projector. He then delivered the same 45–minute talk that he used with secondary school leavers to a class of stunned infants and their equally stunned teacher. Thereafter, this particular NQT made a point of liaising properly, and in advance, with such visitors.

Strategies for making the best use of non-teaching support in the classroom

- Gather information on the role of non-teaching support staff and their expectations of you. Promote a teamworking approach by utilizing the particular skills, talents and expertise of non-teaching colleagues.
- Find out the procedures for briefing non-teaching colleagues.
- Explain what children should be learning and not just what they should be doing.
- Ensure that children understand the adult's role and behave properly when they are with them.
- Prepare lessons that include plans for the work of other adults and review these in lesson evaluations.
- Remember that communication is vital and involves listening as well as talking. Value the different perspectives that other adults bring.

- Develop shared policies on discipline, organization and assessment.
- Avoid stereotypical or negative assumptions about non-teaching colleagues.
- Give specific tasks to parents and volunteers in order to make them feel valued.
- Maintain confidentiality at all times.

The Corporate Life of the Nursery/School

A U D I T

By the end of this section you should

- know about your professional responsibilities in relation to school policies and practices, including those concerned with pastoral and personal safety matters such as bullying;
- know about the structure and function of governing bodies, including their role before, during and after inspections by the Office for Standards in Education (Ofsted).

Many 3–8 settings make use of time outside the normal school day to offer additional activities for the children and the wider community. Student and newly qualified teachers may well find themselves involved in after-school clubs or residential visits. The reader can find commentary on out-of-school activities in Chapter 3. This section, however, is primarily concerned with the development of whole-school documentation, the role of the governing body and Ofsted inspections.

Nursery/School Policies and Practices

Teachers of 3–8 pupils are required to play their part in drawing up, and adhering to, whole-school documentation on a range of matters such as Early Learning Goals, core and foundation subjects in the National Curriculum and generic issues that cut across subjects and areas of learning such as bullying, special educational needs, health and safety, behaviour, and transition to, within and between schools. Such documentation will be composed of policy statements and guidelines, and in the case of National Curriculum subjects and Early Learning Goals will also include schemes of work.

Policies and guidelines

A policy is a succinct description, outlining the overall rationale for teaching a subject or tackling an educational issue. It should be to the point and written in plain English. A policy consists of broad principles which underpin the way in which a subject or issue is approached in a nursery/school. In effect it answers the questions 'What is it?' and 'Why do we do/teach it?'

Guidelines set out how the nursery/school expects staff to approach a subject, area of learning or generic issue with their pupils and they are frequently attached to the policy statements. Guidelines provide a general framework and deal with a range of issues including organization and management, cross-curricular links and assessment. Possible headings for guidelines will vary depending on whether the guidelines in question relate to a National Curriculum subject (e.g. mathematics), the Early Learning Goals (e.g. Creative development) or a generic issue (e.g. bullying). A list of areas that might be included in guidelines for National Curriculum subjects or areas of learning within the Curriculum Guidance for the Foundation Stage is given below, followed by examples of policy statements and guidelines: first, for a generic issue – bullying; and second, for a National Curriculum subject – English.

Possible guideline headings

- Links to the Early Learning Goals or National Curriculum Programmes of Study and Attainment Targets. Links with other subjects.
- How the subject or issue is planned for in the nursery/school.
- Classroom organization, management and teaching methods.
- Marking, monitoring, assessment and recording.
- Continuity and progression across the nursery/school.
- Equal opportunities and multicultural/anti-racist strategies.
- Provision for special educational needs (SEN).
- Provision for children in the Foundation Stage.
- Use and provision of Information and Communications Technology (ICT) and other resources.
- Health and safety.
- Links with cross-curricular elements.
- Links with the wider community.
- The role of the headteacher.
- The role of the subject coordinator.
- The role of parents and other adults.

Eg *Policy and guidelines on a generic issue – Bullying*

Policy statement
. . . . School believes that it is against the interests of all children, the bullied and the bullies, to allow bullying to take place unchallenged. No child can learn properly and achieve their full potential when they feel threatened and vulnerable. We regard bullying as particularly serious and the school will always take firm action against it. In addition, our school believes that we do a long-term disservice to a pupil if we allow him/her to continue to bully others and avoid facing up to the consequences of such actions.

Guidelines

1. Identifying incidents of bullying
Staff need to be aware that there can be a fine line between bullying and boisterous or bossy behaviour. Children being bossy will try to dominate whoever is around at the time

and will often grow out of this behaviour as they mature and develop wider social skills. A bully will *target* younger/weaker children and will display a conscious desire to hurt or frighten these children. A boisterous pupil displays a high-spirited, uncontrolled and not unfriendly presence in the classroom. A bully will *deliberately* set out to spoil other children's activities, displaying hostile, rough and intimidating behaviour.

Bullying can take many forms. It can be physical, emotional or verbal in nature and can involve a single bully or a group of pupils. Possible examples of bullying include
- name calling, malicious gossip and taunting;
- stealing or damaging other children's property and work;
- coercion, threats, extortion and intimidation;
- punching, kicking and other violent behaviour; and
- ostracizing children.

Signs of distress that might indicate that bullying is taking place include
- pupils acting in a withdrawn manner and appearing isolated;
- deterioration in standards of work;
- fake illnesses and a deterioration in attendance and punctuality;
- desire to remain close to adults; and
- apparent unhappiness, anxiety and fear.

2. Reasons for bullying

Bullying can occur in children of all ages and there are a variety of reasons why some pupils become victims of bullying and some pupils become bullies. In some cases the bullies themselves are victims of bullying. The children targeted are often (although not always) timid, anxious or less assertive; in other words, those children deemed unlikely to fight back or resist the bullying, the children who are younger or smaller than the bully, or the children who are loners and not part of a particular group.

The reasons why children are targeted include
- differences in race, sex or social class;
- other differences, including physical disability, general appearance or being new to the school;
- differences in ability, including academic, physical and creative; and
- vulnerability, perhaps as a result of suffering other problems.

Children may become bullies because
- they are themselves victims of bullying or violence;
- they obtain a sense of power and control through the act of bullying;
- they are copying the behaviour of others (either in school, at home or on television and in films and videos);
- they are jealous; or
- they are insecure and have low self-esteem.

3. Strategies for eliminating bullying in the classroom
- Use lots of praise and recognition to reward cooperative, non-aggressive behaviour.
- Encourage the caring side of pupils' development.
- Discuss and promote friendships and cooperation.
- Maintain proper supervision both in the classroom and outside.
- Make children aware that standing by while bullying takes place is to support the bullying.

- Give support to the victim and help him/her to regain and develop self-esteem and confidence.
- Try to find out why the bully is bullying. Do not bully the bully. Help the child to see another's point of view: 'How would you feel if . . . ?'
- Give support to the bully by encouraging and supporting him/her to work positively with other children, for example giving responsibility for looking after someone or something.
- Work to involve parents. Explain why certain actions have been taken and discuss with parents what they can do to reinforce and support the efforts of the nursery/school to resolve the problem successfully. If necessary, help parents to understand the distinction between bossy or boisterous behaviour and bullying. However, make sure that parents know that you take their concerns seriously, are aware of the situation and will take steps to stop their child being made to feel unhappy.
- Serious or persistent incidents should be monitored, recorded and reported to the headteacher or the responsible member of staff.
- In very serious cases bullying needs to be reported to the governing body and if necessary will involve an official complaints procedure.

 Policy and guidelines on National Curriculum subject – English

Subject: English

Date of publication: 2003

1. The aims of English teaching

English is the basic language of communication in this country and throughout much of the world. The mastery of this subject is a prerequisite for educational progress in all other curriculum areas and is vital for pupils' future adult lives as citizens, producers and consumers in society. Through the teaching of English at . . . . School pupils will build on the language opportunities provided in the home and will develop into more proficient and discriminating readers, writers, speakers and listeners.

Pupils will
- be introduced to a wide range of text, materials and information technology resources to enrich and challenge their learning;
- be given opportunities to develop their competence in standard written English; and
- be made aware of the differences between spoken and written forms of language.

2. Interpretation of the statutory orders

The National Curriculum provides the basic framework for our programme of teaching and assessment in English for both key stages.

> In studying English pupils develop skills in speaking, listening, reading and writing. It enables them to express themselves creatively and imaginatively and to communicate with others effectively.
>
> (QCA, 1999, p. 43)

In addition, the school follows the National Literacy Strategy to underpin wider teaching and learning in English. All pupils from Year 1 to Year 6 will experience shared reading and writing tasks, word/sentence level work, individual pupil tasks and guided writing tasks as part of the school's daily literacy hour. Guided reading sessions are also incorporated into the school's English provision on a daily basis.

In English pupils will be taught
- how language works so that they can understand how people write and speak;
- to use formal and impersonal forms of language;
- to adapt writing and speech to a range of different audiences;
- to use conventional letter formation, spelling and grammar;
- to use punctuation;
- comprehension and composition; and
- the meaning of individual words, groups of words, sentences, groups of sentences and whole texts.

3. Planning for English
We have a mixed approach to our planning and teaching of English. In delivering the National Literacy Strategy (NLS) teachers are required to adhere to the national documentation to support their planning. In addition, staff will plan for wider English teaching and learning in their remaining medium-term and lesson plans.

4. Classroom organization and management
The English curriculum is organized into
- learning of reading, writing, speaking and listening in literacy hour lessons; and
- additional and wider learning which goes on throughout the school day and throughout all curriculum areas.

Equal importance is given to these aspects of the English curriculum in terms of organization and management.

5. Teaching methods
The school uses a range of teaching methods in English based on fitness for purpose. These methods include whole-class, group and individual teaching. English can be a collaborative subject and pupils will be taught the skills required to work both as individuals and as members of a team.

6. Assessment, recording and reporting
Marking:
- Feedback to pupils about their own progress in English is achieved through discussion and through marking of work, sometimes done while a task is being carried out.
- Marking should be constructive, continual and consistent.
- Marking should be done sensitively and with discretion so that a child can assimilate a limited number of corrections at one time. This will vary according to age and ability.

Formative and summative assessment:
Formative assessment is carried out mostly by teachers in the course of their teaching through
- hearing children read;
- small-group and class discussions;
- short tests;
- specific assignments; and

- individual discussions with the teacher in which children are encouraged to appraise their own work and progress.

Formal summative assessment is carried out at the end of each National Curriculum Key Stage through the use of SATs and/or teacher assessments. The school also makes use of commercially produced testing systems to measure pupil progress and performance mid-way through each school year.

Recording and reporting:

The records of progress in English kept for each child include
- home/school diaries annotated by the child or parents as appropriate to age and ability;
- a record of books read which takes the form of a reading diary and is maintained by each child;
- a portfolio of written work, dated and annotated with teacher comments and containing one item for each term which shows achievement and progress; and
- reading progression records.

7. Use of ICT in English
This is in line with the school's ICT policy. Pupils will use ICT in English to
- handle information; and
- communicate information.

In addition to the use of class based computer resources, the school's ICT lab is used to support teaching and learning in English.

8. Meeting the needs of early years children
Language development for the under-fives and early years children receives a very high priority at . . . . School. Teaching and learning in the school's nursery and reception settings follow the Curriculum Guidance for the Foundation Stage. Teaching encourages children to extend their vocabulary, speak clearly and confidently and listen carefully. The children are provided with numerous play based opportunities to improve their skills in this area through discussions and conversations, structured role-play activities, listening to stories and poems, singing songs, handling and looking at books, and writing. The children are helped to recognize letters and write simple words including their own names.

Children in the Foundation Stage are introduced to the components of the literacy hour during their final term in reception in preparation for their transition to Key Stage 1.

9. Resources for English
Classroom resources for English include
- a class reading library containing fiction, non-fiction and poetry;
- dictionaries;
- textbooks and workbooks to support comprehension activities;
- a selection of paper and guidelines for writing activities;
- the class computer; and
- speaking books and tape recorders in the early years settings.

Central resources for English are the responsibility of the English coordinator in consultation with staff and the headteacher. The school expects these resources to be kept in good condition and to be replaced when worn. Staff are responsible for returning resources to central areas when they have finished using them.

10. Links with the cross-curricular elements
Links will be made with appropriate cross-curricular elements, particularly Personal, social and health education (PSHE) and citizenship. These links will be identified on the school's schemes of work.

11. Differentiation
At . . . . School we aim to provide for the needs of individual children and the following strategies are used as appropriate:
- Children with difficulties in English receive extra support in the classroom from a specialist teacher and/or external agencies.
- Children are supported within their class by their own class teacher and differentiated work is given as appropriate.
- Extra help is provided in the classroom by non-teaching assistants and parent volunteers.
- Able children are encouraged to develop their full potential by being provided with challenging work appropriate to their needs.

12. Equal opportunities, multicultural education and English as an Additional Language (EAL)
Where children speak English as a second language the teaching will be adapted and differentiated to meet their needs and ensure that they achieve their full potential. In addition, the school provides a range of literature including stories and tales from different cultures and geographical and historical periods.

13. Continuity and progression in English
At . . . . School continuity and progression are ensured by using the National Literacy Strategy in planning for English. In addition, staff use after-school meetings and in-service training days when appropriate to discuss the English curriculum and ensure consistency in approach and standards.

14. Time allocation for English
The 'formal' time allocated each week is 7 hours in Key Stage 2 and 7 hours in Key Stage 1. In addition, pupils will be given opportunities to apply their learning about reading, writing, speaking and listening during linked (integrated thematic) work.

15. Links with the wider community
Opportunities are provided for the children to enhance their learning in English through links with local businesses and organizations, through visits and by inviting parents and other adults into school.

16. The role of the English coordinator
The coordinator, working alongside the headteacher, has the responsibility for ensuring quality in the teaching and learning of English in the school. He/She will take the lead role in the production of whole-school documentation and in addition will support colleagues in the production of short-term planning. He/She has responsibility for the maintenance of resources and equipment, and for the purchase of new equipment and materials. He/She will attend courses, be a resource of subject knowledge and provide in-service training for his/her colleagues.

17. The role of the headteacher

The Headteacher will support the English coordinator in encouraging colleagues to teach English effectively. He/She will be responsible, through the English coordinator, for ensuring that the policy and guidelines are used and for bringing the policy and guidelines to staff for periodic updating. This policy will be reviewed every two years. The next review will begin in . . . . and the revised policy will be in place by . . . . The headteacher will ensure that the school's policy is in line with national policy and that of the Local Education Authority (LEA).

Schemes of work

A scheme of work constitutes long-term planning (see Chapter 3) and gives details about what is taught, where and when across the school/nursery. It provides for the sequence of teaching throughout the nursery/school in order to ensure progression and continuity while avoiding repetition. Schemes are based on relevant national documentation such as the Early Learning Goals, National Curriculum Programmes of Study, and National Literacy and Numeracy Strategies. More specific, medium-term planning for individual classes or year groups is based upon this framework. It is worth noting that with the increasing emphasis on English and mathematics, including the introduction of literacy and numeracy hours, many schools are using commercially produced schemes such as those published by the Qualifications and Curriculum Authority (QCA) to help them deliver the non-core foundation subjects which make up much of the wider curriculum.

Eg

Section from scheme of work for Key Stage 1 Geography

Programmes of Study (PoS) requirements	Year 1 Local area study	Year 1 On the farm	Year 1 Improving the school grounds	Year 1/2 Barnaby Bear	Year 2 Bangladesh
1a Ask geographical questions	•	•	•	•	•
b Observe and record	•	•	•		•
c Express own views	•	•	•	•	•
d Communicate in different ways	•	•	•	•	•
2a Use geographical vocabulary	•	•	•	•	•
b Fieldwork skills	•	•	•		

(Owen and Ryan, 2001)

Governing Bodies

The governing body has responsibility for the overall management and conduct of a nursery/school. The governors are not concerned directly with the day-to-day running of the nursery/school as this is the responsibility of the headteacher; they deal with more strategic issues related to monitoring and evaluation of a school's performance. The exact nature of the governors' responsibilities will vary depending upon whether the nursery or school has *county*, *special* or *voluntary aided* status, and the details of the governing body's duties and powers will be set out in the nursery/school Articles of Government. Some of the areas in which governing bodies have a role to play are listed in the example below.

Issues of school governance

- standards of attainment (including comparisons against national averages)
- health and safety
- racial equality and inclusion
- parents
- links with the community
- the curriculum
- resourcing, finance and budgets
- staffing
- development planning
- premises
- child welfare and discipline
- admissions
- extra-curricular activities

The exact size of the governing body will be determined by the size of the nursery/school, and those elected and appointed to be school/nursery governors will represent a range of interests. Trainee and newly qualified teachers can obtain up-to-date information on the constitution of governing bodies by accessing the Department for Education and Skills (DfES) website (www.dfes.gov.uk).

Categories of governor

- Parent governors are elected by a vote of all parents with a child at the nursery/school, and they too must have a child in the school/nursery to be eligible to stand.
- Teacher governors are elected by the staff in the school and report back to their colleagues on the discussions and actions of the governing body. Schools and nurseries are required to ensure that non-teaching staff are also represented.
- Appointed governors are chosen by the LEA, and any other bodies with authority to appoint, such as the church in the case of voluntary aided schools.
- Community, partnership and sponsor governors are coopted by other governors from a wide variety of backgrounds, the aim being to broaden and strengthen the expertise of the governing body. At least one member of the governing body should be a member of the local business community.

- Foundation governors represent the views of churches or trusts in, for example, voluntary aided schools.
- The headteacher can opt to be a governor or not as he/she sees fit. Whatever the decision, he/she is entitled to attend all governors' meetings.

Each year the governing body must elect a Chair and Vice-Chair to lead meetings and oversee the business of the governing body. Neither the Chair nor the Vice-Chair can be an employee of the school/nursery. In addition, the governing body employs a clerk. The clerk's tasks include arranging meetings, circulating agendas and papers, and taking minutes. Normally, papers will be circulated to members of the governing body prior to meetings to enable the discussion to be chaired more efficiently. Due to the extensive nature of the governors' responsibilities, most nurseries and schools set up a number of sub-committees in order to delegate some of the decision-making and preparatory work.

Range of sub-committees

- finance
- premises
- recruitment and staffing
- curriculum

Once a term, the headteacher must make a report to the governing body. This report is a way of keeping governors up to date with events in the nursery/school, and places issues before the governors for advice or decisions. Curriculum coordinators may be asked to report back to governors on developments in their area of responsibility, particularly when the coordinator is involved in meeting targets set out in a development plan or identified as needing attention by an inspection team from Ofsted. The governors themselves have a duty to keep all parents informed about their actions and the work of the nursery/school. This is done formally through an annual report supported by an annual parents' meeting at which parents can discuss the report and any matters arising from it with members of the governing body. Parent governors and the headteacher are also likely to be approached on a more informal basis whenever an issue of concern to parents arises.

Inspection

It is a governing body's responsibility to ensure that nurseries and schools are prepared to be inspected by teams from Ofsted and that they respond to the findings of these teams. The inspection teams, led by a registered inspector (RI), visit nurseries and schools every four or five years to inspect standards, not to offer advice and support. Not only do inspection teams make a judgement about existing standards, they also comment on the extent to which a nursery/school has improved since its last inspection and on its capacity to improve still further in the future (Ofsted, 2003). In addition to the RI, each team should contain one layperson and *a range of specialisms appropriate to the task*. Not surprisingly, schools and nurseries have no right to choose their own inspection team, although they can request the CVs of team members. Governing bodies can also draw the inspectors' attention to particular aspects of the school/nursery which they would like the inspectors to comment on, and can even ask Ofsted to conduct an inspection, although there is no guarantee that it will do so. Schools deemed to be in special measures as a result of an earlier inspection, for example, may seek to bring forward the next inspection if they believe the outcome will raise them out of special measures.

Pre-inspection

During the pre-inspection period schools and nurseries are sent details of what the inspection team will look at and what some of the team's initial hypotheses are concerning the nursery/school in the *pre-inspection commentary*. Inspection teams also require timetables. Their aim is to see every teacher teaching as broad a range of subjects/areas as possible during the course of the inspection. Nurseries and schools are not required to produce additional documentation for an inspection but before arriving, the inspection team will require copies of all the existing documentation pertaining to the running of the nursery/school which could include

- school/nursery development plans;
- schemes of work;
- policies and guidelines;
- pupils' records;
- details of in-service training for staff during the previous three years;
- the school prospectus;
- the programme of staff meetings; and
- financial details.

Prior to an inspection a questionnaire is sent to all parents by the governors to elicit comments and responses concerning their children's education. The responses are mailed directly back to the inspectors. Once the questionnaires have been sent out, it is then the responsibility of the governors to organize a parents' evening at which the RI will explain the purposes and nature of the inspection and discuss parental views and reactions in the light of the questionnaire responses. No governor or member of staff (including the headteacher) may attend this meeting unless they have a child in the school.

Inspection

The inspection itself will focus upon

- the quality of teaching and learning in the nursery/school;
- the standards of achievement;
- the curriculum offered to pupils;
- the efficiency of school leadership and management;
- partnership arrangements; and
- the development of pupils.

Class teachers are not the only staff to be inspected. The headteacher, deputy headteacher, members of the governing body, the nursery team leader and curriculum coordinators may all be interviewed about their roles. Inspectors will also make comments on the class teachers' ability to deploy non-teaching support staff effectively within the classrooms. Furthermore, inspectors may also make use of pupil interviews. While in school/nursery, inspectors will observe teaching, talk to children and make comments on an observation schedule. Given the focus on standards, inspection teams will be particularly interested in prior attainment and the progress made by children. Consequently, nursery/reception settings will be looked at carefully for data on prior attainment, and Year 2 and Year 6 classes will also be closely examined as a means of gauging pupil progress and achievement.

Inspectors would normally be expected to spend a minimum of 30 minutes observing any lesson and to be present at the start of the session. Teachers need to have their plans and records available. Inspectors award ratings based on their observations during the sessions. The ratings system has changed since its inception and could change again in the future. However, during 2003 a score of 1 denoted excellence, a score in the middle of the range denoted satisfactory teaching and learning, while a score of 6 or 7 denoted a poor or very poor performance. It is worth noting that in the context of an inspection the term '*satisfactory*' indicates competence; it should not be imbued with any of the connotations normally associated with everyday usage of the term. This said, inspection teams will be looking for learning and teaching that is '*good*' or better, rather than satisfactory.

In addition to classroom observations, the inspection team will look at SATs results in primary settings and examine teacher assessments and samples of work that reflect the ability range in classes. This work is examined in order to make judgements concerning continuity, progression, coverage of the Early Learning Goals and the National Curriculum, and the extent to which pupil achievement is in line with national expectations. Towards the end of the inspection the RI, plus other members of the team, will talk to the headteacher and deputy headteacher and give a verbal report on their main findings; they are likely to be quite specific at this stage. This is the headteacher's final opportunity to challenge or query the inspectors' judgements.

Post-inspection

During the post-inspection period the nursery/school receives further reports and has to be ready to respond to the team's findings. Shortly after the inspection the RI plus one or two of the team members will return to report back to the staff and the governors. They will not be quite so specific as they were with the headteacher and deputy headteacher, but they will highlight strengths and weaknesses, and present the governors with a list of areas that need to be addressed. A copy of the full written report will be forwarded to the nursery/school a few weeks later accompanied by a shorter (two-page) summary report which the governors have to send to parents. At this point the report becomes a public document. Parents and others wishing to access copies of the full inspection report can locate them on the Ofsted website (www.ofsted.gov.uk). Once the inspection report has been received, there is a statutory requirement upon the governors to draw up an action plan to address those areas identified by the inspection team as requiring change. Newly qualified teachers with curriculum coordination responsibilities may find themselves leading aspects of this action planning. Even if the governors disagree with an inspection finding they must still institute action to bring about the change required in the final report.

Action plans identify

- clear targets and criteria for success;
- the action to be taken to meet the targets including personnel involved in monitoring, evaluating and controlling the process;
- an indication of the timescales involved; and
- possible funding or resourcing needed.

Eg *Inspection comments and related action plan*

Remarks on teaching and learning in history

107. Attainment in history in both Key Stages 1 and 2 is in line with national expectations. In Key Stage 1 pupils are developing a sense of chronology. They can also give some valid reasons for people's actions and past events. By the end of Key Stage 2 most pupils are able to combine information from a variety of sources and make inferences and deductions. They have a sound general knowledge of the Tudors, Vikings and Ancient Egypt. Progress in both Key Stages is good.

108. Pupils' attitudes to learning history are good. They are interested in the topics and study units, answer questions with enthusiasm and concentrate well.

109. In the small number of lessons observed, the quality of teaching is sound. Teachers' subject knowledge is secure. Individual lessons are well planned with clear learning objectives. More precise references to the PoS would aid both progression and assessment of pupils' attainment and progress.

110. The new coordinator has not yet had time to make a significant impact, nor has she

had the opportunity to benefit from in-service training. The policy and guidelines for the subject need updating to bring them into line with the rest of the school's documentation. The role of the coordinator in monitoring curriculum development and the quality of teaching is not yet in place. The subject is adequately resourced and pupils' work is displayed well. The history curriculum is significantly enriched by school visits.

Eg *Action plan*

Targets	Criteria for success	Action	Member(s) of staff responsible	By when	Completed on
To improve documentation for history in the school	• Produce policy and guidelines for history • Produce scheme of work for history	• Draft action plan to be reviewed/adapted/ approved by staff • Draft documentation to be produced by coordinator • Draft documentation to be reviewed/adapted/ approved by staff	History coordinator All staff	End of Autumn term	
To enhance subject expertise of history coordinator	• Attend LEA training courses for history	• Agree funding for staff training with governors • Obtain copy of LEA Inset provision and apply	Headteacher History coordinator	End of academic year	
To institute monitoring of the history curriculum	• Planning for history is reviewed • History teaching is observed in classrooms • History resources are recorded	• Arrange staff meeting to discuss and agree systems for coordinator to review history planning • Draw up timetable for classroom observations • Conduct audit of history resources across the school	All staff Headteacher/ coordinator in consultation with staff Coordinator	End of academic year	
To make increased use of National Curriculum documentation	• Long term plans clearly state relevant PoS • Medium- and short-term planning is	• Use new policy and guidelines and map out history coverage across the year groups • Check that reference to	Coordinator All staff Coordinator	End of Spring term	

Targets (continued)	Criteria for success	Action	Member(s) of staff responsible	By when	Completed on
in planning for history	based on whole-school plans	relevant PoS appears in planning • Check that lesson objectives are informed by the National Curriculum during peer observation	Coordinator		
To improve assessment and recording of pupil attainment in history	• Class records to include history • Agreement among staff about levels at Key Stages 1 and 2 • Informative reporting to parents	• Create resource of benchmarked history work • Organize moderation meetings • Develop exemplar material to support report writing	Coordinator All staff	End of Summer term	

(O'Hara and O'Hara, 2001)

Coping with an inspection as a student/newly qualified teacher

- Make sure the learning environment is attractive and stimulating for the children.
- Make sure your planning is available for the inspector to look at. Session planners should show clear and appropriate learning objectives.
- The quality of your teaching and the children's learning will be of prime concern to an inspector during an observation. Make sure you consider the different needs and abilities in your class. How are you going to differentiate for them?
- Your questioning and exposition skills are important elements in ensuring that learning takes place. Have you thought through your questions, explanations and vocabulary?
- The structure and organization of the lesson/session needs to be well thought out. Is there a clear beginning, middle and end? How are transition times going to be managed? Are your instructions clear? Is your timing and pacing suitable for the age and abilities of children? Have you made effective use of any adult support in the nursery/classroom?
- You need to maintain the children's interest and enthusiasm and keep them on task. This might be more difficult if you play it safe and plan a staid, completely risk-free lesson. How can you make your lesson interesting and exciting without losing control of events?

Continuing Professional Development (CPD)

By the end of this section you should

- understand the need to take responsibility for your own professional development and to keep up to date with inspection evidence, and research and developments in pedagogy in the subjects you teach;
- be aware of the Career Entry Profile (CEP) and the arrangements for induction for newly qualified teachers (NQTs).

Developing a Reflective Approach to Practice

High-quality teaching and learning can be supported and enhanced by many factors but trainee and newly qualified 3–8 teachers would do well to pay close attention to the need to engage in and draw upon whole-school approaches and to conduct themselves as thoughtful and reflective professionals. Trainee and newly qualified teachers who engage in self-evaluation (critically reflecting on their practice and how to improve it) are likely to master a wider range of effective teaching methods more quickly than those who do not (Bengtsson, 1995). Such evaluation can be used to improve performance over both the long and the short term. Without ongoing self-evaluation there can be no progress that is not accidental or very slow. Reflective teachers evaluate their performance in order to progress more rapidly and in those directions where progression is most needed whether this is to do with knowledge or skills. Reflective practitioners acknowledge that they do not know all the answers and recognize the steep learning curve that confronts them (Moyles and Robinson, 2002), but they accept that to manage learning in the classroom in increasingly effective ways they must also recognize and build on their achievements, while simultaneously identifying and plugging any gaps.

Self-evaluation is not simply a summative task to complete at the end of a lesson or term (reflection *on* action). Good teachers are constantly evaluating their practice including during teaching (reflection *in* action). It is this ongoing evaluation that generates a decision to rephrase something differently in order to communicate an idea more effectively, or encourages a teacher to pick up the pace of a lesson in response to the early signs of fidgeting. Teachers automatically reflect on their practice as they teach but they also need to reflect on it afterwards in order to draw useful lessons for the future. It is a continual process throughout a teacher's career as achievements and gaps change over time. Clearly this longer-term evaluation will be based at least in part on everyday observations and evaluations. However, it is also necessary to move beyond the specific to consider the larger picture. Trainees and newly qualified teachers may wish to use similar headings to structure their longer-term evaluation but ought to avoid wasting time by regurgitating chunks of lesson evaluations. They should concentrate instead on the wider picture and make an accurate appraisal of their performance and issues relating to their future practice.

Evaluating teaching and learning

- When noting down evaluative remarks as evidence for tutors and school mentors, bullet points can provide a manageable and efficient approach.
- Start with what went well. Why did it go well? How do you know? What is your evidence?
- Was there an aspect of the lesson/session that did not go well/as well? Why was this? How do you know? What is your evidence?
- To what extent were your teaching objectives (knowledge, skills, attitudes, new vocabulary) achieved? How do you know? What is your evidence?
- Was the lesson content too hard/too easy/just right? For whom? How do you know? What is your evidence?
- How effective was your organization and management (timing, pacing, resources, transitions)? How do you know? What is your evidence?
- To what extent were good order and a positive learning atmosphere maintained? How do you know? What is your evidence?
- What would you do differently in the future? Why?
- What should the children do next?

Learning from Evidence and the Practice of Others

In addition to a reflective and analytical approach to the task of teaching, trainee and newly qualified teachers can also inform and improve their practice by accessing sources of information on recent educational research, new guidance on practice and ideas for work with children. Professional journals, magazines, professional organizations and government agencies are all useful sources.

Eg ### Useful periodicals

- *Childhood Education*
- *Early Childhood Research Quarterly*
- *International Journal of Early Years Education*
- *Nursery World*
- *The Curriculum Journal*
- *Times Educational Supplement*

Many publications arising from the work of government departments and other agencies and organizations can be located on the internet. These often contain recent press releases, information on circulars and lists of publications. Such sites can be

30

helpful for trainee and newly qualified teachers wishing to keep abreast of the latest thinking about the 3–8 curriculum and good practice generally, for example the Effective Pedagogy in the Early Years (EPPE) project (Siraj-Blatchford *et al.*, 2002) and the Study of Pedagogical Effectiveness in Early Learning (SPEEL) project (Moyles *et al.*, 2002). Furthermore, Ofsted inspection reports can be a useful source of information for trainee and newly qualified teachers wishing to keep up to date with what constitutes quality teaching and learning in the 3–8 age range, or even which jobs to apply for.

Eg

Useful website addresses for inspection evidence and current research and publications on 3–8 education

- British Educational Communications and Technology Agency (BECTa): www.becta.org.uk
- Department for Education and Skills (DfES): www.dfes.gov.uk
- Early Education: www.early-education.org.uk
- National Grid for Learning (NGFL): www.ngfl.gov.uk
- Office for Standards in Education (Ofsted): www.ofsted.gov.uk
- Qualifications and Curriculum Authority (QCA): www.qca.org.uk
- Teachernet: www.teachernet.gov.uk/professionaldevelopment/
- Teacher Training Agency (TTA): www.canteach.gov.uk

Induction arrangements

The introduction of teacher appraisal, performance management and arrangements for the induction of NQTs will ensure that a willingness to learn from the practice of others and the ability to evaluate one's own practice effectively will continue to be important throughout a teacher's career. Trainee teachers are required to complete a CEP towards the end of their initial teacher education. This profile cites aspects of a trainee's practice that are strengths and other aspects where further development would be useful in their first year of teaching. The decisions about what constitute strengths and areas for further development are made in discussion between trainees and trainers; these discussions will be heavily influenced by teaching practice reports from nursery/school.

Eg

Career Entry Profile (CEP)

Transition Point One   Date: 18/6/2003

Note down your response to the questions, where you might find evidence to support your thinking, and/or the reasoning that led you to this response:

Interesting aspects of teaching
- *Encouraging and motivating children to be excited about their learning (Teaching Practice file)*
- *Planning and teaching around physical development/Physical Education (Final placement report)*

Strengths
- *Knowledge and understanding of how young children learn (Course work assignments)*
- *Good organizational and classroom management skills (Final placement report)*
- *Good interpersonal skills (Final placement report)*
- *Use of display (Final placement report)*

Further experience sought
- *Experience of children with EAL (Little opportunity during placements to date)*
- *Wider experience of children with special educational needs (SEN) (Encountered only 1 case of Asperger's Syndrome to date on placement)*
- *Appropriate uses of ICT in nursery and reception classes (Computer was broken on final teaching practice)*

Professional development and aspirations
- *Work with a range of age groups within early years and primary (To widen future employment opportunities)*
- *Develop curriculum coordination skills (To gain management experience)*

___

Summary check – How well have you
- reflected on your broader experience and the relevant skills and expertise you have developed?
- thought about why you are particularly motivated towards some particular aspects of teaching?
- identified why you want to find out more about, or gain more experience and expertise in, some areas of teaching?

(Career Entry and Development Profile 13)

Once appointed, NQTs on full-time permanent contracts will have an induction programme that will last for three terms. Newly qualified teachers on short-term or part-time contracts will spend an equivalent period being inducted, for example an NQT on a 0.5 contract will have an induction period lasting six terms. NQTs do not have to start their induction year immediately but once commenced they are normally expected to complete it within five years (TTA, 2003). Headteachers have overall responsibility for ensuring that NQTs are properly inducted and will appoint an induction tutor whose role it will be to act as mentor during the induction period. Headteachers may decide to take this mentoring role themselves. The CEP forms the starting point for NQTs and their mentors in planning and monitoring the induction year. Newly qualified teachers will have a reduced teaching load in order to facilitate their induction and some of this time can also be used to observe more experienced colleagues in action either in their own school or in another school where effective practice is taking place. The Induction Standards follow on from and are intended to build upon the Professional Standards for the Award of Qualified Teacher Status. Newly qualified teachers are expected to continue to meet consistently the QTS Standards albeit with increased professional competence in an employment context and to meet the Induction Standards outlined below as well.

Induction Standards

Professional values and practice
- Work collaboratively with colleagues to raise standards by sharing effective practice.

Knowledge and understanding
- Show commitment to CPD by identifying areas for improvement and taking steps to address these needs.

Teaching
- Plan effectively to meet the needs of SEN pupils.
- Liaise effectively with parents/carers on pupils' progress and attainment.
- Engage in effective teamwork.
- Direct the work of other adults.
- Secure appropriate behaviour in the classroom.
- Deal effectively with inappropriate behaviour.

(TTA, 2003, p. 17)

During induction, NQTs will be monitored, supported and assessed by their induction mentor and/or headteacher. Lesson observations will be conducted on a half-termly basis and will focus upon a particular aspect of the NQTs' teaching. Such observations will be accompanied by follow-up discussions during which time the NQTs and their mentors can analyse the lesson. In addition, NQTs will be expected to take part in professional reviews of progress in which future targets will be negotiated and set. Summative assessment meetings will take place towards the end of each term.

Agenda for summative meetings

- **End of first term**: Assessing the extent to which the NQT is consistently meeting the Professional Standards for the Award of QTS and is beginning to meet the Induction Standards.
- **End of second term**: Gauging the NQT's progress towards meeting the Induction Standards.
- **End of third term**: Determining whether the NQT has met all the requirements for the satisfactory completion of the induction period.

Student and newly qualified teachers wishing to examine induction materials and procedures in more detail, including supporting documentation such as mentor report forms, can access the information via the Teacher Training Agency's website (www.canteach.gov.uk/).

The Responsibilities and Legal Liabilities of the 3–8 Teacher

By the end of this section you should have a working knowledge and understanding of

- teachers' professional duties as set out in the current School Teachers' Pay and Conditions document, issued under the School Teachers' Pay and Conditions Act 1991;
- teachers' responsibilities and legal liabilities relating to the Race Relations Act 1976, the Race Relations (Amendment) Act 2000 and the Sex Discrimination Act 1975;
- the Health and Safety at Work Act 1974 and teachers' common law duty to ensure that pupils are healthy and safe;
- teachers' responsibilities and legal liabilities relating to the promotion of children's welfare as set out in the Children Act 1989, the role of the education service in protecting children from abuse (DfEE Circular 10/95) and appropriate physical contact with pupils (DfEE Circular 10/95);
- teachers' responsibilities relating to discipline and control, including appropriate physical restraint of pupils (Section 4 of the Education Act 1997 and DfEE Circular 9/94);
- how to establish a presence in the classroom and how to promote positive values, attitudes and behaviour.

The School Teachers' Pay and Conditions Act 1991

The School Teachers' Pay and Conditions Act 1991 sets out the pay and conditions of teachers in England and Wales. The tasks of 3–8 teachers are many and include a wide range of professional duties in common with those of all other teachers. The Act provides for the constitution of a Review Body and defines the powers and responsibilities of the Secretary of State for Education and Skills to make Statutory Orders on teachers' pay and conditions. The function of the Review Body is to consider matters relating to pay and conditions and to report their findings and recommendations to the Secretary of State. It is intended as a way of trying to ensure a rational basis for policy-making based on balanced consideration of the evidence. Although the Secretary of State has the power to override and ignore the Review Body, to do so completely could prove politically embarrassing.

Not only may the Review Body consider issues for itself, but the Secretary of State may also ask it to examine a particular matter and report back within a given period. In such cases those affected – teachers, their unions, school governors and LEAs – have to be given the opportunity to submit evidence to the Review Body. Once the Secretary of State has received the report and advice from the Review Body there is a legal requirement to publish the report and subsequently seek to make a Statutory Order based on that report. In so doing, the Secretary of State has the power to modify or change the recommendations. In addition to seeking recommendations from the Review Body, the Secretary of State also has the power to make Statutory Orders in his/her own right. Whenever a Statutory Order is made, teachers must be paid according to the pay scales laid down in it, and any conditions set out in the Statutory Order become part of teachers' contracts.

Pay

Teachers' salaries are determined by the number of points a member of staff has reached on a pay scale. These points will be assessed and awarded by an LEA if a teacher is employed centrally or if the school/nursery at which he/she is employed does not have a delegated budget. Where a school has a delegated budget, or in the case of grant-maintained schools, it is the governing body's responsibility to make the points assessment. In parts of the country where schools and LEAs are experiencing difficulties with teacher recruitment and retention the basic salary package may be augmented by the offer of additional monies to tempt applicants into the area. If trainee or newly qualified teachers are uncertain as to their points entitlement, their teaching unions will be able to offer advice.

Pay

- Since the introduction of the revised 6–point pay scale, NQTs start at point 1.
- Local Education Authorities and governing bodies can award extra points where recruitment and retention is difficult (in certain parts of the country and in certain subject areas) and in cases of excellence.
- An additional point is added for every year's satisfactory performance until the teacher reaches point 6 on the scale. Scale point 6 is the maximum point a teacher can reach by virtue of experience and qualifications alone. This yearly increment is not automatic and can be withheld by the LEA or governing body if they feel that a teacher's performance is not satisfactory.
- Once a teacher reaches point 6 on the scale he/she can apply for performance to be assessed in order to pass the **threshold**. If successful he/she moves to point 1 on the upper pay scale. Progress in pay rates after this point is performance related and not automatic, with a minimum period between incremental increases of two years. To progress through the upper pay scale teachers have to demonstrate that they have sustained or enhanced their substantial contribution to the working of the nursery/school.

- Many teachers are expected to take on posts of responsibility during their teaching careers and some of these posts can carry additional points, for example English coordinator, Nursery Team Leader, Key Stage 1 coordinator.
- Teachers who wish to advance their career without moving into school management are also able to apply for advanced skills teacher (AST) posts which have their own pay scale.
- Teachers who are primarily engaged in teaching children with SEN are entitled to an extra point on the pay scale and could receive two such points should the governors so decide.

(NUT, 2002)

Conditions of service

Trainee and newly qualified teachers can obtain information on conditions of service from Circular 12/99: School Teachers' Pay and Conditions of Employment which can be located on the DfES website (www.dfes.gov.uk). Teacher unions also provide their members with information and advice on conditions of service which can be accessed through the internet.

Useful website addresses for conditions of service

- National Union of Teachers (NUT) – www.teachers.org.uk
- National Association of Schoolmasters Union of Women Teachers (NASUWT) – www.teachersunion.org.uk

Under the terms of the 1991 Act all teachers must carry out their professional duties as well as any particular duties that can be reasonably assigned to them by the headteacher. The term 'reasonable' will appear repeatedly in the remainder of this chapter in relation to teachers' duties and responsibilities and as you will see, it is invariably open to interpretation. Teachers employed on a full-time basis are expected to work for 195 days (a total of 1265 hours) during the school year (NUT, 1998). Five of these days are allocated for staff and curriculum development. In addition to the 1265 figure, teachers are required to work any additional hours needed to enable them to discharge their professional duties effectively. These additional hours would normally be taken up by tasks such as report writing, attending staff meetings and, of course, planning, preparation and marking. The rest of this chapter deals in more detail with some of the regulations governing many of the key duties listed in the example below.

- Teachers are expected to promote the well-being and educational achievement of individual children, irrespective of ethnicity, gender or social class, and alongside this to maintain good order and discipline in the classroom.
- They must safeguard the health and safety of the children in their care, both in school and on outside visits.
- Teachers are expected to take part in activities such as registration, playground supervision and attending assemblies.
- During teaching, staff must ensure that lessons are properly planned. They must also be prepared to take part in medium-term planning and preparation, and whole-school approaches to the curriculum. This planning and teaching must take individual needs and abilities into account.
- Staff must engage in assessing and reporting on children's progress and attainment, for example recording and reporting on the personal and social needs of children, liaising with parents and working with outside agencies and individuals such as special needs colleagues. For teachers of Year 2 pupils, this will include participating in arrangements for SATs, while in reception it will mean completion of the Foundation Stage Profile.
- Beyond the classroom, teachers of young children are required to take part in appraisal activities aimed at improving their own professional competence and as part of this, to review, from time to time, their current practice and their training and development needs.
- Participation at staff meetings and in-service training days is mandatory for teachers.
- Teachers can also be asked to take part in the selection and recruitment of new staff, mentoring newly qualified colleagues and taking responsibilities across the school for coordinating a curriculum area, which would involve ordering resources, developing documentation and supporting the staff development of colleagues.

Inclusion and Equality of Opportunity

Ethnicity

The Race Relations Act 1976 makes direct or indirect discrimination on the grounds of race, colour, ethnic or national origins illegal. Discriminatory behaviour must be opposed by teachers as it creates barriers and obstacles that disadvantage and exclude children. Direct discrimination is considered to have occurred in any instance where an individual is overtly treated unfavourably, for example racial abuse or bullying in the playground. Indirect discrimination relates to those instances where individuals are ostensibly being treated equally, but where the outcome is actually discriminatory in nature. Indirect discrimination through a school's/nursery's admissions policies, for example, is unlawful. Similarly, a school that insisted that all girls wear skirts might appear even-handed but the policy could be deemed discriminatory by some minority ethnic groups for whom skirts would not be regarded as an appropriate mode of dress.

The Race Relations (Amendment) Act 2000 places an onus upon schools to work actively towards not only the elimination of racial discrimination but also the promotion of equal opportunities and positive relations between staff, pupils and parents of different racial groups. For example, staff may need to be alert to instances where disproportionate numbers of ethnic minority children are located in lower ability groups and to look for ways to tackle this underachievement. At the same time, every parent needs to be able to understand school documents (e.g. handbooks, letters, signs, displays, records and reports) and consequently information may need to be available in languages other than English. Trainee and newly qualified teachers wishing to explore this aspect of their role further may wish to visit the Department for Education and Skills (www.dfes.gov.uk) or the Commission for Racial Equality's (www.cre.gov.uk) websites.

Although the Act seeks to end racial discrimination it does provide for the particular needs of certain groups in society to be met. Ending discrimination should not be equated with treating every child as identical. Dietary and clothing requirements need to be respected, as do religious holidays and festivals. Assemblies provide a valuable opportunity to impart anti-racist values to young children, as do projects and topics such as 'Ourselves' which offer opportunities to raise children's awareness of diversity in society. Resources such as reading and reference books ought to be chosen carefully so as to avoid racist stereotyping and some LEAs have within them organizations such as Development Education Centres which can be an excellent source of multicultural and anti-racist resources covering the whole curriculum. Although the facilities and materials available at such centres vary quite considerably due to differences in funding, trainee and newly qualified teachers would be well advised to find out if such an organization exists in their region and to contact it for resources and advice.

Planning in accordance with the Race Relations Act?

School 'A' has a scheme of work for PSHE/Citizenship and Religious Education (RE) which maps out how the school will approach these areas over a two-year cycle.

The plan identifies the focus for 2003–4 as 'Our Culture' and the focus for 2004–5 as 'Other Cultures'.

Is there a problem with this plan in light of the Race Relations (Amendment) Act 2000?

Developing a multicultural/anti-racist approach in the nursery/classroom

- Spell and pronounce children's names properly.
- Help children to recognize and challenge discriminatory practices and behaviour.
- Help children to begin to understand ideas such as fairness, justice and diversity.
- Guide children in the adoption and use of non-discriminatory language.
- Praise and reinforce non-discriminatory behaviour in children.
- Tackle discriminatory behaviour head-on.
- Demonstrate that you value and respect diversity and individual differences by using pupils' first language where possible and by showing respect for traditions, cultures and protocols.

- Acquire and share knowledge about the historical, cultural and spiritual backgrounds in the local community.
- Enable children to take part in the everyday activities of their local community.

Gender

Tackling attitudes

An NQT working with a class of Year 2 children had planned a simple design and technology activity involving textiles in which the children would be asked to design and make some clothes for a doll. During a discussion with the headteacher about resources, the headteacher cautioned her that some of the boys were likely to be extremely hostile to the idea of any work involving dolls, textiles and sewing, as this would be seen as a girls' activity. After discussing strategies with the headteacher the NQT asked the children to make papier-mâché models of themselves. The children were then asked to make clothes for these figures. The boys did not perceive their models as dolls and were enthusiastic about working with the textiles and sewing materials.

Equality of access

John and Helen (Y1) were asked to produce a piece of writing on the computer. The teacher noticed that John had occupied the seat in front of the keyboard and was monopolizing the activity. The teacher intervened and informed John that it was a joint task and that Helen needed to have a go on the computer too. The teacher then moved on to work with another group of children. John meanwhile sat back in his seat with his arms folded. Helen had to reach across him to get to the keyboard. Before long Helen's exclusion was re-imposed.

Like the 1976 Race Relations Act, the 1975 Sex Discrimination Act makes discrimination on the grounds of sex illegal. Also, like racial discrimination, sex discrimination is identified as being either direct or indirect in nature and both are prohibited. Schools and nurseries must provide an entitlement curriculum for both boys and girls. In part, providing an entitlement curriculum for both sexes concerns access; for example, girls have an equal entitlement to experience with computers and construction kits. However, promoting equality of opportunity for both boys and girls also means addressing the expectations and attitudes that some pupils have acquired. Young children can form strong opinions about *boys'* things and *girls'* things at a very early age and as they get older these attitudes are often linked to job aspirations and life choices in a very limiting way. MacNaughton's work (1997) in Australia on boys' and girls' choices of play areas has shown how there is a tendency on the part of some boys to challenge or deny access to some types of activity such as construction play on male terms. MacNaughton categorized and analysed a number of teacher strategies for dealing with this phenomenon (see below) and found that none of them survived for long once the teacher had moved on to another area or group as previously established patterns of behaviour soon re-established themselves. For MacNaughton, young children are trying hard to be *normal*; therefore, practitioners need to broaden children's ideas of what is normal for boys and girls (1997).

Strategies for dealing with stereotypical behaviour

Sparking the girls' interest
• feminization (luring girls into non-traditional areas with *girls'* things)
• separatism (*girls only* time)

Managing the unacceptable behaviour of boys
• fusion (combining *boys'* with *girls'* areas)
• policing (adult intervention and mediation in the interests of equity)

(MacNaughton, 1997)

Promoting equality of opportunity for boys and girls in the nursery/classroom

• Give frequent, positive and encouraging feedback to both boys and girls across the curriculum.
• Have high expectations of both girls and boys across the curriculum.
• Teach children that certain subjects and areas of learning are not the preserve of one sex.
• Encourage the use of non-sexist language and procedures. Do *sensible* girls always clear up? Do *big strong* boys always do the lifting and carrying?
• Provide a variety of learning materials and ensure that girls and boys have opportunities to develop their skills and confidence in using these materials through hands-on experience.
• Remember that, at times, equality of access will require active intervention. It is important to be aware of how boys and girls interact in lessons; where necessary, tackle the behaviour of some children. Such behaviour could include boys calling out while girls put their hands up, ridiculing wrong answers, groaning at correct answers, playing in an aggressive manner and pushing other pupils, including girls, out of reach of certain equipment and resources.
• Challenge gender stereotypes of the sort sometimes found in books and other resources by promoting positive images of women and men.
• Evaluate and reflect upon your teacher–pupil interactions. Do you give equal amounts of time to boys and girls? Do you respond to boys and girls differently? Are boys *'challenged'* and girls *'helped'*?
• Seek to raise and broaden parental expectations of both boys and girls.

Inclusion of children with special educational needs (SEN)

Special educational needs could include children with a physical disability (e.g. visual or hearing impairment), children with Down's Syndrome, children with

Asperger's Syndrome, gifted and talented children and those with emotional and behavioural difficulties. The range of SEN is, therefore, extremely broad, and the reader should look at some of the references in the further sources of information sections at the end of this chapter and Chapter 3 for more detail on which children may be considered as having such needs. Legislation in recent decades has given increasing prominence to the issue of SEN and how best to respond to such needs to enable all children to realize their full potential.

Research and legislation relating to special educational needs (SEN)

- Warnock Report 1978
- Education Act 1981
- International Convention on the Rights of the Child 1989
- The Children's Act 1989
- Code of Practice for Children with SEN 1994 and 2001

Special educational needs are considered to exist in circumstances where special provision has to be made for a child because

- he/she is affected by a disability which precludes or hampers his/her efforts to avail himself/herself of the educational facilities on offer;
- he/she is experiencing learning difficulties. (A learning difficulty in the context of SEN implies a significantly greater difficulty in learning than that experienced by the majority of children of the same age.); or
- he/she is gifted or talented.

The revised National Curriculum outlines three principles through which to facilitate the inclusion of children with SEN. First, teachers need to set suitable learning challenges. Second, they need to respond to pupils' diverse needs, and third, they must overcome potential barriers to learning and assessment for individuals and groups of individuals (QCA, 1999). The aim is to keep children on task as much as possible, in part through establishing a clear structure in which pupils with SEN are encouraged to review previous work and learning, while new skills and concepts are presented in clear unambiguous ways, and are sometimes modelled by the teacher. Guided pupil practice should help to ensure higher success rates, offering more opportunities for positive feedback to individual children. Finally, teachers need to find ways to facilitate independent pupil practice, whereby children with SEN have the chance to apply new knowledge and skills appropriately (Westwood, 1997).

The notion that children with SEN may not be able to take a full part in the curriculum, because of access difficulties or a belief that child centred approaches involving play are inappropriate as they need more one-to-one practice in mastering basic skills, has been challenged. The trend has been to move from segregation of SEN pupils to integration and more recently to inclusion.

- Segregation – provision for SEN pupils is separate from the rest of the nursery/school population.
- Locational integration – SEN pupils share a site with the rest of the nursery/school population.
- Social integration – SEN pupils share out-of-class activities with the rest of the nursery/school population.
- Functional integration – SEN pupils participate in some of the nursery/classroom activities with the rest of the nursery/school population.
- Inclusion – SEN pupils have equal rights and experience full participation in all nursery/classroom activities with the rest of the nursery/school population.

For inclusion to work, staff (teachers and non-teachers) have to be properly prepared and trained. The management in nurseries and schools has to ensure that staff are pedagogically knowledgeable about working with SEN pupils and also that the philosophical rationale underpinning such practice has been accepted. It is also important for nurseries and schools to have access to sufficient levels of support (external and internal) in the form of expert advice and additional staffing in the nursery/classroom to meet the needs of SEN children properly. Staff in schools also have to maintain their commitment to inclusive practice in the face of competing policy pressures (e.g. SATs scores and league tables). If these preconditions are met then there are benefits for all in an inclusive approach to teaching and learning.

Eg **Benefits of inclusion**

For SEN children and their families	**Children** • are spared stereotyping and the negative images caused by segregation; • may experience certain competences being modelled (i.e. by their peers); • acquire realistic life experiences; and • have opportunities to develop friendships with non-SEN peers.
	Families • feel less isolated; and • can develop relationships with parents of non-SEN children and the wider community.
For non-SEN children, their families and society as a whole	**Children** • have a chance to acquire realistic views of, and positive attitudes towards, their SEN peers; • can learn and practise caring and supportive behaviours; and • are presented with positive role models of individuals achieving in the face of adversity.
	Families • have opportunities to develop relationships with parents of SEN children and their offspring; and • can transmit positive attitudes about SEN to their non-SEN offspring.
	Society • can make more efficient use of limited educational resources.

Ensuring the Welfare, Health and Safety of Young Children

In loco parentis

Being *in loco parentis* must rank very highly on a teacher's list of priorities and all teachers have a common law duty to take good care of their pupils. It is particularly fundamental for teachers of younger (3–8) pupils. As child experts, teachers are presumed to be familiar with the likely actions of their pupils in a given situation and are expected to be able to exercise a degree of foresight. Teachers who fail to prevent injury or harm to a child in their care when the risks could be reasonably foreseen are themselves in danger of being deemed negligent. Unfortunately, exact definitions of what constitutes such negligence do not exist and instead, where accusations of negligence arise, the final judgements are likely to be made on the facts of the case. Teachers of young children therefore need to make every effort to ensure their children's safety and not to expose pupils to unnecessary hazards.

A major problem for teachers trying to exercise this foresight is that no environment, and certainly no 3–8 setting, can be made entirely risk free. Young children will always fall over, bump their heads or trap their fingers from time to time. The only way to prevent all these accidents in schools and nurseries would be to close them. This is clearly a nonsense; indeed, risk management and risk awareness are important skills for children to acquire given that they cannot be supervised 24 hours a day. Consequently, teachers need to reduce the risks to acceptable levels by organizing and maintaining a safe learning environment within the nursery/classroom and by thinking carefully about the children in their care before taking them beyond the nursery/school environment.

Thinking about the children

- Are they mature enough and dexterous enough to handle certain tools and materials?
- Are they strong enough to move certain objects?
- To what extent can they take responsibility for themselves and their actions?
- Do they have any physical disabilities that might put them at risk?
- Are nursery/school rules and conventions (e.g. no running) clearly understood?

Health and safety legislation

In addition to teachers' common law duty to care for their pupils, they are also bound by the provisions of the Health and Safety at Work Act 1974. Under the provisions of this Act all employees, including teachers of young children, must not meddle or interfere with anything provided for the purpose of ensuring people's health and safety. They must also have a care for their own safety at work and the safety of others who might be affected by either their actions or their failure to act. Teachers are required to cooperate with others who have duties under the Act such as the school/nursery health and safety representative and the first aid specialist; failure to do this could lead to disciplinary action or even dismissal. Schools and nurseries have health and safety policies (often based on LEA policies) and staff are expected to be familiar with them.

Eg   *Health and safety in 3–8 settings*

Responsibilities of the headteacher
The headteacher must
- ensure that all staff receive instruction in their duties regarding health and safety matters;
- ensure that all staff are adequately trained to carry out their duties;
- fully understand the school's fire drill procedures; and
- check the nursery/school on a regular basis for health and safety issues.

Responsibilities of teaching and non-teaching staff
- All staff, teaching and non-teaching, must be familiar with the school's health and safety policy, the implications of that policy and any procedures, arrangements and practices relating to it.
- All employees, pupils and others must receive appropriate instruction to enable them to operate in a safe and efficient manner (e.g. fire drills).
- All staff must report to the headteacher any problems, defects or hazards that are brought to their notice.

Responsibilities of the caretaker
- The caretaker is responsible for ensuring that cleaning staff are adequately informed, instructed and trained in the safe use and storage of equipment, cleaning substances and other materials.
- The caretaker must not use, or allow cleaning staff to use, unsafe equipment.

Children's welfare

Under the 1989 Children Act, schools and their LEAs are required to assist their local Social Services departments when those departments are investigating allegations of child abuse. Individual teachers in schools are expected to do what is 'reasonable' in the circumstances to safeguard and promote the welfare of their pupils. As with teachers' common law duty of care, there is no exact definition of what constitutes reasonable. More recently, Circular 10/95: Protecting Children from Abuse (DfEE, 1995) attempted to assist teachers in fulfilling their responsibilities to their pupils under the provisions of the 1989 Act by clarifying what was expected. The main points arising from Circular 10/95 are as outlined below.

- All staff should be alert to signs of abuse and know to whom they should report any concerns or suspicions.

- All schools and colleges should have a designated member of staff responsible for coordination of action within the institution and liaison with other agencies including the Area Child Protection Committee (ACPC).
- All schools and colleges should be aware of the child protection procedures established by the ACPC and, in the case of LEA-maintained schools, by the LEA.
- All schools and colleges should have procedures (of which all staff should be aware) for handling suspected cases of abuse of pupils or students, including procedures to be followed if a member of staff is accused of abuse. Schools' and colleges' procedures should be consistent with those of the ACPC and, in the case of LEA-maintained schools, with those of the LEA.
- Guidelines about procedures to be followed if a member of staff is accused of abuse have been drawn up by the Council of Local Education Authorities and the six teacher unions. A copy has been annexed to the Circular.
- Staff with designated responsibility for child protection should receive appropriate training.
- Schools should develop a child protection policy and make it known to parents.
- In every LEA there should be a senior officer with responsibility for coordinating action on child protection across the authority.

(DfEE, 1995)

The main point for students on 3–8 teacher training courses and NQTs arising from the 1989 Act and Circular 10/95 is that should they suspect a child is being abused, then they must alert the designated member of staff in the school whose role it is to liaise with the various child protection agencies. Students and teachers can obtain a copy of the full Circular through the Department of Education and Skills website (www.dfes.gov.uk).

Eg Identifying abuse

Abuse may take a number of forms.
- **Physical abuse**
A child may suffer actual injuries as a result of the violent actions of others. The results can include tell-tale marks such as cuts, bruises and burns.
- **Physical neglect**
A child's suffering is the result of inaction and a failure to protect, care properly and attend to physical needs.
- **Sexual abuse**
Children are exploited sexually by adults. This is a particularly emotive subject and may result in children being noticeably withdrawn or, paradoxically, highly precocious.
- **Emotional abuse**
This abuse is not physical in nature and may not leave any visible marks, but it is no less harmful to a young child. Emotional abuse can result in children being persistently ill-treated or rejected by those whose duty it is to care for them. It can produce profoundly damaging and long-term effects on the emotional and behavioural development of the child, resulting in excessive 'clinginess' or aggression in the nursery/school.

(Kay, 1999)

Simply because a young child is behaving aggressively or appears withdrawn does not constitute evidence of abuse or neglect of any kind. However, it could be an indicator and teachers of young children need to be alert for the signs, and if necessary try to elicit in a tactful, sympathetic and non-leading fashion some information from a child who has made a disclosure of some kind. Any such discussion must be handled very carefully. Under no circumstances should trainee teachers initiate such a discussion without first referring to their class teacher or mentor. Newly qualified teachers, too, would be well advised to seek the support and advice of experienced colleagues before becoming involved in any case of suspected abuse. Where a child has initiated such a discussion, the main aim for the teacher is to give the child the opportunity to talk and then to listen to what he/she has to say. Open-ended questions are the best way to proceed in order to get the truest picture possible and avoid prejudicing any possible future legal actions.

Eg *A worrying development*

Paul was painting in the nursery. His teacher noticed that he had used only red and black paint and that the picture had a somewhat visceral quality to it. She told Paul that his painting was very interesting and asked him if he would like her to write anything under his picture for him. Paul thought for a moment and then said, 'The daddy hits the mummy with a pan, the mummy stabs the daddy.'

If such discussions between teacher and young child do take place, the teacher must note down the conversation, giving details of the date, time, place, any other people present and what the child said. This written evidence could form part of court proceedings at a future date so it is important to be accurate. Once such a note has been compiled, the teacher must forward the information to the member of staff with responsibility for dealing with suspected cases of abuse or neglect. This designated teacher will then take the process forwards with other agencies and individuals such as EWOs, the local Social Services Department and LEA child protection officers. If there is to be any investigation, it must be conducted by the proper authorities. Individual class teachers, and even designated teachers, are not trained in investigation techniques. Meddling of any kind is likely to cause more harm than good and could result in parents and carers being wrongly accused or someone guilty of abuse escaping the consequences of their actions. The primary role of the teacher therefore is to *be alert for the signs* and to *inform the proper authorities*.

Abuse by staff in the nursery/school

Physical contact is bound to take place continually between staff and children in 3–8 settings. It is not only inevitable, it is also desirable for young children to know that they are valued and cared for by staff who are not cold, distant and aloof. However, when allegations of abuse are made against a member of staff, it is an extremely traumatic experience for the person accused, irrespective of his/her guilt or innocence. Early years teachers and teacher training students must take care at all times to ensure that the inevitable physical contact between themselves and their children is appropriate in nature, and could not be misconstrued as in any way abusive or indecent. Should staff encounter children who are clearly uneasy about physical contact, they would be well advised to avoid any potentially compromising situations, and may wish to place their concerns on record.

In a situation where a young child makes a disclosure suggesting that he/she has been the subject of abuse by a member of staff in the school/nursery, the teacher must initially follow the same procedure as that outlined above. The child must be listened to, and the conversation must be noted down. However, at this stage the allegation and the notes must be reported directly and immediately to the headteacher. Where the subject of the allegation is the headteacher, the teacher has a duty to inform the governors. In cases where allegations are made against members of staff, the headteacher and/or the governors are initially responsible for determining what action, if any, to take.

Possible action arising from allegations of abuse against staff

- The headteacher and/or governors may conclude that the allegation is sufficiently serious to warrant its forwarding to the child protection agencies.
- The headteacher and/or governors could decide that the allegation arose from a lack of judgement or a degree of naïveté on the part of the member of staff concerned, and that the matter would be better dealt with through normal internal procedures.
- The headteacher and/or governors could decide that the allegation is completely unfounded with no evidence to support it and consequently does not warrant either referral or internal disciplinary action.

Any teacher who is the subject of an allegation of abuse has the right to be informed that the allegation has been made and what action the headteacher and governing body propose to take as a result. The only exception to this rule occurs where an objection is made by the child protection agencies such as the police who may not wish the person accused to be informed before they can be formally interviewed. Teachers accused of abuse should seek advice from their union and are entitled to have a union representative present at any subsequent meeting to discuss and investigate the allegation.

Promoting Positive Values and Maintaining Good Order

Schools and nurseries play an important role in helping pupils to grow into responsible adults. In part this is achieved through successfully inculcating in young children a set of values, and promoting what the Education Act 1996 referred to as the *spiritual, cultural, mental and physical development of pupils* (QCA, 1999). Such values include respect for one another, self-respect, honesty, trust, fairness and self-discipline. Everyone involved in the working of nurseries and schools has a part to play in promoting good behaviour and discipline, as without them, teaching and learning will be greatly impaired.

The management in nurseries and schools (governing bodies and headteachers) will take the lead in drawing up the policy on behaviour. Parents are expected to lend their support to the efforts of the nursery/school to maintain good order. It is crucial, wherever possible, that schools draw upon the backing of parents and other carers as the most influential people in the lives of young children. Individual teachers are especially important in translating behaviour policies into reality through their efficiency and professionalism. Good behaviour and discipline are founded on good organization and a professional approach to the task of teaching. Teachers of 3–8 pupils must achieve a balanced approach which takes into consideration the nurture required by young children, while at the same time recognizing the importance of imparting positive social behaviour.

Adopting a positive approach and establishing your presence as a teacher

Many of the day-to-day actions of teachers are fundamental in underpinning attempts to foster good behaviour and discipline among children. The use of praise and recognition promotes consideration and responsibility on the part of children as well as offering an intrinsic reward for good work and behaviour.

Offering praise and recognition

Spot-on.'
'What a good try.'
'I'm impressed.'
'Very imaginative.'
'Well remembered.'
'Quick thinking.'
'I like that.'
'Keep on trying.'
'You have great ideas.'
'Good problem-solving.'
'One more go and you'll be there.'
'You've done better than ever.'
'Your work is really improving.'

(www.practicalparent.org.uk/handyhints)

In some cases, extrinsic rewards such as points, stars or marbles in jars can be used as a strong incentive to promote effort and good behaviour (Wragg, 1993). Providing tasks that are well matched to children's needs and abilities, in sessions and lessons that start and end on time and where interruptions and diversions are minimized or dealt with efficiently, also helps to create a positive learning atmosphere where praise and recognition are attainable by all pupils. Getting to know the children enables teachers to plan ahead and anticipate where and with whom problems might arise in order to develop strategies to reduce the risk. At the same time, giving clear instructions, and using language appropriate to young children, helps to avoid confusion and disruptive behaviour.

Eg   *Ambiguous instruction*

A group of loitering Year 1 children were being ushered good naturedly from the classroom at lunchtime by their teacher who uttered the words 'Go on, hop it you lot.' So they did!

Looking like, and acting the part of, a teacher is an important element in forging professional relationships and maintaining good order. Parents, children and colleagues will make assumptions about students or NQTs based in part on their actions and appearance. Some of these assumptions can facilitate attempts to develop good relationships and good order in the classroom. Children in particular are quite likely to work on the assumption that if it looks like a duck, walks like a duck and quacks like a duck, it must be a duck. Be aware of the assumptions that are being made regarding the look and actions of a teacher; fitting the profile by looking and acting like a teacher is all part of *developing your presence* in the classroom.

Developing your presence as a teacher

- Show consistency in your expectations and actions.
- Radiate a sense of confidence by not hesitating or rushing your speech, making eye contact, and adopting appropriate body postures and tones of voice.
- Exhibit firm, although gentle, insistence when necessary.
- Avoid being overly and inappropriately friendly, especially in the early stages of the year or with older pupils.
- Establish a clear and simple set of rules or conventions within which the activities of the class will take place.

What to do when it all goes wrong

Establishing your presence in the classroom and setting a good example to the children will help to reduce the incidence of unwanted behaviour, but these and other strategies will not eliminate such conduct totally. Teachers who are alert and mobile may spot a situation that is about to deteriorate and may be able to use early intervention, humour or a diversion of some kind to keep children on task. However, the teacher cannot be everywhere at once and all teachers experience instances where children's behaviour will be deemed unacceptable and action of some sort will be required. Where necessary, schools and nurseries have the authority to impose punishment that is reasonable and as before, the term reasonable is subject to interpretation. Teachers of young children have a number of options open to them when trying to deal with unwanted behaviour which include administering punishment, withdrawing pleasurable activities and ignoring unwanted behaviour (Robertson, 1989).

Eg *Strategies for dealing with unwanted behaviour*

- **Administering unpleasantness** might involve the use of reprimands or, in more serious instances, the imposition of sanctions.
- **Withdrawing pleasurable activities** could include the removal of attention such as not listening to and encouraging tale-tellers, or the removal of activities. Teachers need to be careful about always picking games and practical creative activities, as this can carry hidden messages about what aspects of learning are enjoyable and what are not.
- **Ignoring unwanted behaviour** could include rewarding desirable behaviour and denying attention for unwanted behaviour. This can be effective, but it can also be a risky strategy if applied inappropriately. In some situations, for example, other children may provide the desired attention and some actions by children such as racist or sexist abuse simply cannot be ignored. One possible refinement for teachers wishing to utilize this technique is to distinguish between ignoring something completely and deciding against any verbal rebuke or punishment, restricting themselves instead to a slightly shocked look or a raised and very disapproving eyebrow.

Whatever strategy a teacher decides to employ in order to deal effectively with unwanted behaviour, there are some key features of good practice to bear in mind.

Ways to discipline effectively

- **Appropriateness** is crucial, particularly with young children where you are engaged in the care and nurture of pupils as well as in their education. Performance and motivation can be damaged by too severe a punishment or reprimand. Where young children experience unstable care arrangements, where they have been encouraged to adopt conflict resolution strategies based on *might is right*, where adult expectations have been inconsistent with behaviour ignored one day and punished the next, or where pupils have learned that bad behaviour gains adult attention, teachers will need to accept that changing a child's behaviour is likely to take time.
- **Timing** is important. You should try to act before or during misbehaviour. Success in doing this is a powerful statement of your control and awareness. In addition, the immediacy of your actions is much more meaningful and relevant to young children, for whom an incident the day before can be ancient history.

- **Consistency** and **determination** have to be maintained. Every time a rule is broken without comment or penalty makes it harder to enforce that rule in future. Inconsistency on your part will be regarded as unfair by the children and rightly so, and failure to be as good as your word may be seen as ineffectualness.
- **Simplicity** is essential. You should keep any rules or conventions simple unless you want to spend all your time explaining and enforcing them.
- **Fairness** matters. You should never victimize a whole class or nursery for the actions of one individual.
- **Respect** is everything. When you do have to reprimand or punish behaviour, focus on the act rather than the perpetrator. Personalizing matters and humiliating a young child does nothing for that child's self-image; it is degrading for them, constitutes a no-value statement on your part, and in some cases risks open rebellion on the part of the child concerned. Children are far more likely to respond positively to someone they respect and who obviously respects them.

Readers may wish to reflect on the example below and consider to what extent it represents an appropriate, well-timed response to unwanted behaviour.

Eg A punishment fitting a crime?

A student teacher encountered a Year 1 child sitting outside the headteacher's office at breaktime. She enquired as to why he was there. He replied that he was not allowed out to play for six months because he had been 'naughty in the playground'.

While reprimands and punishment play a small role in establishing good order in the classroom when compared to positive discipline and the principles of good classroom management and teaching, this is still a very important role. The examples below represent the more common sorts of behaviour which may require intervention on the part of the 3–8 teacher in order to maintain good order; they range from the very minor to the rather more serious.

Eg Range of unwanted behaviour in 3–8-year-old children

How would you deal with these situations?
- During a class discussion two girls begin to plait one another's hair. In so doing they opt out of the class activity and begin to distract other children who start to join in. An outbreak of hairdressing is about to occur.
- You're reading a story to the class. Matthew is next to you. When you next look around, Matthew has miraculously materialized in a completely different part of the room and is prodding another child.
- You have taken register, explained the morning's tasks and started the children off. It rapidly becomes apparent that chaos is ensuing about your person.
- There is a 'phantom whistler' somewhere in the room.
- Mrs Jones, the peripatetic piano player, is with you in the hall for singing and dancing. Paul and Wayne are pulling faces and objecting loudly at the prospect of having to dance with the girls.
- While moving around the classroom you overhear one individual make a racist remark directly to another child.

- A child comes to you after playtime and claims to have been struck by a child in another class.
- A parent tells you that their child is being bullied at school by a classmate.
- Your class is travelling to the local woods on the bus. Two burly gentlemen, one sporting a rather striking mohican haircut, board the bus and come upstairs to where the children are sitting. Unable to contain herself, and broadcasting on full volume, one of the children shouts out 'Miss! Look at the state of his hair!'
- John and Ali are marched into your classroom at lunchtime by an incandescent lunchtime supervisor, after having suggested that she try something anatomically impossible.
- A child approaches you in the playground and tells you that David has been showing his willie to the girls.
- During the previous week in the nursery Sarah slapped two other children across the face in two separate incidents and was reprimanded. While sitting with a group at the creative table on Monday morning you notice Sarah approach another girl, slap her hard across the face and then scuttle swiftly into the role-play area well away from the now screaming victim.
- Your class are discussing their activities over the weekend with you on Monday morning. Sarah puts her hand up and when asked, tells the class that she has seen a film called 'George' at the weekend and it was really good. When you ask her to tell the class about the film she says that it was all about a huge fish called a shark that went around eating people. The other children start to laugh and catcall.
- The headteacher is reading to the school in assembly. It is a part of the story that is full of dramatic pauses and hushed tones, generating quiet excitement and expectation on the part of the children. Suddenly there is a noise in the midst of your class followed by much sniggering, theatrical wafting of hands, clutching of throats and holding of noses.

The use of force by a teacher

Appropriate restraint?

Simon (Y2) experienced emotional and behavioural difficulties. Simon's teacher had alerted her student teacher to this fact and had made recommendations about how lessons should be organized and managed, particularly in terms of pacing and timing and what could be expected of Simon and his ability to stay on-task. During an afternoon lesson on the Vikings Simon presented himself to the student teacher and made it clear that he had had enough. The student did not realize what was about to happen and instead of trying to divert the impending crisis or offering additional support, he told Simon that he would be the judge of when Simon had had enough. A few seconds later chairs started to fly around the room as children scattered for cover. The student teacher, realizing his mistake, held onto Simon's arms and tried to calm him down by talking to him. He then told Simon that he was going to stop holding Simon's hands and that he wanted him to take deep breaths and then they could talk about how he could help Simon. He let go and Simon grabbed a pair of scissors from the desk and lunged at the student's face.

(O'Hara and O'Hara, 2001)

In extreme circumstances it may be necessary for a teacher to restrain a pupil physically in order to preserve good order in the classroom or to protect everyone's health and safety. It is hard to imagine a situation in most 3–8 settings where considerable force would need to be employed. However, all trainee and newly qualified teachers need to be familiar with the legislation and guidance.

The 1997 Education Act (Section 4) sets out the circumstances when the use of force may be appropriate to prevent a child from

- committing a criminal offence (or in the case of very young children behaving in a way that would be criminal if they were above the age of criminal responsibility);
- injuring themselves or others;
- causing damage to property; or
- behaving in such a way as to undermine good order and discipline in the school/nursery.

In such situations, a teacher may use reasonable force. Once again, the term reasonable is open to interpretation and requires teachers to exercise their professional judgement. In making this judgement about whether or not to use force and how much force to use, teachers must weigh up what they think the circumstances warrant. Clearly, this judgement will be heavily influenced by the very young age of 3–8 children. In an effort to clarify for teachers what sorts of incidents may justify the use of reasonable force, the DfEE published Circular 10/98 which sought to provide additional guidance for schools. This guidance stated clearly that any individual has the right to defend himself/herself against an attack, provided that person does not use a 'disproportionate degree of force to do so'. The Circular also made it quite clear that any teacher is entitled to intervene where pupils are risking their own or others' safety. Circular 10/98 divides the types of incident where force may be necessary into three categories:

1. Where action is necessary in self-defence or because there is an imminent risk of injury;
2. Where there is a developing risk of injury, or significant damage to property; or
3. Where a pupil is behaving in a way that is compromising good order and discipline.

(DfEE, 1998a)

Eg *Range of incidents where force may be necessary*

- Attacks by pupils on members of staff
- Attacks by pupils on other pupils
- Fights between pupils
- Pupils who are deliberately damaging or vandalizing property (or are about to)
- Pupils causing or risking accidents through rough play or misuse of equipment and materials
- Pupils running through school in such a way as to risk injury to themselves or others
- Pupils who leave or try to leave the school premises where those pupils could be at risk if not kept in school
- Pupils persistently refusing to obey an order to leave the classroom
- Pupils behaving in a way that seriously disrupts a lesson.

(DfEE, 1998a)

Having tried to clarify what circumstances might warrant force being used, Circular 10/98 then attempts to assist teachers in interpreting the concept of reasonable, which it acknowledges will always ultimately depend upon all the circumstances of a case.

- Teachers **can**
  – physically block a pupil or get between pupils;
  – hold or restrain a pupil; or
  – lead pupils away.
- Teachers **cannot**
  – use neck-holds of any description;
  – punch, kick or slap a pupil;
  – twist limbs and/or joints;
  – trip pupils up;
  – pull hair or ears; or
  – hold pupils face-down.

Trainee and newly qualified teachers need to be aware that any use of force is illegal if the circumstances do not warrant it, for example using force to prevent very minor incidents. They also need to maintain a sense of proportion as to the amount of force to be used; the guidance calls for the *minimum needed to achieve the desired result* and for teachers to take into account factors such as age, understanding and sex of pupils. Circular 9/94 contains guidance on dealing with children with emotional and behavioural difficulties who may be particularly volatile and whose behaviour can be particularly extreme. However, as with all other pupils, teachers are expected to adopt an essentially constructive and positive approach and to work hard to promote the self-image of such children. Here, too, the application of force should be the last resort, not the norm.

In a situation where a teacher has concluded that force may be necessary, the teacher must tell the pupil concerned to desist from whatever it is he/she is doing and make clear what will happen if he/she does not. When force is used it should be *as well as* communication, not *instead of*. Teachers need to stay as calm as possible and inform the child that restraint or force will cease to be used once the behaviour that caused it has also ceased. In those rare instances (for nursery/infant teachers) where the pupil is particularly large or in other ways is capable of injuring the teacher, then that teacher should clear other pupils from the immediate area to remove them from risk and call or send for assistance. While waiting for this to arrive the teacher should continue to try to resolve the situation verbally, or at least to stop it from escalating. Trainee and newly qualified teachers especially should not be afraid to seek and accept help from more experienced colleagues. It is not a sign of weakness; it is a sign of good sense.

Eg *A no-fuss, effective procedure*
_____

A student teacher was making a preliminary visit to her teaching practice school.
The school contained a number of children who were capable of becoming extremely
disruptive, and in some cases violent, during lessons. The deputy headteacher introduced
her to the school's procedures for dealing with these difficult situations when they
occurred. The procedures included a card system which all staff used. In the event of
disruption or violence in the classroom, the teacher concerned could send a responsible
child to the deputy's room with a card. A yellow card meant 'Please come to my
classroom when you have a few minutes as I need some assistance'. A red card meant
'I need your assistance immediately'.

In addition to situations where teachers have to use force to deal with aggressive
behaviour, there are other situations where, due to a lack of maturity on the part of
pupils, teachers have to react instantly and use force in order to avoid harm befalling
either a child or other people. This can be particularly true for those working with
younger children. On these occasions there may be no time to explain or issue
a warning, and action must be immediate; for example, a reception teacher on an
out-of-school visit when one of the children suddenly jumps into the road and has to
be pulled back quickly; or a young child about to throw a heavy object at another
child in the class without thinking about the likely consequences of the action. In all
cases, the use of force should be the last resort and be used only to protect children
and others, not to punish.

Eg *Don't dither*
_____

A class of Year 1 children were taken on a local walk by their teacher as part of a topic on
'Our School'. The school was situated near a block of flats and the group went up a few
floors to give the children a bird's-eye view of their school and its surroundings. Suddenly
the teacher noticed one of the children holding a large glass marble over the parapet with
the apparent intention of dropping it. She immediately dived forwards, grabbed the
child's hand, drew him away from the parapet, took the marble away from him and spoke
firmly to him about how dangerous such an act could be for passers-by.

The use of force always carries with it the possibility of complaints, and teachers
need to act professionally at all times. Where a serious incident has occurred in
which a teacher has had to use force of some description, this should be reported
verbally and in writing to the headteacher. The written report should include
details of date, time, names, the nature of the incident, a rationale for the use of
force in the circumstances, the pupil's response and any information on injury or
damage suffered.

Having High Expectations of All Children

Adams, J. (1994) '"She'll have a go at anything": towards an equal opportunities policy', in Abbott, L. and Rodger, R. (eds), *Quality Education in the Early Years*. Buckingham: Open University Press.

Commission for Racial Equality, www.cre.gov.uk

DfES (2001) *Special Educational Needs Code of Practice*. London: DfES.

DfES (2003) *Aiming High: Raising the Achievement of Ethnic Minority Pupils*. London: DfES.

Equal Opportunities Commission, www.eoc.org.uk

Working with Parents and Other Adults

Edgington, M. (1998) *The Nursery Teacher in Action: Teaching 3, 4 and 5 Year Olds*, 2nd edn. London: Paul Chapman.

Pollard, A. (1996) *An Introduction to Primary Education: For Parents, Governors and Student Teachers*. London: Cassell.

Strahan, H. (1994) '"You feel like you belong": establishing partnerships between parents and educators', in Abbott, L. and Rodger, R. (eds), *Quality Education in the Early Years*. Buckingham: Open University Press.

The Corporate Life of the Nursery/School

DfES (2003) 'Historic Agreement to Reform School Workforce – Clarke', www.dfes.gov.uk/pns

DfES (2003) Statutory Instrument No. 348, School Governance (Constitution) (England) Regulations (2003), www.dfes.gov.uk/

Kenyon, P. (1998) *Ready for Inspection*. London: Scholastic.

Ofsted (2003) *Handbook for Inspecting Nursery and Primary Schools*. London: Ofsted.

Continuing Professional Development (CPD)

DfEE (1999) *Professional Development: Support for Teaching and Learning*. London: DfEE.

Maynard, T. (ed.) (1997) *An Introduction to Primary Mentoring*. London: Cassell.

Moyles, J., Adams, S. and Musgrove, A. (2002) 'SPEEL: Study of Pedagogical Effectiveness in Early Learning', DfES Research Brief No. RB363, www.dfes.gov.uk/research/

Siraj-Blatchford, I., Sylva, K., Muttock, S., Gilden, R. and Bell, D. (2002) 'Researching Effective Pedagogy in the Early Years', DfES Research Brief No. 356, www.dfes.gov.uk/research/

Teacher Training Agency (2003) *Into Induction 2003: An Introduction for Trainee Teachers to the Induction Period for Newly Qualified Teachers*. London: TTA.

The Responsibilities and Legal Liabilities of the 3–8 Teacher

Children Act 1989: Section 3(5). London: HMSO.

Cowley, S. (2001) *Getting the Buggers to Behave*. London: Continuum.

Development Education Association (DEA), 29–31 Cowper Street, London, EC2A 4AP (Tel. 020 7490 8123).

DfE (1994) *Circular 8/94: Pupil Behaviour and Discipline*. London: HMSO.

DfE (1994) *Circular 9/94: The Education of Children with Emotional and Behavioural Difficulties*. London: HMSO.

DfEE (1995) *Circular 10/95: Protecting Children from Abuse: The Role of the Education Service*. London: HMSO.

DfEE (1998) *Circular 10/98: The Use of Force to Control or Restrain Pupils*. London: DfEE.

DfES (2001) *Health and Safety: Responsibilities and Powers*. London: DfES.

DfES (2001) *Health and Safety of Pupils on Educational Visits*. London: DfES.

Kay, J. (1999) *Protecting Children: A Practical Guide*. London: Cassell.

NASUWT (2002) 'Race Relations (Amendment) Act 2000 and the Code of Practice: Implications for Schools and Colleges', www.teachersunion.org.uk

Roffey, S. and O'Reirdan, T. (2001) *Young Children and Classroom Behaviour: Needs, Perspectives and Strategies*. London: David Fulton.

School Teachers' Pay and Conditions Act 1991. London: HMSO.

Trend, R. (1997) *Qualified Teacher Status: A Practical Introduction*. London: Letts Educational.

Westwood, P. (1997) *Commonsense Methods for Children with Special Needs*, 3rd edn. London: Routledge.

Wragg, E. C. (1993) *Class Management*. London: Routledge.

Knowledge and Understanding

SUMMARY

This chapter deals with the knowledge and understanding expected of trainee and newly qualified 3–8 teachers. The chapter will consider some of the theories concerning young children's development and the impact such theories have on teaching and learning. The chapter goes on to examine the Code of Practice for pupils with special educational needs (SEN) and concludes by examining the various subjects that make up the 3–8 curricula. The chapter uses the six areas of learning set out in the Curriculum Guidance for the Foundation Stage to structure the discussion, and comments concerning National Curriculum subjects, National Literacy and Numeracy Strategies, personal, social and health education (PSHE) and citizenship are incorporated into this framework.

By the end of this chapter you should

- understand how children's development can affect their learning;
- know about the Code of Practice for children with SEN; and
- know about the aims, principles and content of the 3–8 curricula (i.e. the six areas of learning, National Curriculum subjects, literacy and numeracy hours, PSHE and citizenship).

The Foundation Stage Curriculum (Nursery and Reception Pupils)

AUDIT

By the end of this section you should

- know about the principles underlying the Curriculum Guidance for the Foundation Stage;
- have an overview of the six areas of learning contained within the Curriculum Guidance for the Foundation Stage.

During the past decade there has been a plethora of reforms aimed at extending and enhancing early childhood services in the UK including educational provision. The development of an early years curriculum is part of this much wider context, which includes the launch of the Sure Start programme; the establishment of Education Action Zones, Early Years Development and Childcare Partnerships (EYDCPs), Early Excellence Centres; and developments in the training of teachers and others intending to work with young children. The developments in staff training have been paralleled by developments in the early years curriculum resulting in the publication of the Curriculum Guidance for the Foundation Stage (QCA, 2000) which sets out the desired learning outcomes (Early Learning Goals) for children upon completion of their reception year. Those nurseries that are part of the UK-maintained sector, as well as primary school reception classes, are now expected to use the Early Learning Goals to structure their work with pupils aged 3–5. The introduction of these goals was accompanied by the establishment of the Foundation Stage, comprising both nursery and reception settings. This represented a shift of focus for many reception settings who had previously operated in ways little different from Key Stage 1.

The Curriculum Guidance for the Foundation Stage (QCA, 2000) set out a series of *principles* to underpin teaching and learning across the curriculum (QCA, 2000, pp. 6–25). Effective early years education requires not only a relevant curriculum and practitioners capable of implementing it but also practitioners who understand young children and their rapid development. For the Early Learning Goals to be implemented appropriately, therefore, early years teachers need to ensure that

- children have access to rich and stimulating experiences;
- children feel included, secure and valued;
- children get to build on what they already know and can do;
- children are not excluded as a result of ethnicity, gender, ability or social class;
- children have opportunities to engage with both teacher-planned activities and self-initiated activities;
- children have opportunities to experience teaching and learning in both indoor and outdoor settings;

- staff observe and respond appropriately to children, providing well-planned purposeful activities backed up by appropriate intervention; and
- schools and nurseries work closely with parents.

(QCA, 2000)

High-quality early years education can do much to lay the foundations for children's future successes in learning, but the rationale behind such provision concerns more than just preparation for future educational experiences. The education of 3–5-year-old children should be recognized as a distinctive stage in the continuum of learning and be valued in its own right. Education of the under-fives is part of a continuum beginning in the home and moving on to compulsory schooling. The broad aims for early years education are very similar to those for the over-fives, with an additional emphasis on the considerable amount of care that very young children require, care which is intrinsically linked to their education (DfEE, 1997).

Teachers are reminded in the underlying principles that the rate of children's development is different and uneven, and that some children will have had a wide range of experiences before they enter an educational setting of any kind while others will not. Children are not all on the same start line when they enter nursery or reception classes. They will display a range of predispositions and some will have SEN be they physical, emotional, behavioural or cognitive, or they may be gifted or talented in some way. To provide an appropriate curriculum, therefore, early years practitioners need first to bear in mind the children's abilities and experiences to date. Teachers who fail to recognize this fact and so not take it into account when planning and teaching are likely to be less effective and may experience more problems than those who do.

The development of a curriculum for the under-fives has also been influenced by a desire to ensure breadth and balance, and a wish to achieve a measure of continuity with the National Curriculum. The structure, organization and delivery of the curriculum in the early years are often different from what is found in primary settings and ought to be viewed as the best way of addressing the particular needs of 3–5-year-olds during this crucial period of their development (QCA, 1998a). The term curriculum is often interpreted in a holistic and inclusive manner in the Foundation Stage. Learning is not structured using subject boundaries as it is in the National Curriculum. The curriculum in the early years encompasses not just the six different areas of learning but includes all aspects of young children's experiences. The early years curriculum is *everything children do, see, hear or feel in their setting, both planned and unplanned* (QCA in Drake, 2001). This difference is based in large part on social-interactionist/constructivist understandings of how young pupils learn. Young children do not necessarily make the same subject distinctions with which adults seek to organize teaching and learning. In nursery and reception classes activities can offer starting points for learning across a number of areas. The Curriculum

Guidance for the Foundation Stage organizes the Early Learning Goals into six areas of learning which, while frequently corresponding to, do not replicate the subjects in the National Curriculum (Select Committee on Education and Employment, 2000).

The six areas of learning

- Personal, social and emotional development
- Communication, language and literacy
- Mathematical development
- Knowledge and understanding of the world
- Physical development
- Creative development

Although the QCA documentation (2000) retains the same areas of learning as those contained in earlier curriculum models (SCAA, 1996), the Early Learning Goals are more precise. They represent what most children will be expected to achieve by the end of their time in reception classes. The Early Learning Goals are supported by a series of *stepping stones* which set out a model of progression in terms of the knowledge, skills and attitudes that children will need to develop if they are to achieve the anticipated outcomes by the end of the Foundation Stage. Progression through these stepping stones is not age related but it is more likely that younger children will be better described by earlier bands while later bands provide a closer approximation to the attainment of older children.

Eg *Early Learning Goal*

Physical development
These outcomes focus on the development of children's coordination, control, manipulation and movement as well as their appreciation of health and well-being (QCA, 2000, p. 112).

Progression from age 3 . . .

Stepping stones – Yellow band	Operate equipment by means of pushing and pulling movements
Stepping stones – Blue band	Construct with large materials such as cartons, long lengths of fabric and planks Show increasing control in using equipment for climbing, scrambling, sliding and swinging
Stepping stones – Green band	Use increasing control over an object by touching, pushing, patting, throwing, catching or kicking it Retrieve, collect and catch objects
Early Learning Goal . . . to the end of the Foundation Stage	Use a range of small and large equipment

The National Curriculum for 5–8-Year-Olds (Years 1, 2 and 3)

By the end of this section you should

- know about the structure of the National Curriculum and its underlying principles;
- know about the place of literacy and numeracy hours within the primary curriculum;
- know about the framework for PSHE and Citizenship.

The underlying principles of the National Curriculum are based on the Education Reform Act 1988 and the Education Act 1996 and are set out in the current documentation (QCA, 1999) in the form of two interrelated aims and four main purposes.

National Curriculum aims

1. The National Curriculum is a curriculum for all – all children irrespective of their social, ethnic or cultural background, or their ability, need to be helped to learn and to achieve.
2. The National Curriculum concerns the development of the whole child not just academic progress – education must contribute to children's moral, spiritual, social and cultural development as a means of preparing them for the *opportunities, responsibilities and experiences of adult life*.

(QCA, 1999, p. 11).

National Curriculum purposes

1. To establish an entitlement to a range of subjects, and to develop a range of skills and attitudes essential for academic achievement, self-fulfilment and socially responsible behaviour.
2. To establish standards by making expectations clear to all those involved in teaching and learning (children, teachers, parents, governors, society) and to use these standards to measure attainment and set improvement targets.
3. To promote continuity and coherence, to ensure progression in children's learning and to facilitate transition into, within and beyond educational settings.
4. To promote public understanding and thereby confidence in the performance of compulsory education, and to facilitate and inform debates within society about educational matters.

(QCA, 1999, pp. 12–13)

The National Curriculum sets out a broad and balanced curriculum that should be offered to pupils at both Key Stage 1 (children 5–7 years of age) and Key Stage 2 (children 7–11 years of age), and that should be relevant to the needs of the pupils taking it. The curriculum outlined comprises the National Curriculum subjects (core and foundation), Religious Education (RE) for all children over five, and a series of cross-curricular elements and additional subjects which together form the whole curriculum.

Eg *National Curriculum subjects*

Core subjects	Foundation subjects
English	design and technology
mathematics	information and communications technology (ICT)
science	history
	geography
	music
	art
	physical education

(QCA, 1999)

Each subject in the National Curriculum has a Programme of Study (PoS) for Key Stages 1 and 2, which is intended to help teachers organize the curriculum offered to children. Programmes of Study are designed to assist teachers in planning. Each PoS sets out the curriculum content under the headings of *knowledge, skills and understanding* and *breadth of study*. In the case of the core curriculum subjects (English, mathematics and science) this content is further divided into discrete sub-sections.

Eg *Programme of Study (PoS) for science*

- Sc1 Scientific enquiry
- Sc2 Life processes and living things
- Sc3 Materials and their properties
- Sc4 Physical processes.

(QCA, 1999, pp. 78–82)

Each subject in the National Curriculum also has a set of Attainment Targets (ATs), broken down into level descriptions, intended to help teachers make judgements about children's learning and achievements. Attainment Targets are designed to assist teachers in assessment, and teachers are required to use a *best fit* approach when deciding the level that most closely corresponds to a child's abilities.

Eg *Programme of Study (PoS) for Music at Key Stage 1*

- **Knowledge, skills and understanding**
  - Controlling sounds through singing and playing – performing skills (1a–1c)
  - Creating and developing musical ideas – composing skills (2a–2b)
  - Responding and reviewing – appraising skills (3a–3b)
  - Listening, and applying knowledge and understanding (4a-4d)
- **Breadth of study** – Pupils should be taught the knowledge, skills and understanding through
  - a range of musical activities that integrate performing, composing and appraising (5a);

– responding to a range of musical and non-musical starting points (5b);
– working on their own, in groups of different sizes and as a class (5c);
– a range of live and recorded music from different times and cultures (5d).

(QCA, 1999, pp. 124–5)

To be considered at Level 1 for attainment in music, children have to show that they can
- recognize and explore how sounds can be made and changed;
- use their voices in different ways;
- repeat short rhythmic and melodic patterns;
- create and choose sounds in response to given starting points;
- respond to different moods in music;
- recognize well-defined changes in sounds;
- identify simple repeated patterns;
- take account of musical instructions.

(QCA, 1999, p. 35)

Since its inception in 1989 the National Curriculum for Key Stages 1 and 2 has been subject to numerous refinements and modifications, for example the introduction in 1995 (DFE) and then again in 1999 (QCA) of revised documentation with more compact PoS to make it more manageable. In addition, ICT first appeared in the National Curriculum distributed among the various other subjects and was particularly prominent in the PoS for design and technology. During the 1995 revisions it was brought together into what amounted to a *de facto* additional subject in the documentation, with its own PoS and ATs, while still retaining a high degree of relevance for most of the other subjects. However, apart from the changes to ICT the subjects themselves have remained constant throughout the various revisions.

The introduction of the National Curriculum carried with it an inherent tension between the desire to offer pupils a broad and balanced curriculum and the desire to raise standards, particularly in subjects like English and mathematics. This tension has been further exacerbated by developments such as the introduction of targets for SATs results and of literacy and numeracy hours for pupils in Key Stages 1 and 2. The consequences of this initial tension (and subsequent developments) have included pressure on the amount of time available for delivering the non-core foundation subjects necessary for a broad and balanced curriculum. Materials published by the Qualifications and Curriculum Authority (QCA, 1998b) constituted a recognition of this pressure and were an attempt to retain the commitment to breadth and balance by developing more flexible approaches to the teaching of subjects other than English and mathematics.

The Cross-Curricular Elements

The cross-curricular elements were originally envisaged as important areas of learning with relevance across the National Curriculum as a whole, and addressed the broader development of children, key skills and metacognitive skills (learning how to learn). They were not restricted to any one subject area; their purpose was to pull together the broad education of the individual and augment the basic curriculum as set out in the core and foundation subjects (National Curriculum Council, 1990). These elements included cross-curricular themes, skills and dimensions.

Eg

Range of cross-curricular elements

Cross-curricular themes offered opportunities for discussion of values and beliefs as well as adding to children's knowledge and understanding. They included
• economic and industrial understanding;
• careers education and guidance;
• health education;
• education for citizenship; and
• environmental education.

Cross-curricular skills comprised those skills that were relevant (in varying degrees) to all subjects but which were not the preserve of any one subject. They included
• study skills;
• problem-solving skills;
• communication skills;
• numeracy skills;
• ICT skills; and
• personal and social skills.

Cross-curricular dimensions were closely associated with the principles of entitlement arising from the 1988 Education Reform Act. They concerned the ethos and philosophy of education and were designed to promote equality and fairness. The cross-curricular dimensions included
• preparation for life in a multicultural society;
• access (to the curriculum) for children with different learning abilities; and
• equality of opportunity for all.

(National Curriculum Council, 1990)

Since their appearance in National Curriculum Council (NCC) documentation (1990) some of these cross-curricular elements have assumed increasing prominence in education. Information and communications technology has evolved into a National Curriculum subject in its own right. Personal, social and health education and citizenship have a non-statutory PoS attached to them within the revised National Curriculum (QCA, 1999, pp. 136–41), while literacy and numeracy hours now dominate the activities of many, if not most, primary classrooms for nearly half of every day. Other aspects of the cross-curricular elements have, however, retained a status that is lower profile, with, in some cases, little attention being paid to them. Teachers, perhaps understandably, prioritize those areas such as statutory subjects (e.g. English and mathematics) where public accountability is greatest.

Eg *Learning across the National Curriculum in the revised documentation*

- Promoting spiritual, moral, social and cultural development
- Promoting PSHE and citizenship
- Promoting key skills across the National Curriculum
  - Communication
  - Application of number
  - Information technology
  - Working with others
  - Improving own learning and performance
  - Problem-solving
- Thinking skills
  - Information processing skills
  - Reasoning skills
  - Enquiry skills
  - Creative thinking skills
  - Evaluation skills
- Financial capability
- Enterprise education
- Education for sustainable development

(QCA, 1999, pp. 19–23)

Transition to, within and between 3–8 Settings and Curricula

Transition to, within and between nurseries and schools can be a very stressful time for both children and their parents. Frequently, the transition involves a change of culture, personnel and location and where children are moving between nursery and reception and between reception and Key Stage 1, transition can also mean a change of curriculum as children move from the Early Learning Goals to National Curriculum PoS, plus the National Literacy and Numeracy Strategies.

There are a number of significant transition events for pupils between the ages of 3 and 8, as well as the lesser ones that occur at the start of every year when many children move to new classes in the same school.

Transition events
- from home to nursery/reception;
- from nursery to reception;
- from reception to Key Stage 1;

- from Key Stage 1 to Key Stage 2; and
- from one class/teacher to another class/teacher.

Children's ability to make a successful transition from home to nursery, or from nursery to school (becoming happy and successful learners in the process) can have a profound impact on their future development and attainment. Any transition has the potential to make young children feel insecure and nervous. For many 3–5-year-old children, for example, attending nursery or reception for the first time can be a particularly stressful experience; for some, it will be their first experience away from their home. Parents are often referred to in school documentation as key players in supporting the children during these periods. It is worth remembering that parents, too, may be experiencing feelings of anxiety and teachers can play a part in reducing this. Parents may well seek out teachers to air their concerns or ask for information or advice. Teachers can facilitate the process of building partnerships by recognizing, taking seriously and addressing parental concerns.

Nursery and school transition policies seek to offer advice to staff on ways of easing the concerns and anxieties that families may have about transition. The priority for all teachers, whatever the transition, is to help children to become secure and confident in their new environment as soon as possible, and to establish positive and productive relationships with both pupils and parents.

Helping children and parents to cope with transition events

- Provide written information for parents on the curriculum that their children will encounter in the new class. Talk to parents before and during the transition period. If parents are reassured they can communicate that reassurance to their children. They can also offer valuable information that you can use to help make children feel more secure.
- Talk to the children's current teacher prior to receiving a new group. He/She can offer good advice on likes and dislikes, learning dispositions, curriculum strengths and weaknesses, and can also help you to identify those children most likely to be adversely affected by the changes taking place.
- Try to visit your new class in their present setting. What sort of learning environment are they used to? What sort of conventions and routines are they used to? Can you use similar conventions and routines to minimize their sense of disruption?
- Offer to swap places with your new class's current teacher, so that the children can get used to seeing you as their teacher.
- Help your pupils who are moving on to their next class to produce mini-portfolios of work that they can give to their new teacher.
- Make sure you speak positively about the new setting or class that your children will be attending. Do not reinforce or magnify their concerns and worries.
- Where children are moving schools rather than classes, involve older children in the induction process (e.g. provide 'buddies' in the playground).

Special Educational Needs (SEN) and the Code of Practice

By the end of this section you should

- be familiar with some of the characteristics displayed by children who have special educational needs (SEN);
- be familiar with the teacher's responsibilities under the Code of Practice on the identification and assessment of special educational needs;

The Range of Special Educational Needs (SEN)

As the National Curriculum has pupil entitlement enshrined within it, teachers are expected to respond positively to the SEN that many children have during their time in 3–8 settings. These SEN may be physical, cognitive and/or emotional/behavioural in nature and they include pupils who are gifted and talented as well as pupils whose learning is hindered by physical disabilities and/or learning difficulties.

Special educational needs (SEN) in 3–8 settings

Physical disabilities
- hearing impairment
- visual impairment
- arthritis
- asthma
- diabetes
- epilepsy
- cerebral palsy
- cystic fibrosis
- spina bifida
- muscular dystrophy

Learning difficulties
- autism
- aphasia
- dyslexia
- dyspraxia
- emotional and behavioural difficulties (EBD)
- Attention-Deficit (Hyperactivity) Disorder (AD(H)D)

Gifted and talented pupils

There are numerous **physical disabilities** that teachers may encounter in nursery and primary schools. In some cases the condition itself can hamper children's efforts to engage with the curriculum on offer, for example a child with a visual impairment or a child with cerebral palsy. In other cases it is the consequences of the condition such as hospitalization and absences from nursery/school that may impede children's educational progress.

Some children experience **learning difficulties** that can range from mild to severe and from specific to complex. In some cases these learning difficulties are cognitive in nature and often result in problems with core elements in the curriculum, such as English and mathematics. Children who are experiencing learning difficulties of this sort may

- find it hard to understand the language used;
- have a limited concentration span and engage in time-wasting or work avoidance;
- experience problems in transferring and applying knowledge and skills;
- exhibit poor general knowledge;
- find following instructions difficult; or
- display a lack of care and attention when working.

In other cases, however, learning difficulties are actually rooted in problems located elsewhere, such as in children's social and emotional development. SEN in one area can be intimately connected to SEN in another area. Language acquisition, for example, is both a precursor and co-requisite for learning in most, if not all, areas of the curriculum, and an inability, therefore, to make oneself understood is likely to result in considerable frustration and could lead to aberrant behaviour such as withdrawal or aggression.

Some children with SEN are described as **gifted and talented**. Exact definitions of what constitutes *giftedness* or *talentedness* are hard to produce. There is considerable debate over the concept of giftedness and singling out children as gifted has been seen by some as potentially damaging (e.g. raising of expectations that put undue pressure on a child). The arguments can be further complicated by the suggestion that singling out pupils as gifted is an elitist approach to education. However, if there are children in mainstream education who are very able then ensuring that their needs are met ought to be seen as an equal opportunities issue rather than elitism (Ofsted/DFE, 1994).

All teachers encounter pupils who are bright, but terms such as gifted and talented suggest abilities that exceed those of even their very able peers. It is important to be aware of the wider curriculum when considering gifted and talented pupils: a child might be an average reader but an outstanding artist or technologist; they might be quick thinking and creative but have writing skills that are less well developed. Children who are considered gifted and talented are likely to be capable of pursuing their learning in greater depth and at a faster pace than their peers. Children who are thought to be gifted and talented may

- display a good memory for facts, people or events;
- possess good powers of observation;

- like to know how things work or happen;
- be able to follow relatively complex instructions;
- have a wide vocabulary which they use accurately;
- possess good physical coordination and control;
- have a high level of visual and spatial awareness;
- display a high degree of independence, self-sufficiency and initiative;
- be ambitious, setting themselves high goals; or
- display good social skills with older children and adults, and have a well-developed sense of humour, yet they may experience difficulties with their peers.

(Ofsted/DfE, 1994)

Gifted and talented pupils can easily become bored and disruptive, can dominate their more average peers and can be intolerant. They may be sensitive to criticism and rejection, troubled by their difference and may even be tempted to underachieve to conform. Gifted and talented children may also frighten or annoy their teachers. The speed and pace at which these children often work, as well as the high levels of thought, autonomy and independence of which they are capable, can make great demands on already overloaded professionals.

Irrespective of the SEN in question, all teachers need to be aware of the procedures laid down in the Code of Practice for Special Educational Needs (DfES, 2001b).

Following the Code of Practice for Special Educational Needs (SEN)

Wherever SEN are thought to exist, teachers of 3–8 pupils need to be familiar with the Code of Practice for addressing these needs (DfES, 2001b). Special educational needs may be identified when a child starts school/nursery and concern over a child's progress can be registered at this point by teachers, parents, other carers or external agencies. Concerns may also arise at any time during the nursery/school years. Whenever there appears to be cause for concern, the nursery/school SEN coordinator (SENCO) needs to be involved, as do the parents/carers.

The class teacher will take the lead in gathering information and evidence and completing an **initial cause for concern** sheet. Depending on the nature of the cause for concern, teaching staff may also need to seek information from others. For example, when a teacher suspects that a child has behavioural problems, he/she may need to establish a more accurate picture by talking to parents, carers or lunchtime supervisors.

Following the initial cause for concern, teachers are required to monitor the child over a period of time and maintain a record of progress at intervals. Notes and observations need to be carefully collated and dated since they will be shared with and communicated to parents, carers, the SENCO and possibly external agencies.

If, after a term's monitoring, the child seems not to have made any progress, the school must set up an **individual education plan** (IEP) which must be reviewed at least twice a year and preferably termly. The IEP will describe the nature of the child's difficulties and will outline the action(s) to be taken. In some cases the action will involve special provision and may include learning support either from outside agencies or from SEN staff employed by the nursery/school. For the majority of children, early identification and appropriate intervention leads to them overcoming their difficulties.

If the IEP does not result in progress formal assistance can be sought from external support services (Roffey, 2001) which may result in a revised IEP for the child containing new targets and fresh strategies for supporting the child's progress. Having involved the external agencies it may become apparent that the existing provision available to the child is inappropriate or insufficient to help him/her overcome the difficulties in which case the decision is made to request a statutory assessment of the child's needs from the Local Education Authority (LEA) which will result in a formal Statement of Special Educational Needs. At this point the LEA takes responsibility for overseeing and managing the task of addressing the child's needs, albeit still in consultation and collaboration with parents/carers and the school. The issuing of a Statement of Special Educational Needs carries with it the mandatory requirement to conduct an annual review. Children on the special needs register are entitled by law to even greater levels of special provision. For example, children with severe physical and learning difficulties will have support workers who accompany them throughout the school day. Chapter 3 contains further information on the adaptation of teaching and learning to promote the inclusion of pupils with SEN.

Eg Working with the Code of Practice

John, a Year 1 pupil, was deemed to have moderate learning difficulties under the Code of Practice. It was suspected that he was struggling with an attention deficiency disorder: he was easily distracted during lessons, and his poor concentration and attention resulted in him wandering off-task and interfering with other children which often resulted in squabbles. He also had unrealistic expectations of his abilities, leading to frustration and a tendency to give up quickly. His teacher, therefore, tried to plan work for John that was short and focused. In addition, she made sure that John understood the purposes of the sessions and the likely outcomes, and also made sure that he received plenty of praise and recognition for his efforts. During literacy hour sessions, John would work with a special needs support teacher who provided short focused tasks on phonics and reading. John was encouraged to reflect and comment on his own learning and progress as a way of raising his self-esteem and modifying his behaviour by promoting his ability to persevere.

Children as Learners

By the end of this section you should

- have developed some understanding of how pupils' learning is affected by their intellectual, emotional and social development;
- understand the importance of first-hand experience, high-quality adult intervention, cooperation, play and talk in young children's learning.

Various schools of thought have emerged which attempt to understand and explain children's development, and this section deals with the work of psychologists and researchers such as Piaget, Athey, Bruner, Vygotsky and Isaacs. The work of these constructivists/interactionists and social interactionists (Bruce, 1997) has had a significant impact upon current practice in 3–8 settings and is characterized by the idea that children learn best when they are interacting with their environment, with their peers and with adults, and are thus *constructing meaning* in the process.

Jean Piaget and Constructivist Theories of Learning

The Swiss psychologist Jean Piaget made a major and ground-breaking contribution to our understanding of how children think and learn. Through his research he hoped to understand and explain how young children come to make sense of the world around them and to develop ways of operating effectively in it. A key element in Piaget's theories was the idea that children are not passive learners soaking up the wisdom of adults. Instead, for Piaget, children were actively constructing meaning and ideas about how the world works as a result of interacting with it.

Piaget used the concepts of assimilation, disequilibrium and accommodation to explain the process of learning. A child would *assimilate* knowledge as a result of first-hand experience. Subsequent experience would force the child to re-evaluate his/her original ideas in the light of new situations and observations in order to *accommodate* to the new reality. The lack of equilibrium or *disequilibrium* caused by encountering a situation which did not conform to the child's old model (*schema*) of the world was resolved as the child incorporated the new knowledge and experience into his/her existing mental models, thus improving and enhancing them.

For Piaget, progression in intellectual development was the result of the loss, and subsequent restoration at a new higher level, of *equilibrium*. In Piaget's model, the older and more mature the children, the more adept they would be at taking into account increasing quantities of information and exploring increasingly complex strategies to help them solve problems and operate effectively in their environment.

As a result of his observations and experiments Piaget postulated a series of developmental stages which children went through in a regular and ordered sequence. In each of these stages children were refining their thinking in the light of experience. The sequence was invariable; children could not bypass stages or make short cuts to reach more advanced stages. Nor was progression from one stage to the next envisaged by Piaget as a revolutionary, overnight affair, but was instead an evolutionary and more gradual process. He included guidance on the ages at which children go through these stages although he acknowledged that these were only an approximation and believed that while children were travelling the same route they were not necessarily progressing at the same speed. Finally, although the idea did not originate with Piaget, a controversial element in his theories was the notion of readiness. If a child found a problem too difficult then this constituted evidence that the child was not yet ready to learn. In other words, the child's mental schema had not yet reached a level where restructuring was possible.

Piaget's stages

1. **Sensorimotor**. Children are getting to know the world through the physical actions that they can perform (age 0–2 years).
2. **Pre-operational**. Children have not yet acquired fully logical thinking (age 2–7 years).
3. **Concrete operational**. Children can think logically about problems that are concrete, i.e. here and now (age 7–12 years).
4. **Formal operational**. Children are able to think rationally about abstract or hypothetical problems (age 12 onwards).

Chris Athey and schema

Piaget's work on schema has since been refined and expanded upon by researchers such as Chris Athey and Cathy Nutbrown. Athey (1990) and others have observed that as children make sense of the world through interacting with it, some of them appear to exhibit patterns of repeatable behaviour. Through her research Athey was able to identify a number of different schema and suggested four ways in which schema might manifest themselves:

1. through motor actions (i.e. physical movement);
2. through symbolic functioning (i.e. representing something through drawings or letters);
3. through functional dependency relationships (i.e. 'I've done x so that y can happen');
4. through thought.

Athey's, and subsequent, research has suggested that not all children show evidence of exploring schema, and that those who do, do not necessarily follow a set pattern. Furthermore, some children may explore more than one schema at a time. That said, Athey's work on the concept of schema is very useful in understanding how some young children learn, and can help to make sense of nursery/classroom observations of young children's actions.

- A young child is observed running in circles during outdoor play.
- During painting activities the same child likes to paint circles regularly.
- She appears fascinated by artefacts and objects that are circular in shape.
- This child may be showing evidence of a schema. She appears to be establishing connections in relation to circles.

Her teacher takes her on a circle walk around the classroom, provides different shapes to be sorted into categories such as *circles* and *not circles*, talks about properties of circles and looks at books containing circles with the child.

Jerome Bruner, Lev Vygotsky and social-interactionist theories of learning

Like Piaget, Athey and others, Jerome Bruner made an important contribution to understanding cognitive development in children. By using Piaget's ideas and linking these to his own theories Bruner, too, developed a stage model. He was particularly interested in the part played by experience in cognitive development, concluding that careful instruction (guiding a child to new ways of coping with a new problem) could aid the process of maturation (Keenan, 2002).

Bruner's stages

1. **Enactive stage**: understanding through first-hand experience;
2. **Iconic stage**: understanding through images;
3. **Symbolic stage**: children are able to express ideas through words and numbers and have acquired the concept of conservation.

Bruner's research suggested that children were capable of intellectual achievements at an earlier point than that predicted by Piaget as a result of instruction and carefully structured environments. This challenged the idea of readiness. For Bruner, passively waiting for children to become ready to learn may necessitate a very long delay indeed. As a result, the concept of readiness could actually lead to a lowering of educational standards and teacher expectations. While teachers of young children do need to be sensitive to a child's needs, abilities and development, they also need to be prepared to intervene through questioning, guiding and instructing in an effort to extend and challenge thinking. Bruner suggested that there was a social dimension to cognitive development, whereby a child's learning is also influenced and affected by those experiences involving interaction with both children and adults. In Bruner's model, communication and language played a crucial role in learning and cognitive development. Facilitating pupils' progress through the use of appropriate support materials and intervention would provide children with *scaffolding* upon which they could construct increasingly advanced ways of thinking and understanding the world. Bruner also advocated a spiral curriculum for children in which they would revisit topics at regular intervals thus advancing their learning towards higher levels of understanding.

Eg   *A spiral curriculum*
_____

Knowledge and understanding of the world/History

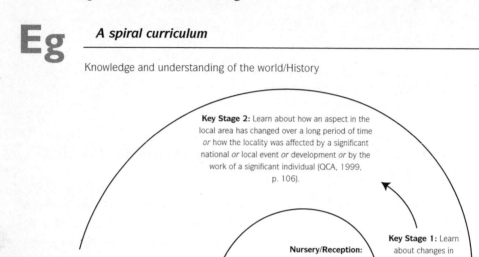

Key Stage 2: Learn about how an aspect in the local area has changed over a long period of time *or* how the locality was affected by a significant national *or* local event *or* development *or* by the work of a significant individual (QCA, 1999, p. 106).

Nursery/Reception: Show an interest in the lives of people familiar to them. Begin to differentiate between past and present (QCA, 2000, p. 94).

Key Stage 1: Learn about changes in their own lives and the way of life of their family or others around them (QCA, 1999, p. 104).

Vygotsky, too, recognized communication and language as centrally important to children's cognitive development (Keenan, 2002; Wood, 1998). In addition, for those taking a Vygotskian perspective, readiness is not simply a question of a child's existing knowledge or schema; it is also influenced by a child's capacity to learn. Like Bruner, Vygotsky also advocated the use of scaffolding to advance children's learning and developed the notion of a *zone of proximal development* (ZPD) to explain his ideas:

Eg   *Vygotsky's concept of ZPD*
_____

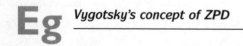

what someone (a child) can do unaided

zone of proximal development

what someone (a child) can achieve with help from someone more skilful/knowledgeable

Susan Isaacs and the Affective Dimension of Childhood

Any explanatory model of childhood needs to make reference to the whole child. Many researchers have pointed out that children are *made up of far more than cognitive capacities* (Zigler in Hyson, 1994, p. ix). Just as there is a relationship between thought and action, so, too, is there a reciprocal relationship between thought and feeling (Bonnett, 1994). Susan Isaacs' work at the Malting House School from 1924 onwards was important in carrying forwards the theoretical basis of early years education. Isaacs' scientifically based inclusion of an affective dimension to the nature of childhood helped to ensure that young children were seen as more than just cognitive beings. Isaacs' work provided a rational theoretical underpinning for the importance of Personal, social and emotional development and the need for children to exercise responsibility and choice in order to develop independence, autonomy and self-control.

This important idea that children are not simply cognitive beings but are also emotional and social beings, and that furthermore there is a connection between growth and development in the first area and growth and development in the second area (Isaacs, 1951), is significant. Anyone involved in teaching young children ought not to underestimate the power of emotions (some subconscious) to motivate behaviour and learning. Memory and learning, for example, may well be enhanced in settings that heighten interest and happiness, enabling greater tolerance of frustration, and promoting perseverance. Bruce's ten principles (1997) and the principles contained within the Curriculum Guidance for the Foundation Stage (QCA, 2000, pp. 6–25) acknowledge the emotional–cognitive link and the positive emotional bases of children's self-initiated learning such as

- satisfied curiosity;
- pleasure in finding out;
- the intrinsic reward of mastery;
- identification with adults and teachers; and
- the impact of adult praise, recognition, confidence and trust.

(Hyson, 1994)

Play as a Vehicle for Learning

For Bruner, play was a phenomenon that everyone could recognize but none could define (*frame*) (in Abbott and Rodger, 1994). Building in opportunities for play is an essential feature of teaching and learning in 3–8 settings. Young children learn well in situations that include an element of doing, and their teachers pay particular attention to the need to offer hands-on experiences including those involving play. As Edwards and Knight commented (1994), it is possible to take the play out of learning (if one must), but impossible to take the learning out of play. Play offers children the chance to learn in contexts in which they are highly receptive. It is much more than simply a recreational time-filler; it is a valuable approach to learning. Through play children

- experience making choices and taking charge of their own learning;
- can test out their ideas and reinforce their learning;
- can act out and come to terms with their feelings;
- can encounter new ideas;
- learn in a very physical way using all their senses;
- can engage in extended exploration; and
- can draw together all of the above to make sense of the world (Bruce, 1997).

While nurseries and many reception classes offer a wide range of play activities for pupils, the choice often narrows as children move through the infant school and into Year 3, frequently becoming restricted to occasional work with construction kits and computer simulations. In addition, an increasingly large distinction is sometimes drawn between playing and working as children get older. Not only does the range of play activities become narrower, but some teachers seem much less willing to allocate time to play. Rather than being seen as an approach to learning, play sometimes appears to be regarded as a luxury that actually takes time away from that pursuit. Although this is not surprising given the emphasis on literacy and numeracy, meeting government-set targets for Standard Attainment Tests (SATs) results and ever-increasing levels of teacher accountability at Key Stages 1 and 2, it is still a great shame as play offers a wide range of potential learning opportunities.

Bruner suggested that play could be either *exploratory* and/or *social* in nature, while Vygotsky felt that *pretend* and *role-play* was particularly valuable in developmental terms. The Curriculum Guidance for the Foundation Stage, meanwhile, refers to the need for children to experience both *structured play* and *free play*. Play can, therefore, be categorized in a number of ways (Macintyre, 2001) and it would be a mistake to think that the boundaries between the different categories are anything other than permeable. Spontaneous child-directed scenarios can emerge from settings that are ostensibly teacher-directed in nature. Similarly, scenarios designed to foster social or imaginative play can also provide opportunities for exploratory play at the same time; for example, some role-play areas incorporate mark-making materials, tools and equipment.

Structured play describes situations that have been planned and initiated by the teacher; these might include role- and pretend play, social or exploratory play opportunities. Games and puzzles can also be used by teachers to structure children's learning by providing pupils with interesting situations in which they can hone their problem-solving skills, cooperate with others, and learn to compete in non-aggressive ways. Increasingly, many games and simulations are available using ICT. Although some schools and nurseries remain to be convinced of the educational worth of such games, it is possible that they may offer children the chance to practise physical skills such as hand–eye coordination; to develop their intellectual potential, demanding memory and planning; and promote social and emotional development by encouraging children to share, take turns, cooperate, negotiate and make decisions for themselves.

In contrast, **free play** is a term used to describe spontaneous play initiated by the children in which they have the chance to interact with their peers in activities that they themselves have devised and through which they can express themselves and explore things that are of special interest to them. Such play can be a powerful method of arousing and sustaining children's curiosity and motivation.

Exploratory play describes children experimenting, often purposefully, with tools, equipment and materials. This could involve sand or water play, using tricycles in the outdoor area, making dens, junk modelling, mark-marking, painting, using ICT or building with construction kits. Exploratory play provides opportunities for children to be creative, to hone their physical skills and to investigate the world around them.

Social play offers children opportunities to learn about and practise the rules, rituals and norms of a society. Truly social play is rare before the age of three with many pre-nursery children still engaging in *parallel* or *associative* rather than *cooperative* play (Parten in Keenan, 2002). Even after the age of three practitioners may still observe children who while in a social context are still operating in non-social ways by engaging in solitary play or by observing the play of others.

- **Associative play**. Children talk to one another and share materials but do not take on different roles within the same imaginary context or work towards completing a joint project. Most common form among 4-year-olds.
- **Parallel play**. A child plays *beside*, rather than *with*, other children. He/She may be using the same toys and materials but children are not interacting. Most common form among 2-year-olds.
- **Onlooker behaviour**. A child watches other children, but does not join in.
- **Unoccupied play**. A child is present alongside other children but does not play with anything and instead watches whatever interests him/her.
- **Solitary play**. A child plays by himself/herself in a way that is different from those around him/her.

(Parten in Keenan, 2002)

Pretend play, **role-play** and **imaginary play** are very effective in providing young children with opportunities to express their feelings verbally as well as practising and reinforcing social skills (Abbott, 1994). Pretend play introduces rules and opportunities to explore feelings and to learn about the social norms expected of people; for example, the 'baby' has to act the part and behave like a baby (Keenan, 2002). Pretend play can encourage children to play at a level beyond their stage in life, for example being a parent, a fire fighter or a doctor. Pretend play also stimulates children's creativity and imagination, for example where the climbing frame becomes

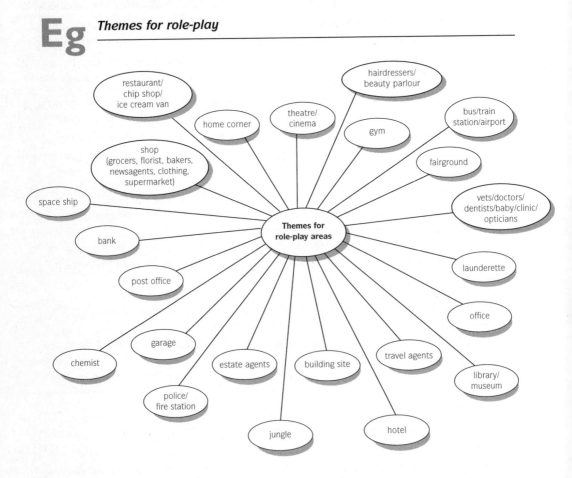

a castle, and can involve small-world play materials using puppets, miniature figures, model animals, houses, farms and cars.

Role- and pretend play scenarios can start from recreating the children's own experiences (e.g. shopping, going to the vets or visiting a café), but setting up role-play areas in the nursery/classroom also offers teachers and pupils the chance to create, and be part of, new and imaginary scenarios (a jungle camp or a fairy story such as 'The Three Bears'). Such play enables young children to practise and learn new or unfamiliar ways of using language, and to come to terms with real-life situations that they might find worrying (for example, going to the dentist). Where the role-play area is connected to themes or topics that are ongoing in the nursery/classroom, opportunities are also created for children to practise and reinforce learning across the curriculum.

Eg *Themes for role-play*

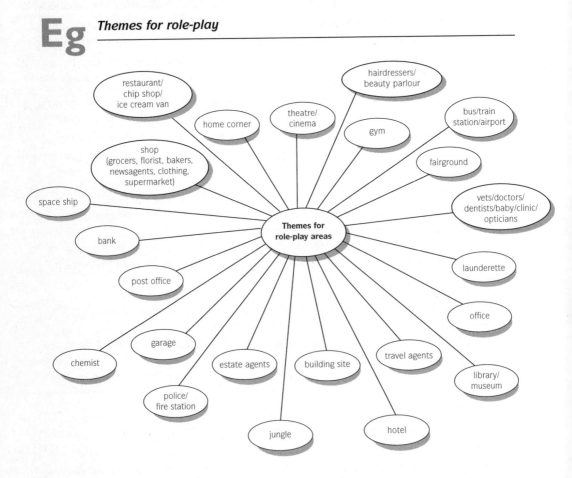

80

- Take play seriously as a vehicle for learning. Plan for it and set out clear educational objectives.
- Utilize outdoor as well as indoor spaces, where possible offering open rather than restricted access to the former.
- Stimulate children's imagination through the experiences offered. For example, enhance the quality of play by ensuring that the role-play area contains plenty of interesting and exciting equipment and materials. Similarly, use trips and visits to real locations (e.g. shops and cafés) to provide children with ideas about ways of behaving and likely events in a given context.
- Provide space, resources and time for pretend play. Where appropriate, real-life artefacts may be better than pretend ones for promoting responsible behaviour. Common artefacts for role-play include tables, chairs, beds, a range of clothing (male, female, multicultural), accessories (purses/wallets, jewellery, hats) and kitchen artefacts (cooker, sink, washing machine).
- Build learning opportunities from across the curriculum into the play activities taking place. For example, water play can provide an excellent context within which to extend children's Mathematical development, or their Knowledge and understanding of the world.
- Be ready to become active participants in children's play from time to time (scaffolding). While it is important not to let involvement become interference, teachers may well have to get drawn into play situations if they wish their learning objectives to be realized. For example, providing access to adults can present children with models of how to use language appropriately, how to listen and how to respond.
- Offer opportunities for children to extend and improve their oral language skills through working in pairs and groups and by providing a wide range of shared experiences.
- Think aloud with pupils, providing opportunities for reasoning, investigating and solving simple problems verbally.
- Encourage children to question and share their ideas.
- Use bilingual teachers and support staff to facilitate the play and talk of pupils with English as an additional language (EAL) or with SEN.
- Use activities rooted in the wider curriculum, such as art and music to develop children's communication and literacy skills.

The work of constructivists like Piaget, social interactionists such as Bruner and Vygotsky, and other researchers such as Athey and Isaacs can be seen informing current practice in 3–8 settings. Development is viewed as largely sequential with things happening in a certain order that is more or less the same for all children, although the rate of development varies widely. These differing rates of development are the product of a range of factors (e.g. biological/genetic, environmental, social and cultural) that can either enhance or inhibit a child's development. Young children are perceived as active learners who benefit from opportunities to play and relevant first-hand experiences in secure and caring environments. Schools and nurseries assist pupils in making sense of the world by exploring objects, materials and feelings in meaningful situations. Children's natural curiosity is harnessed as they are encouraged to ask why and how things are as they are by practitioners capable of scaffolding children's learning. The rest of the chapter uses the areas of learning set out in the Curriculum Guidance for the Foundation Stage (QCA, 2000) to provide an overall structure into which comments on the subjects in the National Curriculum for Key Stages 1 and 2 have been integrated. Although it has no corresponding heading in the Early Learning Goals, the final section on ICT reflects its increasing importance across the 3–8 age range.

Personal, Social and Emotional Development

A U D I T

By the end of this section you should

- know about the teaching of Personal, social and emotional development in the Curriculum Guidance for the Foundation Stage (QCA, 2000, pp. 28–43);
- know about the teaching of personal, social and health education (PSHE) and citizenship in the primary curriculum (QCA, 1999, pp. 19–23, 136–41);
- know about the teaching of RE in the primary curriculum.

This section deals with personal, social and emotional education for 3–8 pupils. It also includes reference to RE, PSHE and citizenship for infant pupils as these are three areas in which the over-fives can be encouraged to increase their skills and sensitivity at this stage of their development. A child's Personal, social and emotional development will affect the way he/she relates to peers and adults. Nurseries and schools seek to help young children develop their understanding of social and personal values, as actively promoting children's Personal, social and emotional development benefits teachers in 3–8 settings by encouraging good behaviour and achievement on the part of the pupils. At the same time, this provides children with strategies for reconciling social and emotional conflicts and offers opportunities for them to establish good interpersonal relationships. These experiences will be of use to them during their continuing education and later as adults.

Eg *The range of development*

- **Social development**. The ability to interact positively with peers, practitioners and others.
- **Moral development**. An increasing awareness of right and wrong and why things are right or wrong.
- **Emotional development**. The ability to control impulses and express feelings in increasingly mature and responsible ways. The ability to understand why one feels a particular emotion coupled with awareness and understanding of the feelings of others.
- **Personal development**. The growth of self-esteem and the acquisition of a set of positive qualities and dispositions including determination, industriousness, creativity, enthusiasm, independence and patience.

Teachers of young children are often building on the work of the family, starting from and continuing the good work done by most parents and carers, and ameliorating the worst effects of the minority (DES, 1992). While most children can begin to develop self-confidence and an understanding of right and wrong through the support of their families, for some, their development in this area is impeded by stressful home circumstances which militate against success. Children whose self-image is poor, for example, may find working successfully as part of a group difficult. Children's home experiences prior to starting nursery/school can have a significant impact on their social and emotional development. In some cases there will have been a failure to meet the child's basic need for affection and security. In other instances conflict in the home can lead to frustration, tension, anger and anxiety in the child. In the case of parental separation, for example, children can not only grieve, but will sometimes experience guilt. Other children will find it difficult to express their emotions or to understand the feelings of others having experienced abusive behaviour on the part of adults. Faced with such experiences practitioners need to be consistent and reliable, for example doing what you said you would do, when you said you would do it within a time-frame meaningful to young children. Practitioners can also model positive emotional management by staying calm and being willing to talk about their own feelings and the feelings of others.

Eg

Modelling behaviour

Adults can model desired behaviours by
- playing/working cooperatively;
- sharing and taking turns;
- dealing positively with conflicts that arise;
- caring about others;
- making decisions and forming opinions; and
- demonstrating independence, confidence and self-reliance.

By the time children reach the Foundation Stage and beyond, most will be able to cope with more than one regular carer provided there is at least some consistency, predictability and regularity. Having a special relationship with one adult can be an important source of security and stability for children and can greatly aid teachers' attempts to promote children's Personal, social and emotional development. In reception and Key Stage 1 settings stability and continuity are provided in part by the class teacher system. Many nurseries, meanwhile, operate a key worker system whereby all practitioners (teaching and non-teaching) have responsibility for certain children, although the teacher retains overall responsibility for the children's well-being and education. Such systems also support teachers' efforts to monitor and assess children's continuing development over time and so help them to respond appropriately to the needs of the children in this and other areas of learning.

Although established patterns of behaviour with others will be in evidence when children start nursery/reception the teacher plays a big part in influencing the continuing development of a child. Practitioners who show children that they are accepted and respected are more likely to promote self-esteem. For a child to learn and develop positively and to their full potential they need to feel secure, cared about, valued and successful. Self-esteem is an important contributory factor in children's social and emotional development which in turn underpins their progress elsewhere in the curriculum. Children with low self-esteem and impaired social or emotional development may struggle in their relationships with others, may be less willing to try new things as a result of a fear of failure, may find it much harder to pay attention, becoming easily disheartened, and can find praise and recognition hard to accept, having become convinced that they are *rubbish* at certain tasks. Children with greater self-esteem are more likely to

- attempt to acquire new skills;
- experiment/try things out/be prepared to make mistakes;
- take criticism without feeling emotionally crushed;
- feel good about joining in with others;
- cope with losing/not always getting their own way;
- be enthusiastic and willing to persevere if at first things do not go as they would like.

Practitioners need to let the children know that they like and respect them by listening to them; by offering opportunities for them to exercise choice and decision-making skills; by offering opportunities for success, mastery and achievement; and by offering praise and recognition. Even occasional disapproval of children's actions does not detract from this acceptance and valuing of them as individuals. Practitioners also need to be willing to mediate between children to ensure that discriminatory or anti-social behaviour or comments on the part of peers do not undermine their sense of worth.

Eg *Monitoring young children's Personal, social and emotional development*

Nursery	Reception
Will approach/participate in some activities and move around without adult intervention	Will participate and persevere in activities of their choice for 5–10 minutes
Are becoming aware of routines and session organization	Are becoming aware of school routines and organization as regards each session and each day
Are able to locate own coat and some equipment with help	Are able to locate equipment necessary for a specific task
Can follow simple instructions with guidance	Can follow simple instructions
Will confidently pursue activities they enjoy at the start of the session	Settle in the classroom confidently each morning with minimum staff support

Play confidently in all areas	Have a positive self-image
Are naturally curious about the learning environment	Are developing natural curiosity and questioning skills
Can concentrate on teacher-directed activity with adult support for five minutes	Can concentrate for ten minutes with small amounts of adult support
Are able to listen and respond in specific situations, e.g. action songs	Can listen and respond appropriately to questions in a group
Are beginning to share and take turns and have an awareness of others	Show simple cooperative play
Are easily motivated and show interest in nursery activities	Are well motivated and interested
Are beginning to make links between activities and their own experiences	Are beginning to make links and will find something seen or discussed on their own
Pay attention and are able to focus in a 1 : 1 situation	Pay attention and are able to focus with support or in a small group

Promoting pupils' Personal, social and emotional development

Aims	Strategies
1. Help children to develop an understanding of their position and role within their family context.	1. Encourage children to develop an awareness of their position in the family: • Name family members. • Describe family roles and responsibilities. • Seek information and clarification about family members. • Develop family trees/maps. • Talk to them about family events/activities.
2. Help children to become increasingly aware that they are part of a larger community.	2. Help children to learn about their local community: • Elicit children's knowledge and understanding of where they live. • Ask children to identify and describe features of their neighbourhood. • Discuss community rules relating to road safety, littering, signs and symbols. • Talk to children about people from/in other parts of the country/world.
3. Encourage children to develop positive relationships outside the family context in nursery/ school enabling them to participate as members of a group.	3. Teach children that cooperating, taking turns, waiting and becoming less egocentric are all valued behaviours. Encourage them to • help and look after others (parents, peers, pets); • take turns; • line up and move sensibly as a group/class; • listen to other children and adults; • share with others;

KNOWLEDGE AND UNDERSTANDING

- talk about fair and unfair behaviour;
- show consideration to others in the group;
- show respect for others in their class and in their surroundings.

4. Increase and extend children's self-awareness and independence.	4. Encourage children to take increasing responsibilities, to develop increasingly realistic expectations of themselves and to exercise increasing control over their own learning experiences, their environment and their resources.

Encourage them to
- exercise choice over activities/food;
- dress themselves after dance/movement;
- go to the toilet independently;
- look after their possessions properly, for example hanging up their coats after outdoor play;
- resolve disagreements amicably and independently;
- express themselves confidently;
- try new things and have a go;
- tidy up after themselves;
- tell the truth;
- look for alternative/independent solutions to problems.

Personal, Social and Health Education (PSHE) and Citizenship

Eg *Purposes of education*

Dear Teacher,
I am a survivor of a concentration camp.
My eyes saw what no man should witness:
Gas chambers built by learned engineers;
Children poisoned by educated physicians;
Infants killed by trained nurses;
Women and babies shot and burned by high school and college graduates.
So I am suspicious of education.
My request is:
Help your students to become human. Your efforts must never produce learned monsters, skilled psychopaths, educated Eichmanns.
Reading, writing and arithmetic are important only if they serve to make our children more human.

(Pike and Selby, 1988)

Personal, social and health education and citizenship appeared in 1990 as part of National Curriculum Council (NCC) documentation for cross-curricular elements and were revised in 1999 to form part of the non-statutory guidance accompanying the National Curriculum for Key Stages 1 and 2 (QCA, 1999, pp. 136–41). They are not subjects but important cross-curricular themes with their own non-statutory PoS. Personal, social and health education and citizenship formalize the work primary teachers have always done in fostering responsibility, care and concern in children. In some ways they build on the work done by early years practitioners under the heading of Personal, social and emotional development. However, PSHE and citizenship also provide a framework within which children can be introduced to topics such as sex and drugs education as well as some of the systems and institutions of the society within which they live. Their purpose is to help children become informed and responsible citizens as they grow up by

- contributing to the spiritual, moral, social and cultural development of pupils as set out in the original Education Reform Act 1988 (NCC, 1990);
- fostering active participation by pupils in their local communities and encouraging them to take an interest in issues in the wider world; and
- fostering respect for different national, religious or ethnic groups and encouraging a commitment to democratic institutions and procedures.

Work on PSHE and citizenship in primary settings is intended to ensure that children

- have an understanding of the nature of community (different communities, organization, the family, serving the community, public services, pluralism, multicultural Britain);
- know about democratic approaches to society (reconciling competing needs and ideas, diversity and interdependence among groups in society, politics); and
- understand their rights and responsibilities in society (social and moral aspects of behaviour, law, work and leisure).

Personal, social and health education and citizenship does not mean that subjects such as politics, economics, sociology, human biology, environmental sciences or law have to be added to the primary curriculum. Instead, teachers are expected to look for opportunities to help children to learn about these things as part of their everyday work in school. For example, a visit to a local industrial museum to learn about the conditions of workers in the past offers opportunities to discuss notions of fairness, right and wrong, and social justice with children as part of their history work. Similarly, work in geography on distant locations offers children the chance to think about and discuss similarities, diversity and interdependence today, while work in design and technology offers opportunities to consider issues such as sustainable (e.g. wind farm) versus consumptive (e.g. coal fired power station) technologies. In addition to the integration of PSHE and citizenship themes into existing activities, the scheme of work to accompany the non-statutory PoS (www.standards.dfes.gov.uk) also offers ideas for interesting activities on discrete themes such as 'Making choices', 'Taking part', 'People who help us' and 'Animals and us'.

- Exercise
- Diet
- Family life/relationships
- Substance abuse (drugs/household chemicals)
- Personal hygiene
- The environment and human health
- Disease (spread and control)
- Safety (road safety, personal safety)
- People who help us to stay safe and healthy (fire service, police, doctors, nurses and other health professionals)

Circle Time

Circle time is one way of promoting self-esteem and fostering caring relationships in groups and classes of children. As such it is often used as a vehicle through which to promote Personal, social and emotional development, PSHE and citizenship. It works best when used in an ongoing and proactive fashion rather than as an *ad hoc* response to unwanted incidents. Circle time activities can help children to acquire the sorts of social skills necessary to be able to live and work together in a more harmonious fashion and offer pupils the chance to experience *being trusted, being respected, being successful, being praised, being listened to, listening to others, cooperating* and *working constructively in groups* (Curry and Bromfield, 1995). Circle time can offer teachers interesting and fun ways of helping children to

- develop strategies for dealing positively with their feelings;
- cope with change;
- deal with conflict;
- solve problems; and
- develop tolerance towards their peers.

The structured nature of these activities (they often require children to adhere to certain rules and conventions) may make them more demanding for some of the youngest (nursery) children and care should be taken with younger children not to *overdwell* by keeping children sitting still for too long (10–15 minutes may be sufficient at any one time). Circle time requires children to adhere to some simple rules which themselves provide useful personal and social training, for example *when other people are speaking we listen*. With some 3–8 children this rule may be particularly challenging and some practitioners introduce a special object such as a sea shell or teddy bear which gives the holder the right to speak. For other 3–8 children the prospect of speaking in front of a large group may be particularly daunting and one rule for circle time ought to be that '*I do not have to say anything until I am ready*'. All children have the right to decline to contribute until such time as they feel confident enough to do so. Once again, some practitioners use special objects to encourage contributions, for example giving shy and reticent children a puppet or doll which can *talk for* the child.

Eg *Circle time with Year 2 children*

Level	Purpose and activities	Example
Warm-up games	Practising/reiterating the rules and conventions, for example turn-taking, sharing, listening *'My name is . . .'* *'My favourite colour/animal/food is . . .'* *'My best friend is . . . . . . because . . .'* *'I'm good at . . .'* *'Something nice that happened to me was . . .'* *'Everyone with black hair get up and change places.'* *'Everyone wearing green get up and change places.'* Building confidence and trust by providing affirmation for the participants; fostering an awareness of others, listening skills and imagination.	A group of twelve children and their teacher sit together on the carpet. The children are in a circle. There is a gap in the circle. The child on the right of the gap has to ask someone to come and sit next to them. (Rule: Boys must pick a girl and girls must pick a boy.)
Introducing the theme	Exploring feelings, empathy, problem-solving and conflict resolution *'I feel happy when . . .'* *'It makes me angry when . . .'* *'. . . . . is fair/unfair because . . .'* *'. . . . . is right/wrong because . . .'* *'I want to try to . . . . . today'*	The teacher tells the children that they are going to be thinking about things that make them sad and what they can do to help other people who are sad. The teacher says, 'I feel sad when . . .' The child on the right tells the group what makes him/her sad and so on around the circle. (Rule: Everyone must start with the phrase 'I feel sad when . . .')
Developing the theme		The teacher groups the children into threes and asks the children to think about what they could do if they see someone who is sad. The teacher spends time with each group, offering encouragement and sharing ideas.
Plenary/ conclusion	Checking on learning and offering praise, recognition and encouragement for the future	The children re-form the original circle of twelve and the teacher chairs the feedback session in which children can report to the whole group on their ideas and

Level	Purpose and activities	Example
		suggestions. Children who are reluctant to comment in front of everyone else are not forced to do so.
		A short finishing-off activity praising one or two children in the group by giving them a round of applause. Finally, recognizing the efforts of all the group by getting everyone to give themselves a pat on the back.

Running circle time activities with infants

- Do not make the group too large with younger infants, and do not make the task too complicated.
- Remember the age and maturity of the children. Having to sit still and passively for long periods is likely to provoke considerable disruption and undermine the purposes of the activity.
- 'Little and often' can be a useful motto for those working with younger pupils. These children are likely to benefit from more frequent, shorter sessions that encourage greater participation.
- Simple rules and conventions can be introduced to help get circle time activities up and running with the minimum of fuss, for example developing special signs and signals for gaining children's attention, or passing an object around the group which confers the right to speak on the holder.

Religious Education (RE)

The moral dimension of RE offers considerable potential for overlap between this subject and the more secular area of Personal, social and emotional development. Both are concerned with helping children to develop notions of correct and incorrect forms of behaviour. RE can provide opportunities to help children develop their understanding of what it means to be fair, considerate, courageous and truthful, through introducing children to some of the stories associated with a range of religious faiths. However, RE also incorporates cultural and spiritual dimensions (Edwards and Knight, 1994). These aspects of RE involve both concepts (such as life after death, creation and miracles) and knowledge and understanding of the many different religions in Britain today including Christianity, Islam, Hinduism, Judaism, Buddhism and Sikhism.

Promoting knowledge and understanding of different religions with young children

- Visit the Commission for Racial Equality's website (www.cre.gov.uk), which contains pages offering information on ethnic and religious groups in Britain plus their history.

- Seek specific information on different world religions by contacting regional or national organizations direct or by accessing suitable websites (e.g. www.multifaithnet.org/)
- Celebrate a range of religious festivals such as Eid, Diwali and Christmas.
- Tell stories as ways to celebrate, and introduce young children to, the diversity and range of religious ideas and beliefs.
- Present religious ideas with respect if they are not to become indistinguishable from nursery rhymes and fairy stories. Unlike 'Goldilocks and the Three Bears', religious events and stories are underpinned by important articles of faith and belief.
- Invite visitors of different faiths to explain to children what it means to live life, for example as a Muslim or a Christian.
- Discuss any special books associated with different religious faiths, for example the Bible, Qur'an or Torah.
- Liaise with local representatives of different faiths; have clear learning objectives for planned visits and discuss them with these representatives.
- Visit places of worship to look at the structure, architecture, designs and objects (both functional and symbolic). Encourage the children to reflect on
  - protocols, conventions or actions upon entering a place of worship;
  - sights, sounds and smells in the place of worship, including signs and symbols, songs and chants, incense and perfumes, colour, pattern and design used in the construction of the place of worship;
  - special areas and/or artefacts within the place of worship, for example holy books or objects;
  - their feelings and emotions while in the place of worship.

Communication, Language and Literacy

AUDIT

By the end of this section you should

- know about the teaching of Communication, language and literacy in the Curriculum Guidance for the Foundation Stage (QCA, 2000, pp. 44–67);
- know about the teaching of English in the National Curriculum (QCA, 1999, pp. 42–58);
- know about the National Literacy Strategy (NLS) and its relationship with English in the National Curriculum (QCA, 1998b).

This area of learning forms a huge part of the 3–8 curricula. Not only do Communication, language and literacy in the early years and English in the primary school have a distinct identity of their own, but they are also involved in some way in almost every other activity that takes place in nursery/school. There can be few aspects of the 3–8 curricula more important for children's future educational achievements and opportunities in life. This section will deal with the areas of speaking and listening, reading and writing. It will identify some of the key issues that 3–8 teachers need to consider and direct readers to further sources of information that they ought to familiarize themselves with in order to meet fully the Standards for initial teacher training.

Speaking and Listening

Teachers recognize the fundamental importance of language development, for both the children's future adult prospects and their educational achievements. Oral language is the basis for literacy, and as a result teachers give significant consideration to both the quantity and quality of talk. Adults are constantly putting young children into situations where they need to pay attention, and listening carefully (individually, and in group and class situations) is an essential learning skill, albeit one that can prove a challenge for some young pupils. Many children entering nursery/reception classes are relatively skilled in speaking and listening, having had experience of listening to stories, learning rhymes or singing along with songs on the radio or television at home. At the same time, some of their peers are lacking in confidence and can be reluctant to communicate. They may have difficulty in listening attentively for even the shortest of periods, and may also have only a very limited vocabulary. Other children may be fluent speakers and listeners, but not in English. This wide range in ability results in a great deal of time spent in providing opportunities designed to promote speaking and listening (Burnett and Myers, 2004).

As children move through the 3–8 age range they should

- gain in confidence in their use of spoken language;
- be able to demonstrate listening behaviour;
- be able to use spoken language to describe, question, recall and recount their experiences;
- increase their ability to comprehend spoken language; and
- become more skilful in articulating and expressing their feelings and ideas verbally.

Eg *Dealing with a reluctant speaker*

When Matthew joined the reception class he was very reluctant to contribute verbally in front of his peers and others, so much so that he would approach the teacher and whisper any questions or requests in her ear. His teacher realized that she would need to make Matthew feel secure and raise his confidence through patience, praise and quiet encouragement. The process took a great deal of time but by the end of the year Matthew felt able to join in group discussions and answer questions with support.

The ethos and environment in 3–8 settings play a crucial part in fostering children's speaking and listening skills. It is vital that young children have the confidence to talk. Conversations with peers and adults can improve children's abilities to describe, to remember, and to develop and clarify their thoughts and ideas. Discussions such as these also foster the ability to listen to the ideas and observations of their peers and others, as well as providing opportunities to introduce new vocabulary. Listening to stories can be a powerful way to introduce new words, extend children's experience of language and help them to become more familiar with the rhythms, patterns and structures of language. Offering less threatening opportunities for children to express themselves verbally such as daily chats and discussions with small groups and individuals can be particularly rewarding for children who find talking in large groups (e.g. whole-class situations) difficult and are thus reluctant to contribute. Familiar topics for discussion may further bolster children's confidence such as experiences in the home, activities in the nursery/school, and observations and events in the local environment. Puppets, telephones and masks can also be introduced to help some children overcome their anxieties about speaking in front of others.

Questioning by teachers is valuable in promoting good dialogue and interaction with and among pupils, and children need to be allowed the opportunity to ask questions as well as answer them. More open-ended questions can provide opportunities for children to talk at length on a topic. Such questions offer more children the chance to respond and can be a good way of challenging more able pupils. Closed questions, meanwhile (where there is one correct answer and what is being sought is more clearly defined), can offer greater security for some children. Having asked a question, teachers should not be tempted to cut off the reply through impatience. Those teaching the 3–8 age range have to be prepared to wait and avoid jumping in too quickly to answer their own questions. Prompting can be helpful when children are making an effort to express themselves verbally, but if done too often or too quickly it can be frustrating for a child who knows the word(s) he/she needs, but just wants a second or two to remember and arrange them. At the same time, teachers need to be sensitive to children who are genuinely struggling and be ready to support them when necessary.

Increasing pupil confidence in speaking and listening

- Encourage children to ask and answer questions; seek information and clarification; retell and share personal experiences; participate in group discussions; and to work cooperatively and collaboratively with their peers, in pairs and groups, during activities such as circle time.
- Establish speaking and listening conventions such as 'hands up' and reward appropriate behaviour with praise and recognition.
- Read stories to the children, look at and talk about books.
- Issue simple instructions to encourage children to demonstrate attentiveness and respond appropriately to the speaker, for example when getting changed for dance and movement, washing hands before lunch, or putting on aprons before painting. These routines and procedures, while being effective as class management strategies, are also an important part of the learning process.
- Introduce musical activities, nursery rhymes, action games and songs (e.g. 'Simon'/'Susan Says') to provide listening skills practice.
- Create role-/pretend play areas in the classroom where children can use their verbal communication skills through participation in imaginary play, acting out a variety of roles and make-believe situations, and organizing and planning scenes using various props (e.g. telephones/mobiles) or small-world figures.

KNOWLEDGE AND UNDERSTANDING

• Look for opportunities to develop speaking and listening skills across the whole curriculum (e.g. using tape recorders to record science investigations or history/geography field trips).

Reading and Writing

Reading and writing are interdependent areas of learning. As with speaking and listening the range of ability in terms of reading and writing in 3–8 settings can be very wide. Some children upon entering nursery are able to recognize their own name in print and to engage in mark-making on paper which closely resembles writing. A few may even be able to read and write simple words such as their own names. By the time children move on to Key Stage 1 they should have improved their understanding of the functions of print, be experimenting with it, be using books and a variety of texts for pleasure and information, and be actively seeking and engaging in literary experiences.

Below is a broad brush model of the stages that young children go through in becoming readers and writers. Trainee and newly qualified teachers will need to refer to the Further Sources of Information section (p. 129) in order to appreciate more fully this area of children's learning.

1. **Emergent readers/writers**, while taking part in shared activities with the teacher, are beginning to realize that writing and drawing are different means of communication, and that speech can be recorded in print and that print can be turned back into speech. They are beginning to learn some of the letter shapes, to write their names and to recognize familiar logos and signs in their local environment. They can move on to identify a handful of the more common words encountered in books such as 'is', 'and', 'the', and are also learning to recognize these words in isolation. Establishing attractive and stimulating reading and mark-making areas are important strategies in fostering a positive approach to reading and writing at this stage of children's development.

2. **Beginning readers/writers** are able to write their own name plus a small number of common words. They are also learning to recognize an increasing number of these common words such as 'in', 'my', 'her'. They are starting to join in much more with reading and discussion of stories, are beginning to blend sounds into words, can play I-spy games, and can match a range of words and letters by sight.

3. **Developing readers/writers** are beginning to read and write independently. They are able to use the context of a text and initial letters in their efforts to establish meaning, and can read and write individual letters as well as an increasing range of words, for example 'dog', 'cat', 'red'. As the children progress they become increasingly adept at using the context of a text to predict meaning and to work out more complicated phonic blends. They can read and write words

with consonant blends (st, fr, sk, and, sl), consonant (ch, sh, th) and vowel (ea, oi) digraphs and are aware of the silent 'e' (like, come). They have a more extensive and increasing sight vocabulary. Although children's reading and writing development are interrelated it is worth remembering that developing readers and writers may be able to read more complex words than they can spell.

4. Fluent readers/writers have successfully achieved the basic competences. They can select books on the basis of interest and need. They can read and write words involving silent letters, longer word endings and polysyllabic words, and they can self-correct in reading.

Promoting reading and writing in 3–8 settings

- Set up a reading area in the nursery/classroom. Offer a wide range of texts to appeal to the widest possible audience and extend pupils' experience (e.g. fiction, picture books, touch and feel books, books with flaps, dual language texts, poems and rhymes, reference and non-fiction books, 'books' that the children have written themselves). Display the books attractively to encourage children to select them (e.g. using book boxes to present front covers rather than spines). Provide comfortable seating and carpeting to encourage children to spend time in the area. Include audio materials and ICT equipment such as story tapes and talking books.
- Provide opportunities for children to select books for individual needs and interests, and to request favourite stories in order to help them to become increasingly enthusiastic about using books for pleasure and information.
- Encourage children to read and reread simple texts that are known/familiar to them.
- When trying to help children to become increasingly knowledgeable about the functions of print, provide opportunities for them to see that written language has meaning, for example by reading familiar signs, labels and names.
- Encourage children to seek information about the meaning of print, attempt their own writing and share texts.
- Set up a writing or mark-making area in the nursery/classroom. Give the children a wide range of good quality mark-making resources to encourage their involvement and to demonstrate the status such activities have in the teacher's mind (offer a wide variety of pencils, pens and crayons, and good quality paper). Provide a range of real-life writing materials and artefacts (e.g. printed stationery, envelopes, labels, greetings cards, forms, tags, stamps, post box) to help pupils see that writing has a purpose. Include scissors, tape, paper clips, stapler, notice board and marker pens. Give children access to a computer or other word-processing equipment (e.g. the concept keyboard).
- Take care not to rush the youngest children prematurely into formal approaches to reading and writing. In many nurseries, for example, reading and mark-making areas are set up to encourage children to engage in and enjoy the earliest stages of reading and writing in more informal settings. Socio-dramatic role-play areas such as 'The Travel Agents' or 'The Post Office' also offer opportunities to foster purposeful reading and writing activities, as well as the obvious potential for speaking and listening.
- Model purposeful reading and writing for the children (e.g. signing your name, writing a list/birthday card/letter, looking for information on a topic). Young children often get some of their earliest ideas about reading and writing from watching and copying adults around them whom they see reading and writing themselves.

KNOWLEDGE AND UNDERSTANDING

The National Literacy Strategy (NLS)

The NLS (DfEE, 1998b) was introduced in response to perceived shortcomings in literacy levels among pupils in compulsory education, although the rationale was hotly contested both at the time and since (Burnett and Myers, 2004). The NLS is not compulsory and schools retain the right to introduce their own literacy programmes; however, the majority use the NLS framework. Nor is it a scheme of work for English in the National Curriculum as it focuses primarily upon reading and writing, although elements of speaking and listening are inevitably involved in its implementation. As a result schools are expected to conduct teaching and learning in English in addition to that undertaken as part of the NLS.

The NLS documentation sets out programmes of work for each year group, covering pupils from reception to Year 6 and provides teachers with guidance on lessons and assessment. Specific guidance is offered for reception teachers in an attempt to establish a seamless transition from Foundation Stage to primary settings. Reception teachers are able to break literacy hours down into more manageable portions for younger children and to teach the different parts at different times of the day. It is quite common, however, for reception pupils to be introduced to full literacy hours during their final term in reception as a way of preparing them for the curriculum they will encounter upon entering Key Stage 1.

The NLS comprises three interrelated strands: word level work, sentence level work and text level work. Using the NLS framework teachers are expected to cover a range of work within a given term and to choose texts and writing tasks to facilitate the teaching and learning programme. In practice this placed a great deal of pressure on teachers and many schools utilize commercially produced schemes to support literacy hour lessons.

The approach set out in the NLS is for dedicated literacy lessons on a daily basis which incorporate direct, whole-class teaching as well as a range of independent/individual work and guided group tasks.

Eg *Literacy hour format*

15 minutes	15 minutes	20 minutes	10 minutes
Introduction and shared text level work as a class	Word level or sentence level work as a class	Individual reading/writing tasks and guided reading/writing tasks with the class teacher supervising two guided reading/writing groups per lesson	Plenary as a class to consolidate and check on learning

(DfEE, 1998)

The timescale of one hour is quite tight and many primary teachers have raised concerns about issues such as children being repeatedly unable to complete written work in the 20 minutes allocated, and the difficulties in trying to carry out guided reading activities in dynamic, busy and, sometimes, noisy classroom settings. Concern has also been expressed over what to do where children find particular elements difficult to grasp when the NLS has the teaching programme for a term already mapped out. In some Year 2 and Year 6 classes in particular, the NLS can evolve at certain times of the year into preparation sessions for the SATs and tests during the Summer term. Chapter 3 contains exemplar material showing planning for the NLS.

Children with English as an Additional Language (EAL)

Many schools and nurseries have pupils for whom English is an additional language (EAL). These children are far from being part of a homogeneous group. Such pupils may be bilingual or even multilingual; alternatively, they may be at the very earliest stages of English acquisition. They may have very diverse backgrounds linguistically, socially and culturally, and may well have different levels of language competency both in their home language(s) and in English. Failure to appreciate this diversity could result in teachers concluding, wrongly, that children have behavioural problems of some kind, or are less motivated or less intelligent than their English-speaking peers. Many bilingual pupils are capable of achievement as high as, or higher than, their monolingual peers even before fluency in English has been mastered, particularly in subjects such as mathematics or art where an incomplete grasp of English is less of a barrier to accessing the curriculum (DfES, 2003a).

Recognizing and supporting the breadth of bilingual children's language skills and understanding will make a positive contribution to their learning of English and their success in education generally. At the same time, it is essential for all children to make progress in mastering English in the interests of their future achievements in school and, later on, their opportunities as adults. Bilingual children learn English best in mainstream settings in which they are supported in the acquisition of English across the whole curriculum and alongside English speaking peers. In this way bilingual children encounter English in subject specific and meaningful contexts, which speeds up their access to the curriculum (Burnett and Myers, 2004; DfES, 2003a).

Supporting the Communication, language and literacy skills of bilingual pupils

- Provide a learning environment in which children feel able to utilize the full range of their linguistic repertoire and feel confident that their first language has a legitimacy in the classroom (Barratt-Pugh, 1994). Bilingual support staff can be particularly effective in helping teachers to achieve this. Where such staff are available children can benefit from the additional support in taking in and understanding the spoken word, and can be encouraged to express themselves clearly and appropriately. Such support can help children overcome feelings of isolation and frustration where much of what goes on in the nursery/classroom may pass them by.

- Learn key words and phrases in order to be able to *meet and greet* parents and children using their first language.
- Provide resources including books, posters and ICT software that are free from cultural bias and negative, stereotypical images.
- Use dual-language books and tapes to give parity of esteem to other languages.
- Provide play equipment such as clothing, construction kits and artefacts that reflect a wide range of cultural experiences.
- Use a range of teaching techniques and devices to assist bilingual children in reading and writing, for example introducing writing frames or providing collaborative reading experiences.
- Ensure that displays, labelling and written communication with children and their families reflect the diversity and variety of young children's home languages. Once again bilingual support staff can be an invaluable resource enabling schools and nurseries to do this.

Mathematical Development

A U D I T

By the end of this section you should

- know about the teaching of Mathematical development in the Curriculum Guidance for the Foundation Stage (QCA, 2000, pp. 68–81);
- know about the teaching of mathematics in the primary curriculum (QCA, 1999, pp. 60–74);
- know about the National Numeracy Strategy (NNS) and its relationship with mathematics in the National Curriculum (QCA, 1999).

Like Communication, language and literacy/English, mathematics is a powerful means of communication with importance and application across the curriculum. The inclusion of mathematics in the 3–8 curricula provides opportunities to improve and increase children's powers of logical thinking, their ability to calculate, represent, explain and predict, as well as developing their spatial awareness. Many day-to-day nursery and school experiences, including play, provide opportunities for children to learn mathematical concepts and ideas including

- recognizing and using numbers;
- comparing and recognizing relationships;
- ordering and sequencing;
- sorting and classifying;
- establishing invariant properties;
- using mathematical language;
- using mathematical knowledge to carry out simple number operations and solve practical problems.

Number

From birth, children are surrounded by ideas in number form. Number concepts which develop in the early years are the result of both teaching and informal experiences. Children come to attach meaning to number names as a result of frequent use in different contexts, such as sorting activities with beads and cotton reels, matching activities with collections of natural objects, counting games, and songs and rhymes involving numbers. Much early number work concerns correspondence and conservation, while using number names encourages the beginnings of understanding cardinal and ordinal numbers.

Early number exercises

- Make number collections
- Thread coloured beads following a sequence card
- Number rhymes and songs
- Count on/back
- Number 'jumps'
- One more than/less than
- Number patterns
- Simple number bonds, 1–5 leading to 5–10
- Number trails inside/outside the nursery/classroom
- Collecting groups of objects (e.g. 4 bricks, 3 leaves, 5 cars)
- Counting to 5, counting to 10

Teachers of younger pupils need to appreciate the importance of children understanding number, and to avoid confusing this with formal number operations and recording. Hughes (1986) presents a revealing insight into children's use of written arithmetic and suggests that there may be a disturbing discrepancy between children's use of symbols in the classroom and their ability to apply them elsewhere. Time is needed for children to relate their concrete understanding of number to the abstract written symbols.

Helping children with number

- Offer pupils activities leading to counting. Without the ability to count, progress in children's general mathematical development will be severely limited.
- Take advantage of the myriad of counting opportunities that present themselves during the course of any day in a nursery/classroom, such as 'How many . . . ?', 'Who is second/third?', 'Who has the most/least?' and 'Is it the same as/more than/less than?'
- Assist children to develop their skills in mental number work and provide opportunities to develop their understanding and skills still further through practical work. Encourage children to try out their own mental strategies. Many strategies can lead to the 'right answer'.
- Emphasize the importance of thinking mathematically (understanding, interpreting and communicating solutions) as well as standard calculation procedures.

- View computational skills as tools. Children need not only the ability to perform a particular numerical operation, but also knowledge of when it should be employed. Many teachers will be familiar with questions such as 'Is it an add, Miss?' as some children struggle to make sense of written symbols, particularly operator signs such as + and -.
- Offer children opportunities to record in a variety of ways.

Providing Practical Experience of Mathematics

Although mathematical operations such as addition and subtraction are crucially important, real and relevant contexts within which children have to exercise their mathematical skills are equally valuable. Practical mathematical experiences can include work on shape and space, measurement, number work and logic. Many everyday activities in 3–8 classes provide opportunities to think logically and solve practical problems using mathematics. Using everyday routines and situations provides real contexts for the use of mathematics, for example sharing out biscuits at milk time. The skills of prediction, classification and sequencing can be encouraged through questions such as 'What will happen?' and 'Why do you think?' during structured play activities. Furthermore, everyday sorting and classifying activities can be useful in developing early logic. Children's logical thinking begins to develop as they start to distinguish differences and similarities in things, making comparisons and arranging them systematically.

Practical mathematics tasks

- Find and match bricks in the construction kits that are the same.
- Compare (two objects to begin with).
- Work with foodstuffs; follow simple recipes.
- Look for 'big' leaves and 'little' leaves in the environment.
- Pass the parcel 'quickly' and 'slowly'.
- Run on the spot in PE for a 'long' time and a 'short' time.
- 'Which is the biggest/smallest?'
- 'Which container holds the most sand/water?'
- Position and reposition play figures, for example behind, in front of, on top of.
- Sort and classify objects according to type; for example, sort toy animals or cars as part of small-scale structured play activities.
- Sort and classify objects according to shape, for example two-dimensional card cut-outs, three-dimensional construction bricks.
- Sort and classify objects according to colour, for example beads, bobbins.
- Sort and classify objects according to size, for example containers in sand and water play.
- Sort/group each other, for example 'Who's got laces on their shoes?', 'Who's got brown hair?'

Providing a practical dimension to mathematics

Offer children activities which require them to

- make direct comparisons (e.g. small and large, long and short);
- sequence more than two objects;
- measure (e.g. mix and combine materials such as foodstuffs or paint);
- utilize their estimation skills when measuring and/or comparing;
- move and handle a range of equipment and objects as a way of improving their spatial awareness of, and developing an appreciation of, patterns and relationships in shape and number;
- engage in structured play activities, including outdoor play and work with construction kits, to develop their awareness of shape and space.

Mathematics and the Wider Curriculum

Linking mathematics with other curriculum areas provides further opportunities for skills to be used in practical and meaningful situations, for example measuring and marking out in design and technology, or using simple charts to record scientific observations. Teachers need to be adept at drawing mathematical experiences out of activities that are ostensibly creative, scientific or physical in nature.

Establishing links with Communication language and literacy/English is of prime importance. A great many stories, poems and songs that are used with young children provide ways of exposing pupils to mathematical ideas, knowledge and understanding, for example 'There Were Ten in the Bed'. The relationship between language and mathematics is particularly important. When children fail to understand what is being asked of them they will not be able to complete the activity they have been given. Adult–pupil talk provides numerous opportunities to encourage young children to think mathematically about

- number – 'Have we got enough?'
- measurement – 'Which is longer?'
- logic – 'Why did that happen?'
- spatial awareness – 'Which brick will fit in there?'
- mathematical language – 'Whose is the tallest/heaviest?', 'Who's got the most/least?'

Eg *Multiple opportunities for mathematical learning throughout 3–8 curricula activities*

- Matching objects in collections (leaves, seeds).
- Making sets of up to 10 objects (e.g. 6 cars, 10 bricks).
- Sorting clothes in the home corner (hats, coats, gloves).
- Counting out objects (plates and cups in the home corner, sweets/biscuits at snack time).

- Creating different structures/shapes with the same number of Lego bricks.
- Practising songs and rhymes which involve counting by rote ('Currant Buns in The Baker's Shop').
- Using mathematics in socio-dramatic role-play (setting up the Three Bears' House in the home corner).
- Providing games which have the potential to reinforce mathematical learning (e.g. rolling dice, playing cards, completing jigsaws, matching shape games, lotto and snap).
- Baking and measuring out ingredients for simple recipes.
- Practising positional and directional language using small-world play equipment or programmable vehicles such as the Pixie or Roamer.

Promoting mathematical skills, knowledge and understanding in 3–8 settings

- Set up a numeracy table/area in the nursery/classroom. The resources could include counting materials (beads, buttons, number lines); blocks, shapes, sorting games and jigsaws; measuring equipment (rulers, metre sticks, scales and balances, clocks and timers); maths books and stories with a mathematical theme; writing/drawing materials.
- Provide opportunities for the acquisition and reinforcement of mathematical knowledge through practical work. Observe and talk about numerals around the classroom (e.g. using the clock, plastic coins, number lines, telephone numbers in the role-play area, talking about page numbers in books). Accompany the children on maths trails and visits in the local environment (looking at bus numbers, numbers on houses and cars, buying items in a shop).
- Provide opportunities for young children to engage in discussions on mathematical topics as a means of improving their understanding.
- Offer counting and number games to provide opportunities for children to engage in skills practice and for you to explain mathematical ideas.
- Use the medium of structured play with a wide range of materials and equipment such as sand, water, construction kits and toys to provide investigative, measuring and problem-solving mathematical experiences.
- Remember the importance of opportunities for consolidation and reinforcement, rather than rushing into, and insisting upon, formal recording too quickly, especially with younger children.

The National Numeracy Strategy (NNS)

As with the NLS, the NNS (DfEE, 1999) was introduced to tackle perceived underachievement, this time in relation to mathematics. In the same way, schools have the right to introduce their own numeracy programmes; however, as with literacy the majority use the NNS framework. Unlike the NLS the NNS does form a scheme of work, for mathematics in the National Curriculum, covering as it does all aspects of the National Curriculum Programmes of Study (QCA, 1999).

The NNS documentation sets out yearly programmes of work for each year group, covering pupils from reception to Year 6, and provides teachers with guidance on lessons and assessment. As with literacy, specific guidance is offered for reception teachers in an attempt to bridge practice between early years and Key Stage 1 provision. Reception teachers are able to break numeracy hours down into more manageable portions for younger children with some aspects being taught to the class and other work broken down into group tasks to be delivered simultaneously or sequentially throughout the day as the teacher deems fit. Once again, as with literacy, it is quite common for reception pupils to be introduced to full numeracy hours during their final term in reception as a way of preparing them for the curriculum they will encounter upon entering Key Stage 1.

The NNS comprises five strands. The first three (numbers and the number system, calculations and solving problems) correspond to the PoS for Number (QCA, 1999, pp. 62–3, 67–70). The remaining strands (shape, space and measures and handling data) relate to the remaining PoS for mathematics in the National Curriculum. Using and applying mathematics is integrated into each of these strands.

As with the NLS the approach set out in the NNS is for dedicated numeracy lessons on a daily basis which incorporate direct teaching, and interactive and oral work in classes, groups and with individuals. The NNS (DfEE, 1999) suggests lessons of 45 minutes' duration for Key Stage 1 pupils and 50–60 minutes for Key Stage 2 children, and there is a strong emphasis throughout the NNS on mental calculation.

Eg

Numeracy hour format

5–10 minutes	30–40 minutes	10–15 minutes
Introduction involving oral work and mental calculation with the class	Main teaching activity involving whole-class work and pupil activities in groups, pairs and/or individual work	Plenary with the whole class during which time the teacher is expected to identify pupil misconceptions and progress, summarize key concepts and make links to other work

(DfEE, 1999)

As the NNS maps out a set amount of content to be covered each year, lessons where children struggle to grasp the concepts or skills being taught can put pressure on teachers to meet all the objectives in the time available. Consequently, the NNS objectives are set out in both plain and bold text and teachers are expected to prioritize those in bold. Chapter 3 contains exemplar material showing planning for the NNS.

Knowledge and Understanding of the World

AUDIT

By the end of this section you should

- know about the teaching of Knowledge and understanding of the world in the Curriculum Guidance for the Foundation Stage (QCA, 2000, pp. 82–99);
- know about the teaching of science, design and technology, history and geography in the National Curriculum (QCA, 1999, pp. 76–89, 90–5, 102–7, 108–15).

Young children are fascinated by the natural phenomena and manufactured objects that they see around them on a daily basis. By introducing practical activities which enable children to use their senses, nursery/reception teachers can help to lay some of the foundations for understanding in geography, history, technology and science which their primary colleagues can build on as the children enter Key Stage 1 and 2. Pupils need opportunities to

- identify the features of living things, objects, materials and events in the natural and made world, including looking closely at similarities, differences, patterns and change;
- gain information about why things happen and how things work;
- talk and think critically and creatively about their observations and begin to record them with adult support;
- select and use materials and equipment, and take turns and cooperate when using equipment; and
- use technology to support their learning.

Science

First-hand experiences and observations of the world around them provide primary children with opportunities to foster positive attitudes towards investigation and experimentation, such as curiosity and perseverance (Farmery, 2002). This can relate to a range of topics including materials and their properties, similarities and differences, patterns and changes, living things and forces. At the same time first-hand experiences also present opportunities for younger children to acquire a range of skills and experiences useful in their future National Curriculum science work, including

- critical thinking (asking and answering questions about why and how things happen, predicting);
- problem-solving and investigating;
- observational skills;
- measuring, sorting and classifying; and
- hypothesizing (talking about their observations, identifying cause and effect).

Terms such as investigation, enquiry or experimentation may suggest a more formal approach that may not be particularly appropriate for children at the younger end of the 3–8 age range. Younger children are unlikely to plan fair tests, take standard measurements or form scientific hypotheses. For Davies and Howe (2003) the role of the teacher in the Foundation Stage is to encourage imitation, broaden children's knowledge and to challenge their thinking and ideas. They suggest the term '*exploration*' may offer teachers a better description of early science activities.

 Range of exploration

- Guided exploration (child-initiated or adult-initiated with the adult intervening to question/suggest ways forwards)
- Structured exploration (adult-initiated with the adult deliberately scaffolding concepts, skills and attitudes).

(Davies and Howe, 2003)

Eg **A taste of science**

A class of Year 1/2 children had been doing work on the theme of 'Ourselves'. They had been investigating the five senses. The children had a small selection of plastic pots each of which held a similar-looking white material – sugar, salt, icing sugar, self-raising flour and cornflour – to be identified by smell, touch and taste. They described what the substances smelled and felt like and one of the children said that the salt and sugar were 'all crunchy'. The teacher asked the children to look very closely at the different materials to see if they were really that similar. During the subsequent discussion the teacher introduced the words 'powder' and 'crystal'. The children then compared the tastes. Some were easily identified (salt and sugar), while others (flour and cornflour) were unknown to the children. One child then asked what would happen if they mixed in some water. The teacher seized the opportunity to extend the children's learning further in the area of materials and their properties. They were asked to predict what would happen and then she added some water to the pots and stirred the mixtures. The children noticed that some of the substances seemed to disappear. The teacher asked the children to taste the liquids and the children observed that they could still taste the sugar and salt even though they had apparently disappeared. The teacher then introduced the word 'dissolve'.

When engaged in science activities, children should be encouraged to become increasingly responsible for handling equipment and resources safely and sensibly. This could include selecting and collecting objects to see if they will float or sink, putting magnets back where they came from with their keepers attached, and keeping their work area reasonably tidy. When children are making these choices and exercising their decision-making abilities, they need to do so in an environment that is inherently safe.

Using equipment safely

- Do not allow children access to hot materials or sharp tools without close adult supervision.
- Remind children about the hazards of tasting or smelling strange materials and liquids.
- Use plastic containers not glass ones.
- Use water based glues not solvents.
- Warn children of the dangers of mains electricity.

Science activities provide a wealth of cross-curricular learning opportunities. Personal, social and health education and elements of citizenship can be fostered by studying health related or environmental themes, as well as encouraging young children to work harmoniously and sensibly with their peers. Praise and recognition can make children aware that listening to others, offering ideas and observations, carefully following instructions and considerately sharing tasks are all valued behaviours. At the same time, encouraging and assisting children in recording science activities provides opportunities to foster the development of their mathematical and literacy skills, as well as providing teachers with concrete evidence with which to support the assessment, recording and reporting of children's learning.

A written account is not always the most suitable method for recording science work. Having to write up experiments and investigations upon completion can be problematic with very young children, not to say inappropriate on occasions. Some investigative work with young pupils may not warrant a permanent record and in such cases they can be encouraged to talk about their work and their observations. Many young children will be emergent writers, and to produce written work at the end of science tasks could well reduce their interest in and enthusiasm for the subject. Some investigations could be recorded in an ongoing rather than a summative form, such as keeping a daily record of the weather or the growth of cress seeds. Where a written account is appropriate, teachers can act as scribes for those children who need this level of support. Other options for recording science work in ways that best suit the task include pre-prepared charts and simple tables, diagrams, pictures, photographs, tape recordings and cooperative or group reports.

More 3–8 science activities

- **Sound and music**. Make shakers using rice and peas, or 'guitars' using boxes and elastic bands.
- **Magnets**. Which materials are attracted to magnets? Can children move objects with a magnet at a distance, for example through the tabletop, through a sheet of paper?
- **Investigating soaps and detergents**. Make bubbles and get things clean.

- **Light and colour**. Make shadows using torches. Mix powder paints. Test a range of fluorescent and luminous materials in a range of light conditions as part of a road safety project. Conduct a science walk around the school/nursery looking at the use of colour in the local environment (e.g. shop fronts, road signs and traffic lights).
- **Materials and their properties/similarities and differences**. Introduce children to different sorts of paper (writing paper, newsprint, cards, wall papers and gift wrap), and encourage them to describe the different properties such as texture, colour and pattern. Test the properties of the different types of paper in a range of contexts, for example wet and dry.
- **Living things**. Visit a local park and collect objects such as Autumn fruits and leaves. Talk about the seasons to raise children's awareness of range and diversity. Use a commercially produced database with Key Stage 1 children to find out about animals as part of a project on pets. Grow seeds and discuss the needs of living things.
- **Patterns and changes**. Bake bread and conduct other food activities in which the properties of materials are changed. Thaw ice and evaporate water.
- **Forces**. Roll toy cars down ramps at various angles and measure the distances travelled over different surfaces with Key Stage 1 pupils. Water play with nursery/reception pupils, testing objects to see which ones float and which ones sink, or making floaters sink and sinkers float.

Design and Technology

There are many links between science and design and technology but they are not one and the same thing (Davies, 1997). Young children need opportunities to develop their technology skills by designing and making, as well as developing their scientific understanding by observing and investigating the world around them. Local walks and visits provide opportunities for children to observe the wider *built* or *made* environment, including such things as street furniture, machines and buildings. Imaginative and investigative play can be also be used to develop children's interest in the technological products they see around them. Much design in the early stages of a child's education is changeable, based on trial and error; this often runs concurrently with making and the products themselves can be ephemeral in nature, such as sand structures. Although even quite young pupils are able to engage in planning their work orally, using simple pictures, or by listing the materials they will need, designing in more traditional ways such as through drawing can prove more of a challenge. Children's drawing skills may be insufficient for the task, their knowledge and understanding of the tools and materials may lead to unrealistic proposals and some find it hard to appreciate the purpose of two-dimensional design work (Fleer, 2000).

Evolution of a child's idea

During a nursery placement a student teacher was asked to work with children engaged in a construction activity using junk materials and paint. She asked one child about his model and he replied that it was a fire engine. Later in the session the student teacher praised the construction (a series of cardboard boxes, glued together and painted bright red). 'That's a fantastic fire engine you've made.' 'It's not a fire engine,' the child replied indignantly, 'it's a lighthouse.'

A good range of low-cost and no-cost materials (e.g. cardboard boxes, yogurt pots, lolly sticks) are invaluable in giving children opportunities to select and make decisions. At the same time, augmenting such materials with more sophisticated commercially produced resources such as construction kits gives pupils a chance to model with an accuracy that would otherwise be far beyond them. Work with textiles and food can be particularly useful; this allows opportunities to design and make with materials that are accessible, exciting, easily worked and that offer a wide range of possible outcomes. Introducing textile and food activities can also provide opportunities to introduce a multicultural dimension to the 3–8 curricula but teachers should familiarize themselves with the food rules of different cultures and faith communities in order to do this properly.

Some ideas for food activities

- Taste different breads and fillings and then make sandwiches.
- Taste a variety of breads then bake bread. Add different ingredients and flavourings to the dough.
- Make a green salad or fruit salad.
- Make butter.
- Make fruit yogurt by adding fruit to a plain yogurt base.
- Cook eggs in different ways.
- Make vegetable soup.
- Make a pizza.
- Make drinks (e.g. tea, coffee, cocoa, fruit juice, milkshakes).
- Make festive foods and food presents.
- Add beans, salad ingredients and dressings to rice, bulghar wheat or cous-cous.
- Make baked potatoes with different fillings.
- Make a Teddy Bears' Picnic meal.
- Make different coloured peppermint creams.

Children's health and safety is an important factor in design and technology activities where potentially harmful tools and equipment may be involved.

Health and safety in design and technology

- Trainee and newly qualified teachers should consult the nursery/school health and safety guidelines when planning design and technology activities.

- Children should be shown how to handle tools properly.
- Certain tools and equipment should only be used under adult supervision. Young children can use knives but only under close supervision. All such tools must be stored out of reach when not needed.
- Some tools should be used only by the teacher or another responsible adult.
- When working with food, discuss healthy eating and make sure that surfaces are clean, hands have been washed and that pupils with allergies (such as nut allergies) have been identified.
- When using heat sources children should not move hot liquids. Microwave ovens provide opportunities to make some dishes more safely, easily and quickly.

Eg *Establishing clear boundaries*

The woodwork bench in the nursery had a range of soft timber offcuts, two pots of nails, two hammers, two saws and two vices. Teaching and non-teaching staff taught the children how to hold and use the saws properly and safely, how to put timber in a vice and how to use a hammer to drive a nail into wood. When an adult was present in the area children could opt to experiment with the tools and materials. When no adult was present a thick blanket was placed over the whole bench and children knew that the activity was off-limits.

Eg *Avoiding unnecessary risks*

A reception teacher was setting up a structured play area in her classroom. The theme was 'The Launderette' and the children were constructing some of the artefacts to go into the area, gaining experience of handling tools and materials in the process. One group was making a washing machine from a large cardboard box. They drew around a plastic plate to show where the door needed to go but the card was too thick for scissors, so the teacher did the cutting for them using a craft knife which was always kept securely locked away. Children were not allowed to use it, even under supervision.

As with early science work, work in design and technology can contribute to children's learning in other areas:

- Children can begin to hone their abilities in reasoning and thinking logically as well as their interpersonal skills such as cooperation, sharing and negotiation.
- Children's aesthetic awareness can be promoted by encouraging them to make things that are artistically appealing as well as purely functional.
- Designing and making activities can give children the chance to apply knowledge and skills gained in English and mathematics, for example measuring before cutting, 'buying' materials with budgets and discussing their plans.
- Design and technology can also be used to support children's learning in science, for example collecting moving toys (e.g. battery powered, mechanically powered using clockwork motors, or stored energy in springs) and investigating what makes them work.

Textile equipment
- large needles (some pre-threaded)
- variety of threads, silks and wool
- hessian and binka fabrics, felt, patterned offcuts
- scissors (for textile use only; paper blunts scissors quickly)
- miscellaneous materials (ribbon, elastic, buttons, feathers, beads and sequins)
- baskets for storage

Work with food
- utensils (knives, mixing bowls, wooden spoons, whisks)
- crockery and cutlery
- foodstuffs (flour, fat, milk, vegetables, fruit, salt, yeast, sugar, eggs)
- heat source/microwave
- cold storage (fridge)
- hygienic work surfaces/chopping boards

Work with more resistant materials
- tools (scissors, hole punchers, staplers, pliers, vices, hammers, bench hooks, glass paper and/or hobby sanders, saws, drills and glue guns for use under supervision only)
- joining materials (good quality PVA adhesive, sticky tape, masking tape, string, paper fasteners, elastic bands, nails)
- more resistant materials (dowelling, soft timber, balsa, wooden wheels)

Work with less resistant materials
- range of paper and card
- plastics and acetates (drinking straws, cotton bobbins, plastic bottles and containers)
- junk and purchased materials (cardboard boxes, card wheels, lolly sticks)
- clay and other malleable materials (plasticine, play dough)

Design equipment
- rolling pins, moulds, stamps
- drawing/colouring materials
- scissors

Construction equipment
- large-scale kits (Bau Spiel, Tac-Tic, large wooden blocks)
- small-scale kits (Lego, Duplo-Toolo)
- instruction sheets (remove for free play; include for more directed tasks)
- extension materials for small-scale play activities (plastic figures, floor maps)
- extension materials for large-scale play activities (role-play materials)

Geography and History

Geography and history can be fascinating for young children. Although at first glance teachers may find it hard to relate their adult understanding of these subjects to their practice in early years settings, a great deal of potential exists in the Foundation Stage for using geography and history to make the curriculum relevant to young children while simultaneously laying the foundations for later learning at Key Stages 1 and 2 (Campbell and Little, 1989; Edwards and Knight, 1994; Turner-Bisset, 2002).

Geography is much more than simply memorizing and locating different places; it is a way for children to study the world around them. Geography involves knowledge and understanding about the interaction between the environment and people, as well as developing a set of enquiry based skills (Owen and Ryan, 2001).

Eg *Geographical concepts and skills*

- Pattern.
- Processes and systems.
- Similarities and differences.
- Asking questions.
- Collecting information.
- Interpreting and presenting information.
- Drawing conclusions.

While younger children may find it hard to represent their geographical understanding and ideas using conventional means, their comprehension of place may be much more advanced (Sowden *et al.*, 1995). The picture below was drawn by a reception child following a visit to another school. This child's developing sense of place is clear from the use of arrows and non-standard symbols to represent particular points on his journey as well as more formal symbols such as the compass.

Eg *Reception map*

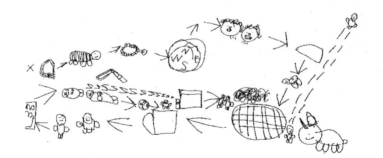

History involves more than mastering a prescribed set of names, dates and past events in the correct sequence. History offers children a way of understanding the past (O'Hara and O'Hara, 2001) through the introduction of key concepts and enquiry skills as well as the assimilation of particular pieces of information or facts.

Historical concepts and skills

- There was a past.
- The past was different from the present.
- There was an order or sequence to the past.
- In many cases (although not all) objects and information from the past remain and can help us to make sense of what things used to be like.
- Find out about other periods, asking and answering questions.
- Interpret historical events.
- Organize and communicate historical information.

(Edwards and Knight, 1994)

Children who are still coming to terms with concepts such as earlier than, later than, yesterday, today and tomorrow are not incapable of understanding the concepts of time or alternative places, provided teachers introduce them to these ideas in ways that are appropriate and manageable for them (Turner-Bisset, 2002). Beginning by asking questions such as 'What did you do yesterday?' or 'Where are you going at the weekend?' is one way of introducing the concepts of place and time to young children. Working back to consider the family also puts these curriculum areas into a meaningful context. Teachers may initiate discussions on different generations in a family, or different places that children have visited or lived in. Moving on to consider the local area, exploring what it was like in the past or how it has changed, allows children to move beyond the immediate and the personal and begin to see themselves as part of a larger community. Finally, teachers can broaden the curriculum to consider the more distant past and locations, including periods beyond living memory, as well as national and international locations.

Some early history

It was the start of the new school year in the nursery. All the children brought photographs of themselves as babies or toddlers with them and nursery staff took new pictures of the children using the digital camera. A display of the images was mounted and children were encouraged to talk about themselves and how they had grown and changed.

In geography, learning can occur when you

- talk about and examine the immediate environment, including where the children live;
- read stories such as 'The Shopping Basket';

- make three-dimensional maps in the sand tray;
- use roll-out road maps in small-world play;
- look at photographs, including aerial photographs of local places;
- go on local walks to introduce children to appropriate terms such as 'semi-detached', 'valley' and 'church';
- look at plan views of the classroom/school;
- make memory maps of how children came to school;
- use secondary sources to find out about more distant places;
- introduce children to maps of all kinds;
- talk to the children about distant locations or local events that they have seen in the media.

In history, learning can occur when you

- talk about past and present events in the children's own lives;
- talk about time and the passage of time, for example using clocks and watches, discussing how the children's activities may change at different times of the day, week or year;
- interview older relatives about how things used to be;
- make family timelines and albums;
- collect and display artefacts from previous times (coins, stamps, posters, tickets);
- discuss and compare past and present artefacts (collecting toys that parents and grandparents may have kept from their own childhood and comparing them with toys today);
- look at and discuss old photographs and postcards of the local area;
- visit local historical sites to consider how and why people and places have altered over time;
- use secondary sources to find out about the more distant past.

Physical Development

By the end of this section you should

- know about the teaching of Physical development in the Curriculum Guidance for the Foundation Stage (QCA, 2000, pp. 100–15);
- know about the teaching of Physical education in the National Curriculum (QCA, 1999, pp. 128–33).

Children's Physical development involves the acquisition of gross and fine motor skills. Between the ages of 3 and 8 children make considerable progress in their coordination, manipulation and muscular control (Sharman *et al.*, 1995). Gross motor skills include the ability to sit, walk, run, climb, balance, throw, catch, kick and pedal. Fine motor skills include the ability to grasp, hold, pick up, stick, cut and thread.

- To encourage children to develop positive attitudes and confidence about themselves and their physical abilities;
- To ensure that children are safe and secure both physically and emotionally;
- To provide an environment that allows children to develop a degree of autonomy and independence; and
- To promote progress in Physical development across a broad range, including gross and fine motor control, hand–eye coordination, body awareness, sensory awareness, spatial awareness, safety awareness, hygiene and healthy living.

Physical development is a major part of the 3–8 curricula as children's Physical development is intimately connected to their intellectual and academic progress. Pupils who have not been able to practise using their bodies with increasing levels of skill can experience difficulties in other areas of learning as they progress through nursery and school. Growing confidence in their physical abilities can in turn promote a growing confidence and self-esteem across the curriculum.

By the time children enter nursery and reception classes most already have an understanding and awareness of their bodies and physical competence, and many everyday activities can contribute to their Physical development and sense of growing independence (e.g. dressing and undressing, cleaning teeth, feeding self using a knife and fork, combing hair, fastening shoes, or washing hands and faces). However, the point at which children develop many of these physical skills can vary greatly, so practitioners need to be aware of those whose development seems to be slower than others and those who have physical difficulties. A child's physical development not only has importance in and of itself but can also contribute to their sense of self-worth and emotional well-being through the sense of satisfaction gained from doing something well and with skill, such as catching or hitting a ball, cycling, or creating a recognizable image with a paint brush.

Health and fitness form a central part of Physical development (QCA, 2000, pp. 100–15), the PE PoS (QCA, 1999, pp. 128–33) and the non-statutory PoS for PSHE (QCA, 1999, pp. 136–41). When promoting good health practices teachers need to help pupils to improve their understanding of how their bodies function and how to keep them healthy. Safety, too, is essential and teachers of young children have a legal obligation to keep pupils safe (see Chapter 1), an obligation that is much easier to fulfil if the children themselves are conscious of safety issues.

Promoting positive attitudes towards safety, health and fitness

- Require children to demonstrate appropriate hygiene practices such as washing their hands before going to lunch or after visiting the toilet.
- Talk to children about different foods and the food–health connection.
- Talk to children about the positive effects of exercise.

- Teach children about the need to warm up and cool down, and help them learn about appropriate posture and use of their bodies.
- Give children opportunities to discuss safety and what it means, for both themselves and their peers. Such discussions could include revisiting and restating rules and conventions that help to create a safe environment, for example avoiding household chemicals and medicines, and crossing the road safely with an adult.
- Encourage children to exercise their judgement and be assertive enough to be able to say no to others when their safety is at risk, as well as identifying and reporting unsafe resources and situations to their teachers.
- Insist on appropriate clothing. Wearing the right clothing is one way to avoid accidents in PE. Teachers can reinforce this idea by changing into sports clothing themselves, even if it only involves putting on a pair of trainers.
- Teach children to use, manipulate and move equipment safely (e.g. carry mats in fours).

The physical education, dance and movement, and play activities that they enjoy in nursery or reception constitute much more than ways of letting young and active children burn off excess energy. Many play activities, for example, involve a mixture of both gross and fine motor skills, for example construction/block play. Play can provide excellent opportunities to promote Physical development. Sand and water play offers children the chance to extend and improve fine motor control as well as being a way to introduce pupils to scientific and mathematical ideas, to foster language and Creative development, to encourage cooperative learning and personal and social development. Play with apparatus in the outdoor area or hall provides opportunities to develop gross motor control, hand–eye coordination or to engage in role-play. Outdoor play not only promotes children's Physical development but also enhances their development across the curriculum including their personal and social development, creative development and knowledge and understanding about the world.

Providing play opportunities for nursery and reception pupils

Water play
- Science and maths. Funnels, jugs, containers, water wheels, ice cubes, coloured water, washing-up liquid for bubbles.
- Language/Creativity. Plastic figures, boats.
- Health, hygiene and safety. Aprons, bucket, mop, cloths.

Sand play
- Science and maths. Spades and trowels, buckets, containers, spoons, rakes, damp and dry sand.
- Language/Creativity. Plastic figures, toy vehicles, toy animals.
- Health, hygiene and safety. Aprons, sweeping brush, dustpan.

Note: It is important to change the water or sand regularly and to ensure that equipment for clearing and cleaning up is readily to hand.

Creative play and mark-making
- Drawing and writing materials.
- Painting using different brushes and different kinds of paint.
- Collage activities involving cutting and sticking.
- Work with malleable materials, for example play dough, clay, plasticine.

Outdoor play
- Climbing and balancing apparatus.
- Crates, wooden boxes, cubes.
- Barrels, tunnels.
- Planks, beams, slides.
- See-saws, rockers.
- Large building blocks.
- Hard and padded surfaces (mats under climbing apparatus).
- Surfaces to promote games and play (hopscotch grids, targets on walls).
- Tricycles, bicycles, scooters, wagons.
- Games apparatus (e.g. balls, bats, bean bags, quoits, hoops, rings).

Note: As with any activity involving potentially dangerous equipment, outdoor play needs proper adult supervision. This supervision includes not merely observing children during their play, but also creating a play environment that is not inherently dangerous.

Physical Education (PE)

As children move through the 3–8 age range and into primary school at the age of 5 they are introduced to more formal PE lessons. Effective provision in PE offers children a range of indoor and outdoor activities that encourage them to respond confidently to physical challenges in a safe environment and enable them to become increasingly competent in the use of their bodies. Physical education can do much to increase children's ability to engage in both cooperative and independent learning, as teachers encourage children to

- show consideration for their surroundings and peers;
- collaborate, share and negotiate with other children; and
- follow rules and play fairly.

Physical education involves children in planning, performing and evaluating physical activities in a range of contexts, including gymnastics, games and dance. Games help pupils to develop their physical skills and understanding of simple tactics and rules. In dance and movement children have the chance to develop actions, appreciate concepts such as fast and slow, learn to make effective use of personal and general space, and have opportunities for creativity and composition, for example moving like an animal. In gymnastics they learn and develop actions and movements that contribute to the development of their gross motor control and hand–eye co-ordination as they move from floor work to apparatus work.

Helping children to become increasingly proficient at planning and performing in PE

- Encourage and support children in taking calculated risks and offer praise for showing confidence and enjoyment in physical activity.
- Teach a range of physical skills and techniques.
- Be alert to children's capabilities and confidence and do not introduce tasks prematurely (e.g. forward rolls) that will undermine confidence and enthusiasm.
- Promote positive attitudes towards health and fitness and an increased awareness of safety principles.
- Promote both cooperative and independent learning.
- Ask children to respond to tasks and try different ways of completing them.
- As pupils become more skilful, provide opportunities for them to start to link and combine actions and movements, and plan more complex movements, sequences of movements and tactics in games (rolling, bouncing, throwing and catching balls).

Helping children to evaluate their own and others' achievements in PE as a means of improvement

Ask children to
- copy the actions and movements of their peers;
- describe their own and others' actions and movements;
- identify and comment on good work; and
- compare actions and movements, suggesting modifications and improvements.

Creative Development

A U D I T

By the end of this section you should

- know about the teaching of Creative development in the Curriculum Guidance for the Foundation Stage (QCA, 2000, pp. 116–27);
- know about the teaching of art and music in the National Curriculum (QCA, 1999, pp. 116–21, 122–7).

The Curriculum Guidance for the Foundation Stage uses the term Creative development to describe work in the realms of art and music. However, it would be a mistake to think that creativity is restricted to the realms of art, music or drama. Creativity can manifest itself in any area of the curriculum (Craft, 1999; Prentice, 2000). This said, young children respond well to sensory experience and the chance to experiment with tools, materials, sounds, shapes and colour. Creative work in art and music allows children to express their ideas and feelings, and to make sense of the world in a very practical way. It gives them experience of making choices and decisions, and promotes independence and perseverance. Through subjects such as art and music pupils can develop their imagination, use materials creatively and appreciate beauty.

Music

Music is a means of expression that has both cognitive and emotional dimensions (QCA, 1999); it introduces children to aspects of different cultures past and present and offers them the opportunity for practical hands-on work. Young children get great pleasure from playing and listening to music. Music is particularly useful as a way of helping children to acquire the vital learning skill of listening and it should be valued for the opportunities it offers to underpin learning in other areas of the curriculum such as mathematics (time, tempo, rhythm) as well as for its inherent worth. In 3–8 settings, a music table or trolley offers children first-hand experience of a range of sounds and instruments.

Setting up a music table in the nursery/classroom

Provide
- a range of instruments (tambourines, drums, cymbals, triangles, shakers, bells, chime bars, wind instruments, home made);
- tape recorders and blank tapes for children to record and listen to their compositions;
- taped songs, tunes and rhymes;
- song books;
- ICT music packages and electronic keyboards.

Although there is a technical element to music, teachers who do not possess technical skills can still be effective in helping children to enjoy and gain confidence in their creative musical abilities. Listening and responding to a range of musical expressions, including music from different cultures and periods, as well as discussing their feelings, helps to promote appreciation, knowledge and understanding, for example of the difference between loud and quiet, fast and slow. Learning and singing rhymes and songs with accompanying actions, and using bodies as instruments (e.g. clapping, tapping, clicking fingers), are also enjoyable and useful activities.

Singing songs and rhymes

- One, two, three, four, five, once I caught a fish alive
- Pat-a-cake, baker's man
- Incy Wincy Spider
- Row your boat
- I'm a little teapot

- I hear thunder
- Ring a ring o' roses
- If you're happy and you know it
- The wheels on the bus
- Heads, shoulders, knees and toes
- Nicky, knacky, knocky, noo
- A sailor went to sea, sea, sea
- Oh, we can play on the big base drum
- Hokey Cokey

Most children do not start formal instrumental music instruction before they are 8 or 9 years old. They should, however, be given opportunities to perform and compose music informally and to experiment with and learn about the different sorts of sounds made by a range of instruments (percussion, string, wind). The instruments on offer to pupils in 3–8 settings can be commercially produced or home made. Real instruments ought to originate from a wide variety of different cultures and locations to extend pupil's musical knowledge and understanding (Leeds City Council, 1996). Music also offers teachers multiple opportunities to introduce new technologies into teaching and learning (e.g. computer software packages, programmable keyboard toys, tape recorder/listening stations and CD players) all of which allow children to compose and/or listen to music.

Making simple instruments

- Shakers (boxes, plastic pop bottles, tins, thick paper bags, peas, beans, pasta shells, rice, buttons).
- Drums (ice cream containers, plastic tubs and bowls, tins).
- Chimes (metal objects on string such as knives and forks).
- Pluckers (boxes/tins with elastic bands stretched across the top).

Art and Design

Through art children can explore, experiment and work with two- and three-dimensional materials in an imaginative manner, develop their abilities to handle tools and equipment safely and effectively and learn useful techniques with which to express themselves. Art with young children should value and emphasize the process as well as the product; the ability to mix the paints and understand colour and texture, for example, are important concomitants to the imaginative and expressive aspects of the subject. Art offers excellent opportunities for the development of fine motor control, and knowledge and understanding about the world as children are given opportunities to observe carefully, record natural and manufactured objects from a range of cultures and locations, and express their ideas and feelings visually (Myer, 2002).

Progression in drawing and painting

By the time children reach the age of 3 many are beginning to want to draw rather than simply scribble. They often begin by trying to represent people they know, with end-results often reminiscent of a 'Mr Man'.

   As children get more practice and become more proficient, their drawings and paintings begin to include more detail; a person may now be shown to have a body or fingers. Children start to make decisions about what they will draw or paint prior to doing so, rather than deciding what a drawing or painting represents afterwards. By the time pupils are ready to move on from Key Stage 1 to Key Stage 2, most are able to incorporate a number of different objects in their pictures and include a rudimentary sense of perspective with houses, trees or clouds in the background.

It is important to remember that children's abilities in art vary, just as they do in other areas. Some pupils may be adept and experienced in the use of textiles, paints or malleable materials; others will be less assured. Some pupils may be competent at drawing and thus capable of representing their observations and ideas at a level normally associated with older children. Others may have had fewer opportunities to experiment with drawing materials and, therefore, their pictures may be less well crafted than those of their peers.

   The examples on pages 121–2 illustrate the sort of progression that can be seen in children's drawing skills. They are, however, intended to be indicative and should not be seen as definitive.

Providing art materials and activities in 3–8 settings

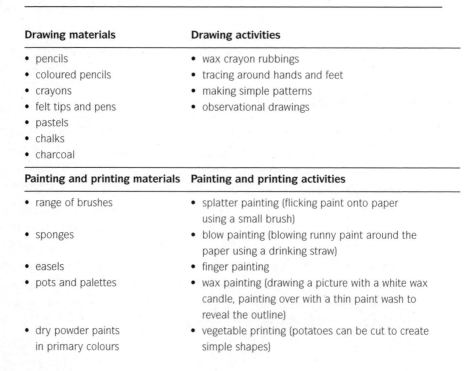

Drawing materials	Drawing activities
• pencils	• wax crayon rubbings
• coloured pencils	• tracing around hands and feet
• crayons	• making simple patterns
• felt tips and pens	• observational drawings
• pastels	
• chalks	
• charcoal	

Painting and printing materials	Painting and printing activities
• range of brushes	• splatter painting (flicking paint onto paper using a small brush)
• sponges	• blow painting (blowing runny paint around the paper using a drinking straw)
• easels	• finger painting
• pots and palettes	• wax painting (drawing a picture with a white wax candle, painting over with a thin paint wash to reveal the outline)
• dry powder paints in primary colours	• vegetable printing (potatoes can be cut to create simple shapes)

age 2½

age 3

age 4

age 5

KNOWLEDGE AND UNDERSTANDING

age 6

age 7

age 8

- ready mix paints
- block printing (using Styrofoam, clay, plasticine or cotton bobbins)
- body printing (hands, feet, fingers)
- symmetrical printing (drip paint onto one half of the paper and fold over to create the final pattern; alternatively, drape painted string onto one half of the paper and then fold)
- poster and powder paints in black, white and primary colours (offering children the chance to experiment with a wide range of effects and to learn how to mix their own colours)
- watered down or thickened paints (using PVA adhesive, flour and water or wallpaper paste – avoid fungicidal pastes)

Three-dimensional materials	Three-dimensional activities
<ul><li>malleable materials for exploring form (clay, plasticine, play dough. Play dough recipe: 2 parts plain flour, 1 part salt, 1 part cold water and 1 tablespoon vegetable oil)</li><li>boards</li><li>rolling pins, cutting tools, stamps</li><li>collage materials</li></ul>	<ul><li>collage</li><li>mobiles</li><li>mosaics</li><li>greetings cards</li><li>folding and cutting doilies to make snow flakes</li><li>colour and scent play dough for variety using food colourings and essences (make sure this does not tempt young children to consume it)</li></ul>

Information and Communications Technology (ICT)

By the end of this section you should

- know about developmentally appropriate uses of Information and Communications Technology in nursery and reception classes (QCA, 2000, pp. 92–3);
- know about the teaching of Information and Communications Technology in the National Curriculum (QCA, 1999, pp. 96–101).

Although this does not form a separate area of learning within the Curriculum Guidance for the Foundation Stage, using ICT is given a more overt form within the National Curriculum, towards which young children are working. As the example below shows, ICT involves more than just the computer; it incorporates any technology related to information, control and communication, including television, radio, audio tape, video, programmable toys, mobiles, photocopiers or faxes (O'Hara, 2004).

124

Nursery – Autumn term

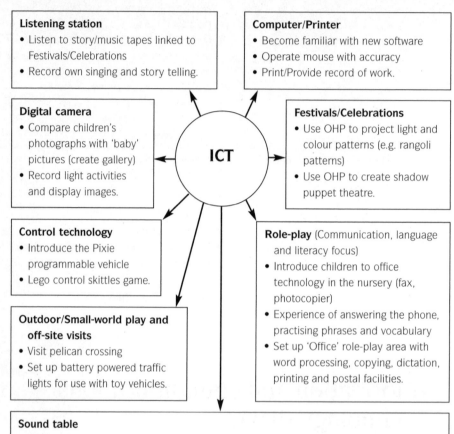

Listening station
- Listen to story/music tapes linked to Festivals/Celebrations
- Record own singing and story telling.

Computer/Printer
- Become familiar with new software
- Operate mouse with accuracy
- Print/Provide record of work.

Digital camera
- Compare children's photographs with 'baby' pictures (create gallery)
- Record light activities and display images.

ICT

Festivals/Celebrations
- Use OHP to project light and colour patterns (e.g. rangoli patterns)
- Use OHP to create shadow puppet theatre.

Control technology
- Introduce the Pixie programmable vehicle
- Lego control skittles game.

Role-play (Communication, language and literacy focus)
- Introduce children to office technology in the nursery (fax, photocopier)
- Experience of answering the phone, practising phrases and vocabulary
- Set up 'Office' role-play area with word processing, copying, dictation, printing and postal facilities.

Outdoor/Small-world play and off-site visits
- Visit pelican crossing
- Set up battery powered traffic lights for use with toy vehicles.

Sound table
- Musical keyboard
- Battery operated electronic/programmable toys (trumpet, saxophone, guitar, music mat).

(O'Hara, 2004)

Using ICT in 3–8 classes provides opportunities for interactive learning, the promotion of fine motor control, personal and social development and the development of reasoning skills. Using ICT in a variety of ways and contexts helps children to become increasingly familiar with it, and increasingly confident and positive about their skills as users (Sharp _et al._, 2002). Teachers need to ensure that all pupils have opportunities to use ICT in the nursery/classroom, that they take account of any home use or other previous experience of ICT, and that they seek opportunities to use ICT to extend and enhance learning across the curriculum.

Increasing children's familiarity and confidence with information and communications technology (ICT)

- Place a computer and/or other ICT equipment (e.g. walkie-talkies, listening stations, mobile phones) in the role-play area and integrate this with structured play activities on different themes such as 'The Travel Agents', 'The Bank', 'The Ticket Office' or 'The Theatre'.
- Use off-site visits to draw attention to the use of ICT in the real world (e.g. the library, supermarket bar codes, concept keyboards in shops and fast food outlets).
- Send and receive faxes and e-mails with children.
- Introduce children to the world wide web as an information source.
- Use programmable toys such as the Roamer or the Pixie.

125
___

Eg Young children can be surprisingly knowledgeable about information and communications technology (ICT)

C (Aged 4) to adult: 'You want to see on the computer, I've got a *folder*!'
Adult: 'Have you? On that computer?' (Points to the nursery PC)
C: 'No, on my computer at home.'
Adult: 'Oh. What's in your folder?'
C: 'Woody.'
Adult: 'Woody?'
C: (Withering look) 'Woody! Buzz Lightyear! Woody!'

D (Aged 4) enters the nursery creative area carrying a mobile phone from the role-play area. She places it next to her on the table while she begins to paint. After a few minutes she picks up the phone and begins to press the buttons.
Adult: 'What are you doing, D?'
D: 'I'm *texting* Julie.'
Adult: 'Oh. What's your message?'
D: 'To see if she can pick me up from nursery.'
D places the phone back on the table and starts painting again. A few minutes later she stops again, places the phone to her ear and starts talking.
D: 'Hello, Julie, are you picking me up from nursery or is my mum?' (Pauses for the imaginary reply) 'Oh, okay.'
D then returns to her painting.

(O'Hara, 2004)

Young children are increasingly enthusiastic and proficient users of ICT; the majority have experience in the home (e.g. telephones, televisions, PCs) and all will encounter it in their local environment (Kerawalla and Crook, 2002). Some parents may not be fully aware of the place of ICT within their children's education or appreciate its relevance; teachers may need to alert parents to the value of these experiences and discuss how to help children get the most out of ICT activities at home. Such discussions would also give teachers a chance to find out about the extent of their pupils' previous experience and skills before planning to use ICT.

Eg *Parents supporting children's learning in information and communications technology (ICT)*

- Spending time with and showing interest in the child – drawing children's attention to the use of ICT in the home (programmable washing machines, video timers) and in the world around them (pelican crossings, bar code readers in the local library).
- Listening, talking to and asking questions of the child – using technical vocabulary and expressions such as 'CD', 'mouse', 'program'; explaining the relationship between the mouse and the pointer on the computer screen; reading information together from a screen; listening to taped stories and music together; stopping/pausing a video to talk about the characters or events.
- Developing children's practical skills – giving children the chance (with supervision where appropriate) to switch things on and off, change channels, play, rewind, fast forward and record, changing CDs, using the mouse, clicking and double clicking.
- Encouraging the child to find out, explore, solve problems and try out new things – seeking information using CD-ROMs or the internet (see www.naeyc.org or www.ictadvice.org.uk for guidance on using the internet).
- Playing with the child – using programmable or battery operated toys, computer games, musical keyboards, taping and playing back the child's own songs.

(O'Hara, 2004)

Increasing children's information and communications technology (ICT) skills

- Allow time for young children to master skills.
- Give children experience of as wide a range of ICT applications as possible in and out of the nursery/school, not just the computer.
- Provide regular and frequent turns at operating ICT equipment as this will be much more effective at increasing skills and confidence than infrequent but long turns.
- Use commercially produced software to introduce children to the keyboard in a structured and systematic fashion.
- Remember that keyboard skills will also develop as a consequence of using the computer in a variety of purposeful contexts, for example writing stories.
- Use concept keyboards to replace the computer keyboard or to supplement it, with software that can be closed in nature or open ended (allowing teachers to design their own overlays for their pupils).
- Introduce children to the mouse. Young children can become proficient quite quickly. Drawing packages are particularly useful in providing them with lots of practice.

The use of ICT in the nursery/classroom offers considerable potential for enriching and enhancing the whole curriculum (Sharp *et al.*, 2002). There is a clear correspondence, for example, between Communication, language and literacy/English and the strand of ICT associated with the communication of information. Information and communications technology can provide valuable tools for reinforcing the essential first-hand and practical mathematics experiences of young children. Children's Creative development may be underpinned and enriched through the inclusion of an ICT dimension; it may also provide yet another context within which young children can progress in terms of their personal and social development through being encouraged to work collaboratively with others (Cooper and Brna, 2002).

Using information and communications technology (ICT) to support learning across the 3–8 curriculum

- Integrate ICT resources into socio-dramatic role-play areas to extend and enhance opportunities for speaking, listening, reading, writing and the application of number (e.g. a travel agents that contains a telephone, a mobile phone, a fax machine, a photocopier, an electronic cash register and a computer showing images of holiday destinations on a timed loop using PowerPoint).
- Point out instances of ICT during visits and local walks (e.g. traffic light sequences, burglar alarms, CCTV cameras, speed cameras).
- Speaking and listening can be enhanced through the use of audio-taped stories, while promoting collaborative (paired) work using ICT requires the children to contribute verbally to the completion of the task.
- Talking books can be used to support early reading as the children can hear the words on the screen. Software that involves matching objects to letters and finding the correct letters, such as 'My World', can also support reading. For older/more able pupils there is software to reinforce phonics.
- Writing can be supported through the use of ICT. Editing and redrafting benefit in particular from open-ended (generic) software. Software is also available that will demonstrate letter formation on-screen, and children can use the keyboard or a concept keyboard to produce emergent writing.
- Pupils' facility with number can be advanced through the use of simple operations software and the use of ICT in meaningful contexts, for example the electronic calculator or cash till in the role-play shop.
- Work on shape, space and measurement can be supported through the use of shape naming programs, finding the positions of objects in packages like 'Albert's House', and work with the Roamer or other programmable devices.
- Using drawing and painting packages offers advantages for young children in terms of the quality of the finish and the opportunity to edit their art work in a way that does not require excessive use of materials or result in messy outcomes.
- Music keyboards, music mats, toys and software exist which enable young children to play and compose tunes, and raise their appreciation and awareness of a wide range of different types of music.

The teacher plays an important role in organizing and managing positive ICT experiences for all children in the nursery/classroom; he/she must be ready to step in and intervene if necessary. It is easy to become complacent, blinded by the obvious enthusiasm of some pupils coupled with the presentation of the resource, to the need to monitor and ensure quality in teaching and learning. To be effective, ICT needs to be integrated appropriately into the curriculum. Using content-rich software (see example below) of the kind commonly found in 3–8 settings should not result in an absence of teacher/adult intervention. Unsupported involvement with unsuitable or undemanding drill and skill software packages is unlikely to provide much in the way of intellectual and creative challenge for children (Edgington, 1998). Equally, while ICT suites can be a valuable resource for the delivery of ICT in the National Curriculum, moving whole classes of nursery or reception pupils to designated ICT suites may result in experiences that are inappropriate given the ways in which young children learn. There may be practical difficulties in terms of staffing and young children may spend far longer in front of a computer screen than is advisable from a health and safety point of view (Caruso Davis & Shade, 1994; Pierce, 1994; Siraj-Blatchford & Siraj-Blatchford, 2002).

Adult input on content-rich software

Three nursery children are sitting in front of a computer using a software package that claims to help children with number recognition. Whenever the right number is matched to the right image the children are rewarded with a flashing screen and a simple jingle.

Closer observation shows that the children are not using their knowledge of number at all and may not even be aware of the purpose of the task. Instead, they are systematically matching every number to every image using a process of trial and error until they have cleared the screen of all the numbers and images.

Good problem-solving perhaps but are these children really reinforcing their number recognition? Quality adult input could have helped them to make the most of the technology and to understand what was being asked of them.

Organizing and managing information and communications technology (ICT) in the classroom

- Well-targeted teacher intervention will help children to get the most out of their ICT experiences. Do not rely on the technology to do the teaching; ICT is a tool not a teacher.
- Group children of similar ability, personalities and dispositions together to generate lively and rewarding discussion, where the pace tends to be agreed and children are less likely to be excluded.
- Use mixed ability pairs, particularly where there is a lot of reading to be done.
- Use children with previous ICT experience as an asset in groups, especially with younger children.
- Be alert to experienced children denying access to others. The warning signs include children making unilateral decisions; children monopolizing equipment; children operating equipment too quickly for their partner(s) to follow or understand; children bossing other children, generating disagreements and squabbles; and children being excluded or ignored by their peers.
- Try to observe the children soon after they have started working with the equipment so that there is time to intervene at an early stage.
- Be prepared to alter groupings to ensure that pupils have positive collaborative experiences while working with ICT.

- When organizing computer resources make sure there is a range of generic (open-ended) as well as content-rich software (Sharp *et al.*, 2002).
- Younger children work well in pairs in front of a computer. While threes are possible, more than three tends to lead to exclusion and lack of space to sit comfortably.
- Ensure that children have a clear role when working together on a computer. Encourage children to have a turn in different roles to avoid individuals monopolizing control of the machine. The centre seat (the one in front of the keyboard) is where control is maintained. A change of role ought to be accompanied by a change of seat. There are only really three roles possible when working on a computer:
  1. operating the keyboard;
  2. reading the screen;
  3. recording any information.

(Ellis, 1986)

FURTHER SOURCES OF INFORMATION

The Foundation Stage Curriculum (Nursery and Reception Pupils)

Anning, A. (ed.) (1995) *A National Curriculum for the Early Years*. Buckingham: Open University Press.

Edwards, A. and Knight, P. (1994) *Effective Early Years Education: Teaching Young Children*. Buckingham: Open University Press.

QCA (2000) Curriculum Guidance for the Foundation Stage. London: QCA.

Rodger, R. (1999) *Planning an Appropriate Curriculum for the Under-5s*. London: David Fulton.

The National Curriculum for 5–8 year olds (Years 1, 2 and 3)

DfEE (1998) *The National Literacy Strategy*. London: DfEE.

DfEE (1999) *The National Numeracy Strategy*. London: DfEE.

QCA (1999) *The National Curriculum: Handbook for Primary Teachers in England Key Stages 1 and 2*. London: QCA.

Children as Learners

Bruce, T. (1997) *Early Childhood Education*, 2nd edn. London: Hodder and Stoughton.

Hyson, M. C. (1994) *The Emotional Development of Young Children: Building an Emotion Centered Curriculum*. New York: Teachers College Press.

Keenan, T. (2002) *An Introduction to Child Development*. London: Sage.

Macintyre, C. (2001) *Enhancing Learning through Play: A Developmental Perspective for Early Years Settings*. London: David Fulton.

Miller, L., Drury, R. and Campbell, R. (eds) (2002) *Exploring Early Years Education and Care*. London: David Fulton.

Nutbrown, C. (1994) *Threads of Thinking*. London: Chapman.

Sayeed, Z. and Guerin, E. (2000) *Early Years Play: A Happy Medium for Assessment and Intervention*. London: David Fulton.

Selley, N. (1999) *The Art of Constructivist Teaching in the Primary School: A Guide for Students and Teachers*. London: David Fulton.

Wood, D. (1998) *How Children Think and Learn*, 2nd edn. Oxford: Blackwell.

Personal, Social and Emotional Development

Curry, M. and Bromfield, C. (1995) *Personal and Social Education for Primary Schools Through Circle Time*. Tamworth: Nasen.

Dowling, M. (2000) *Young Children's Personal, Social and Emotional Development*. London: Paul Chapman.

Hughes, E. (1994) *Religious Education in the Primary School: Managing Diversity*. London: Cassell.

Multifaithnet, www.multifaithnet.org/

Communication, Language and Literacy

Browne, A. (1996) *Developing Language and Literacy 3–8*. London: Chapman.

Burnett, C. and Myers, J. (2004) *Teaching English 3–11: The Essential Guide*. London: Continuum.

Campbell, R. (2002) 'Exploring key literacy learning: own name and alphabet', in Miller, L., Drury, R. and Campbell, R. (eds), *Exploring Early Years Education and Care*. London: David Fulton.

Marsh, J. and Hallet, E. (eds) (1999) *Desirable Literacies: Approaches to Language and Literacy in the Early Years*. London: Chapman.

Merchant, G. (1998) 'Teaching primary English', in Cashdan, A. and Overall, L. (eds), *Teaching in Primary Schools*. London: Cassell.

Parke, T. and Drury, R. (2002) 'Who's listening? Who's teaching? Good circumstances for the language development of young bilinguals in early years settings', in Miller, L., Drury, R. and Campbell, R. (eds), *Exploring Early Years Education and Care*. London: David Fulton.

Whitehead, M. (1999) *Supporting Language and Literacy Development in the Early Years*. Buckingham: Open University Press.

Mathematical Development

Anghileri, J. (ed.) (1995) *Children's Mathematical Thinking in the Primary Years*. London: Cassell.

Askew, M. (1998) *Teaching Primary Mathematics*. London: Hodder and Stoughton.

Cameron, S. (1998) 'Teaching primary mathematics', in Cashdan, A. and Overall, L. (eds), *Teaching in Primary Schools*. London: Cassell.

Duncan, A. (1996) *What Primary Teachers Should Know about Maths*, 2nd edn. London: Hodder and Stoughton.

Edwards, S. (1998) *Managing Effective Teaching of Mathematics 3–8*. London: Paul Chapman.

Haylock, D. (2001) *Mathematics Explained for Primary Teachers*. London: Paul Chapman.

Jennings, S. and Dunne, R. (1997) *Mathematics for Primary Teachers: An Audit and Self-Study Guide*. London: Letts Educational.

Orton, A. and Frobisher, L. (1996) *Insights into Teaching Mathematics*. London: Cassell.

Thompson, I. (ed) (1997) *Teaching and Learning Early Number*. Buckingham: Open University Press.

Knowledge and Understanding of the World

Davies, D. and Howe, A. (2003) *Teaching Science, Design and Technology in the Early Years*. London: David Fulton.

Farmery, C. (2002) *Teaching Science 3–11: The Essential Guide*. London: Continuum.

Fleer, M. (2000) 'Working technologically: investigations into how young children design and make during technology education', *International Journal of Technology and Design Education*, **10**, 43–59.

Fran, M. (1995) *Teaching Early Years Geography*. Cambridge: Kington.

Johnsey, R. (1998) *Exploring Primary Design and Technology*. London: Cassell.

O'Hara, L. and O'Hara, M. (2001) *Teaching History 3–11: The Essential Guide*. London: Continuum.

Owen, D. and Ryan, A. (2001) *Teaching Geography 3–11: The Essential Guide*. London: Continuum.

Ritchie, R. (2001) *Primary Design and Technology*. London: David Fulton.

Rogers, G. and Wallace, J. (2000) 'The wheels on the bus: children designing in an early years classroom', *Research in Science and Technological Education*, **18** (1), 127–36.

Ryan, A. and Jones, J. (1998) 'Teaching the foundation subjects: geography and history', in Cashdan, A. and Overall, L. (eds), *Teaching in Primary Schools*. London: Cassell.

Sowden, S., Stea, D., Blades, M., Spencer, C. and Blaut, J. M. (1995) 'Mapping abilities of four year old children in York, England', *Journal of Geography*, May/June, 107–11.

Turner-Bisset, R. (2002) 'The essence of history in the early years', in Miller, L., Drury, R. and Campbell, R. (eds), *Exploring Early Years Education and Care*. London: David Fulton.

Wiegand, P. (1993) *Children and Primary Geography*. London: Cassell.

Wood, L. and Holden, C. (1995) *Teaching Early Years History*. Cambridge: Kington.

Physical Development

Bilton, H. (1998) *Outdoor Play in the Early Years*. London: David Fulton.

DfE (1995) *Physical Education*. London: HMSO.

Heald, C. (1998) *Physical Development*. Leamington Spa: Scholastic.

Manners, H. K. (1995) *A Framework for Physical Education in the Early Years*. London: Falmer Press.

Wood, E. and Attfield, J. (1996) *Play, Learning and the Early Childhood Curriculum*. London: Chapman.

Creative Development

Allen, R. (2002) 'Drawing as a language in the early years', in Miller, L., Drury, R. and Campbell, R. (eds), *Exploring Early Years Education and Care*. London: David Fulton.

Craft, A. (1999) 'Creative development in the early years: some implications of policy for practice', *The Curriculum Journal*, **10** (1), 135–50.

Gentle, K. (1993) *Teaching Painting in the Primary School*. London: Cassell.

Glover, J. and Ward, S. (eds) (1998) *Teaching Music in the Primary School*, 2nd edn. London: Cassell.

Myer, C. (2002) *Not Just Pictures: Children Developing Creativity through Art*. London: The British Association for Early Childhood Education.

Prentice, R. (2000) 'Creativity: a reaffirmation of its place in early childhood education', *The Curriculum Journal*, **11** (2), 145–58.

Information and Communications Technology (ICT)

Crompton, R. and Mann, P. (eds) (1997) *IT across the Primary Curriculum*. London: Cassell.

Kerawalla, L. and Crook, C. (2002) 'Children's Computer Use at Home and at School: context and continuity', *British Educational Research Journal*, **28** (6), 751–71.

O'Hara, M. (2004) *ICT in the Early Years*. London: Continuum.

Sharp, J., Potter, J., Allen, J. and Loveless, A. (2002) *Primary ICT: Knowledge, Understanding and Practice*. Exeter: Learning Matters.

Siraj-Blatchford, J. and Siraj-Blatchford, I. (2002) 'Guidance for Practitioners on Appropriate Technology Education in Early Childhood', www.ioe.ac.uk/cdl/DATEC

Teaching

SUMMARY

Chapter 2 dealt with the need for 3–8 teachers to have a good knowledge and understanding of the curriculum and children as learners. However, knowing what needs to be taught is insufficient on its own to make someone effective as a teacher. Teachers of 3–8 pupils must also be good planners, managers and communicators, and they must be able to deploy a range of effective strategies in the nursery/classroom that facilitate teaching and learning.

By the end of this chapter you should

- know about planning and target-setting with Foundation Stage and lower primary pupils;
- know about monitoring, assessing and reporting on pupils' learning;
- know about differentiating lessons and responding to the needs of individual children, including pupils with special educational needs (SEN);
- know about classroom organization and management; and
- know about effective teaching strategies.

An Overview of the Role of the Teacher

In addition to the need for opportunities for children to learn through play and first-hand experience, social interactionists such as Bruner and Vygotsky also argued convincingly of the need for high-quality interactions between adults and children as a means of fostering children's personal, social, physical and cognitive development. The teacher must provide a suitable learning environment and plan an appropriate curriculum. He/She must help the children to get the most from this environment through his/her teaching and interactions with pupils. The teacher must also monitor and assess pupils' progress in order to inform future planning and provision.

Teachers therefore need to be effective at organizing and planning a learning environment conducive to children's development. This includes setting up the physical environment to facilitate learning (e.g. organizing props and equipment, providing time for exploration and the deployment of available staff). It also includes planning and decision-making about the knowledge, skills and understanding to be covered.

Having planned the content and established the context teachers then have to teach. They can help children to learn by modelling and explaining problem-solving skills which children can practise on their own, as well as introducing knowledge and skills to extend pupils' learning. With younger children this means actively participating in their work and play as a co-player/co-learner, offering ideas and knowledge to help children sustain the learning. Sayeed and Guerin (2000) advocate mediated learning experiences (MLEs) whereby an adult and child interact in relation to an activity. In accordance with a child's needs the adult adapts the frequency, order, content, location and intensity of the activity. The adult arouses care, curiosity and alertness in the child and helps him/her to understand the activity so that he/she can be successful in it. Teachers have to be able to mediate between the children themselves and to mediate between the physical environment and the children (Jones and Reynolds 1992 in DECS, 1996).

In an MLE the child:	In an MLE the adult:
Selects an activity	Helps the child to select an activity and reduce its complexity
Focuses on relevant aspects	Exposes the child to the activity repeatedly
Perceives and understands similarities and differences	Reinforces learning
Transfers learning to a new situation.	'Bridges' by connecting the child's past, present and future experiences.

(Sayeed and Guerin, 2000)

Teachers must also be capable of monitoring children's progress and assessing their achievements and their needs. This means collecting, organizing and recording data on pupils' learning and using observations and samples of work to make judgements about their progress. Monitoring and assessing children's progress provides teachers with information on possible misconceptions and gaps in knowledge and skills, and these assessments inform subsequent decision-making about future learning opportunities as well as providing the basis for feedback and reporting to parents and others.

Teachers therefore need to be able to

- plan stimulating and interesting activities at an appropriate level for young children;
- offer a broad and balanced curriculum that promotes children's academic, social, physical and emotional development;
- employ alternative forms and methods of assessment;
- use assessment information on pupils' attainment in teaching and in planning future lessons and sequences of lessons;
- record children's progress and achievements;
- report to parents and others on pupils' progress including reports on Standard Attainment Tests (SATs) and the Foundation Stage Profile;
- take into account and respond to the differing needs, abilities and previous experiences (including home experiences) of children;
- provide a high-quality learning environment which motivates and stimulates children and supports their learning; and
- manage a class effectively.

Planning

A U D I T

By the end of this section you should

- know about the planning of lessons and sequences of lessons;
- know how to develop clear learning purposes/objectives.

Why Plan?

Much of children's learning takes place in relatively unstructured contexts outside the nursery/school, for example at home or through the media. Teachers, however, are engaged in building on children's previous learning in a more organized fashion, based on the Early Learning Goals or National Curriculum Programmes of Study (PoS); planning is an essential skill which they all must master in order to be able to do this. There are many distractions in 3–8 settings which may deflect from planning, but without a clear plan to begin with, these distractions will come to rule. It is very hard as a teacher to think on your feet if you are already thinking on your feet. This is not to say that planning should act as a straightjacket; good teachers are able to spot opportunities for unplanned learning when they occur and good planning does not preclude this. Paradoxically, good planning actually makes it easier for teachers to be more responsive and flexible and to make calculated detours, enabling them to adjust their timing and modify their intentions much more easily.

Effective planning provides a clear focus and purpose for lessons and schemes of work. It assists teachers in focusing on their own practice, making it easier to reflect on events, to modify future teaching, to anticipate children's needs and to have responses ready. An absence of effective planning, however, can have serious consequences for teaching and learning. It can lead both to teacher inefficiency and ineffectiveness in the classroom and to learning that is, at best, patchy and uncoordinated. Good planning helps teachers to avoid wasting time and missing learning opportunities. Lessons and activities that are planned are far more likely to be satisfying and successful than those that are not.

Planning to Teach the National Curriculum

The School Curriculum and Assessment Authority (SCAA) identified a number of different levels of planning (SCAA, 1995). The following section gives a brief outline of the progression through long-, medium- and short-term planning using National Curriculum Programmes of Study, National Literacy and Numeracy Strategies and includes examples from primary settings.

Long-term planning: schemes of work

Long-term planning provides broad frameworks outlining the curriculum to be taught during a child's time in the school. Long-term planning of this sort ought to reflect school policies and the whole staff should be involved in developing and approving final versions. Schools draw up schemes of work to cover the full range of National Curriculum subject areas, to address coherence, continuity and progression across the various subjects and between year groups and Key Stages. Schemes of work contain

- the content that needs to be covered within the different year groups (based on National Curriculum Programmes of Study or National Literacy/Numeracy Strategy statements);
- the organization of that content into manageable and coherent sections;
- identification of any real links between the various aspects of the curriculum; and
- the balance between, and time available for, the various subjects and areas of learning.

Long-term planning may also be used by schools in areas such as transition between nursery and school, induction arrangements for new children, and themes, festivals and visits to be incorporated into the curriculum at various times during the year.

Readers are advised to refer to the comments in Chapter 1 concerning policies and guidelines for further information on this aspect of long-term planning.

 Long-term planning

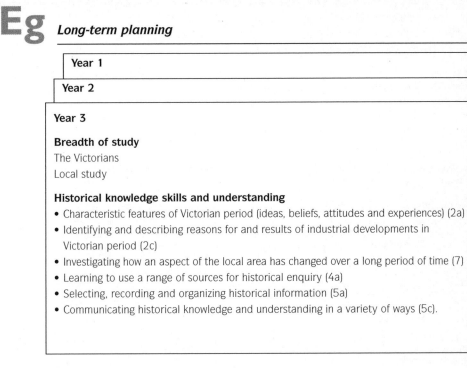

> **Year 1**
>
> **Year 2**
>
> **Year 3**
>
> **Breadth of study**
> The Victorians
> Local study
>
> **Historical knowledge skills and understanding**
> - Characteristic features of Victorian period (ideas, beliefs, attitudes and experiences) (2a)
> - Identifying and describing reasons for and results of industrial developments in Victorian period (2c)
> - Investigating how an aspect of the local area has changed over a long period of time (7)
> - Learning to use a range of sources for historical enquiry (4a)
> - Selecting, recording and organizing historical information (5a)
> - Communicating historical knowledge and understanding in a variety of ways (5c).

(O'Hara and O'Hara, 2001)

Medium-term planning

Medium-term planning covers the details of the programme to be taught to a particular year group normally over a term or half-term period. Such planning is based on the school's long-term plans. It should involve the whole year group team within a school. Medium-term plans show where work is continuing, blocked or linked in nature (SCAA, 1995).

Eg *Medium-term planning outcomes*

- **Continuing work**. Work drawn from a single subject area and ongoing across the year.
- **Blocked work**. Work drawn from a single subject, taught within a set period of time, characterized by a tight subject focus with a discrete body of knowledge, skills and understanding.
- **Linked work**. Work drawn from two or three subject areas, intended to increase the coherence of the curriculum by building on common or complementary knowledge, skills and understanding across the subjects involved.

(SCAA, 1995)

Medium-term plans

- state the learning objectives drawn from the long-term plans indicating progression through the programme;
- indicate the resources needed where some form of advance action will be required, such as booking loan materials from libraries and museums;
- suggest teaching methods and ways of organizing the children; and
- include opportunities for assessment.

Eg *Medium-term plan – geography*

Learning objectives (inc. NC PoS)	Assessment of outcomes Criteria:Mode:	Activity and organization
Where do I live? How do I get to school? NC Geog 1d, 4a, 7a,	**Criteria**: Do children know and understand their own address? Draw conclusions from a graph? **Mode**: Work produced and observations	Children to write their own address and display them onto a large map of the area. Discuss with the children who live the furthest/nearest to school. With the children carry out survey and complete a graph of how children travel to school.
How do I get to school? NC Geog 1d, 2e, 3b	**Criteria**: Can children draw a simple map? **Mode**: Children's work	Children to draw a map of their route from home to school and then describe to a partner, following the map.
What can we see in the local area around school? NC Geog 3a, 3b, 3c	**Criteria**: Can children recall physical and human features in their locality? **Mode**: Observation/Questioning	Children to look at pictures of the locality and describe the features. Children to group them in sets, near and far, buildings and features, and place them in the sequence they are seen on the route to school.
What was my school like long ago? NC Geog 1a, 5a,	**Criteria**: Can children ask geographical questions? **Mode**: Observation	Children to prepare questions to ask the visit or about the school and the local area. Listen to speaker and look at a range of artefacts, photographs and pictures.
What are our immediate surroundings like? NC Geog 1c, 2b, 5b	**Criteria**: Can the children: Describe features of the local environment? Express their opinions on the features? Identify changes in the locality? **Mode**: Questioning	Walk around the local area and school using a map (take digital photographs) to identify main features and changes. Discuss: the quality of the features and the environment; what the children like or dislike about the local area.
What are the changes taking place in our area? NC Geog 3c, 4b, 5a	**Criteria**: Can children identify how things change for better or worse over time? **Mode**: Observation/ Questioning/Work	Discuss the changes taking place using the photographs. With help of the children mark these on the large map. Discuss whether the children think these changes are good or bad. Draw a plan how they would like the school and local area to look in the future.

Pupil outputs	Special resources needed	Links
• Write address • Represent various types of travel on a graph	Large map of area Computers	Maths ICT
• Draw a map showing the route • Recognize where places are	Large map of area	Literacy
• Identify sequence of features seen on their route to school • Describe the features	Pictures of locality	
• Prepared geographical questions • Used secondary sources of information	Visitor to bring artefacts, pictures and photographs	History
• Use a range of words and photographs to show their view on the environment • Know about the changes • Use digital camera	Additional adult support Digital cameras	ICT
• Realize that the process of change is continual • Develop understanding of chronology • Draw a plan	Photographs/ pictures	History

Short-term planning

This focuses upon daily and/or weekly teaching and assessment. Short-term planning is derived from medium-term planning but is more specific and detailed, showing

- clear learning purposes;
- key skills, concepts and vocabulary to be introduced or reinforced;
- the nature of any adult intervention;
- how activities are to be differentiated;
- clear progression through the lesson from introduction to conclusion;
- the resources that will be needed;
- how and what is to be assessed; and
- where feedback to children will be given.

Lessons need clear objectives or learning purposes which indicate what the children are going to learn or practise. There may be many possible activities that would allow children to achieve a particular learning objective. Trainee and newly qualified teachers need to be clear about the distinction between the purposes of a lesson and the activity that the children will do, and sharing these learning purposes with them can help to achieve intended outcomes. Learning purposes, moreover, should not be too numerous. It is both inappropriate and unreasonable to expect pupils in this age group to meet large numbers of learning objectives in any one lesson or session.

In addition to learning purposes, teachers also need criteria by which to assess the children's achievements in order to gauge the extent to which the purpose of the lesson or session has been met. Such criteria can be devised by considering what a child might do or say to demonstrate achievement. For primary pupils, these criteria for assessment can be drawn from National Literacy Strategy (NLS) statements, National Numeracy Strategy (NNS) statements and from National Curriculum level descriptions.

The process of planning lessons enables practitioners to rehearse their ideas in their mind's eye prior to teaching and learning taking place. It also results in a written *aide memoir* which can act as a prompt sheet in relation to key teaching points, the sequencing and ordering of tasks and the organisation of resources. The act of producing lesson plans therefore makes it more likely that learning objectives will be met. That said, such plans ought not to constitute a strait-jacket whereby practitioners forge relentlessly on to their objectives irrespective of the impact on the children. Good practitioners are constantly observing the children and will adjust and amend their plans in response to the interests and needs of the children or in response to unplanned for events. These ongoing observations also play a crucial part in ensuring that subsequent planning is well matched to the needs and abilities of the children.

The planning cycle

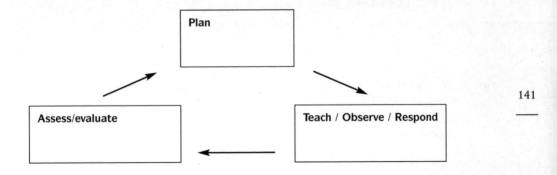

Literacy weekly plan

Literacy Weekly Planner

Class: 3   **Year**: 1   **Term**: Autumn 2003 2nd half   **Week Beginning**: 3 November   **Teacher**:

Phonic, spelling and vocabulary	Grammar and punctuation	Comprehension and composition
4. To discriminate and segment all three phonemes in CVC words. 9. To read on sight other familiar words; (house, little, then, three, once, so).	6. To begin using the term sentence to identify sentences in text.	7. To re-enact stories in a variety of ways, e.g. through role-play and puppets. 5. To describe story settings and incidents and relate them to own experience and that of others.

	Whole-class-shared reading and writing	Whole-class phonics, spelling, vocabulary and grammar	Guided group tasks	Guided group tasks
Mon	Introduce text: *Three Little Pigs*. Cover, title, familiar words.	Using large letters, show an object and children to make the word.	Guided reading White group	Familiar reading Yellow group
Tues	*Three Little Pigs*. Talk about story setting and incidents. Children to give input.	Read familiar words (house, little, then, three, once, so).	Guided reading Blue group	Familiar reading Green group
Weds	*Three Little Pigs*. Children to sequence the events in the story and me to write it on the whiteboard.	Use whiteboards to get children to write CVC words and practise letter formation.	Children to write and sequence the important events that happened in the story.	—————
Thurs	*Three Little Pigs*. Show a section of text without full stop and capital letters. Identify sentences.	Read familiar words; (house, little, three, then once, so).	Children to identify sentences. Put in full stops and capital letters.	—————
Fri	Handwriting in writing books.	CVC words (house, little, then, three, once, so).	Handwriting in books.	—————

Tasks

	Guided	Familiar	Phonics	ICT	Role-Play	
Mon 11.30	White	Yellow	Blue	Green	Red	Phonic work – children to complete CVC Worksheet on 'e, o, u'
Tues 9.50	Blue	Green	White	Red	Yellow	ICT – children to write familiar captions from the *Three Little Pigs*. Using familiar words (house, little, three, then, once, so)
Weds 9.50	Red	White	Yellow	Blue	Green	
Thurs 1.15	Green	Blue	Red	Yellow	White	Role-Play – children to re-enact the story of the *Three Little Pigs* using masks and puppets
Fri 1.15	Yellow	Red	Green	White	Blue	

Group tasks			Plenary
Phonics work Blue group	ICT Green group	Role-Play Red group	Look at ICT and phonic work
Phonics work White group	ICT Red group	Role-Play Yellow group	Look at ICT and phonic work
		→	Read a selection of the children's writing
		→	Check sentences for full stops and capital letters
		→	Re-read the story of the *Three Little Pigs*

Literacy hour session plan

Session Planner

Day: Wednesday	Subject: English – Literacy hour	Class: 3 Yr 1
Date: 5 Nov 2003	Theme: The Three Little Pigs	(Set/Group) Whole class

Lesson Objective/s:	NC/NLS/NNS ref:
• Discriminate and segment all three phonemes in CVC words • Identify and describe characters, events and settings in fiction • Use their knowledge of sequence and story language when they are retelling stories and predicting events • Sequence events and recount them in appropriate detail • Encourage children to use the text they read as models for their own writing • Write familiar words and attempt unfamiliar ones	NC KS1 En En2– 3a, 3b En3 – 1b, 1f, 2a NLS – word level objective 4

Time	Teaching strategies	Pupil tasks and learning outcomes	Support adult/s
Start:	Settle the children on the carpet in their literacy places.	Children to sit on the carpet in their literacy places.	

10.50 am   Whole class – word work

• Explain task – children to listen carefully to words so that they can identify the phonemes (letters) and then write the word accurately on their whiteboard. Look at the word they have written and check letter formation. (Stress the importance of letter formation.) • Hand out whiteboards, pens and cloths to the children. • Read list of words, stressing phonemes. Each time wait for all children to finish then get the children to hold up their board and show the word. Check letter formation. • Collect whiteboards, pens and cloths.	• Children to pass along the whiteboards, etc. • Children to listen carefully and then write the word concentrating on the formation of their letters. • Children to hand in equipment.	NTA to assist with distribution and collection of equipment.

11.05 am   Whole class – text work

• Ask the children to identify week's story. • Ask the children to recount events in the story. • Introduce the idea of putting the events in order of occurrence. Check children's understanding of ordering/sequencing events. Discuss. • Introduce the pictures from the story and explain that we need to put them in the correct order. Ask individual children for contributions. • Introduce group/independent work.	• Children to think about the what the answer might be before putting up their hand with a suggestion. • Children to make suggestions about the meaning of 'ordering'.

Group or independent work

Children to sit in their literacy groups. Children to think about the order of the important events within the story. Children to

- choose four key events in the story;
- draw a picture of the event;
- write a sentence to explain what is happening.

White group – independent work
Blue group – independent work

Green group – teacher supervised work.
Yellow group – teacher supervised work.

Red group – series of pictures from the story, to be ordered. The children to talk through the story with NTA before choosing four key events and completing worksheet with support.

Children to think about the story and the important events, reflecting on what was done as a class.

Children to choose four of the main events and record them in the correct order, drawing a picture and then writing an accompanying sentence.

NTA to work with Red group.

Extension

More able children to write their own ending for the story.

Session
ends:
Plenary

Individual children to show their work to the rest of the class, reading what they have written.

Assessment
Criteria: Can the children
- discriminate and segment all three phonemes in CVC words;
- sequence events and recount them in appropriate detail;
- write familiar words and attempt unfamiliar ones.

Mode:
Outcome and observations of individual children

Resources and vocabulary
- Whiteboards, pens and cloths
- Large pictures from the story
- Five sets of small pictures from the story
- pencil/pencil crayons

Vocabulary
- order or sequence
- familiar words, house, little, three, then, once, so

Numeracy Weekly Plan

| | Mental/Oral | | | |
	Objective	Activity	Vocabulary	Objective
Mon	Respond rapidly to oral questions, phrased in a variety of ways: Take 1 away from 4 4 take away 1	Children to show the number that is 1 less than a given number. Use number fans.	Fewer, less than, take away, subtract, difference between, Equals	Understand addition as • combining sets to make a total; • steps along a number track.
Tues	Respond rapidly to oral questions phrased in a variety of ways; 3 add 1 Add 1 to 4	Children to show the number that is 1 more than a given number. Use number fans.	More, add, sum, total, altogether, equal, sentence	Record simple mental additions in a number sentence using the + and = signs.
Weds	Respond rapidly to oral questions phrased in a variety of ways: Take away 10 from 20 What's 10 less than 40	Children to identify the number that is 10 less than a given number, using large number grid.	Fewer, less than, take away, subtract, difference between, Equals	Understand that addition can be done in any order.
Thurs	Respond rapidly to oral questions phrased in a variety of ways; 3 add 1 Add 1 to 4	Put a variety of numbers on the floor, children to make a circle. Give children addition problem, then they have to find the answer on the number cards.	More, add, sum, total, altogether, equal, sentence	Put the larger number first and count on in ones.
Fri	Record simple mental additions in a number sentence using the + and = signs.	Children to record a practical problem in a number sentence using the + and = signs. Use whiteboards.	More, add, sum, total, altogether, equal, sentence	Understand that addition can be done in any order, but also understand that putting the larger number first and counting on it easier.

146

MAIN ACTIVITY

Lower achievers	Middle achievers	Higher achievers	Resources	Plenary
Practical addition problems: How many children are having sandwiches? How many are girls?	Then show how this is recorded.	Identify what language is used.	Number fans	Talk about different ways of counting, e.g. putting the number in your head. Discuss language and signs to be used.
Children to respond to oral questions.	Write the number sentence, including the answer on whiteboards		Paper Dice – dotted numbers 1–6, and 1–12	Get the children to ask the class some of their number sentences. Talk about + and = signs.
Children to be given 2 dotted dice. Shake dice and make a number sentence	Children to be given 2 dice with numbers 1–6. Shake the dice and write a number sentence.	Children to be given 2 dice, 1 with numbers 1–6 other with numbers 6–12. Shake dice and write a number sentence.	Number fans Whiteboards, pens and cloths.	
Use dominoes to show that addition can be done in any order.	Turn the domino around so that the children can see this.	See if the children can predict the answer.	Whiteboards Dominoes	Talk about doing addition in any order. Talk about adding larger number together (2 + 16).
Children to use dominoes to make an addition problem of their own.	Children to record the number sentence on white boards.			
Identify which is the larger number.	Give children two numbers and ask them compare them.		Differentiated worksheets. Large numbers for physical number	Give more practical problems. Talk about what the children have learned about putting the larger number first. Do weather chart.
Differentiated worksheet with number sentences.	Children to rearrange the number sentence, putting the larger number first.	Once the sentence is arranged children are to work out the answers.		
Give children a variety of number problems.	Ask the children how they did the addition.	Encourage them to put the larger number first.	Whiteboards Digit cards Squashy boxes.	Recap on everything learned throughout the week. (Counting on in ones. Addition in any order. Put the larger number first.)
Use digit cards face down. Pick two numbers add them together. Use objects to help them count.	Use squashy cards to make an addition problem.	Use squashy cards to make an addition problem.		

Numeracy hour session plan

Session Planner

Day: Friday	Subject: Numeracy	Class: 3 Yr 1
Date: 14 Nov 2003	Theme: Addition	(Set/Group) Whole class

Lesson Objective/s:
- Record simple mental additions in a number sentence using the + and = signs
- Understand that addition can be done in any order, but to also understand that putting the larger number first and counting on, is earier.

NC/NLS/NNS ref:
NNS KS1 Calculations
24 –29
32–41

Time	Teaching strategies	Pupil tasks and learning outcomes	Support adult/s

Mental/Oral

Give the children a variety of practical problems. Individual children to write problem as a number sentence on class whiteboard, ensuring that they have the + and – signs.

Example of questions:

If I have 5 sweets and I buy 3 more, how many sweets will I have altogether?

If I have 4 sweets and (name) gives me 5 more, how many sweets will I have in total?

Children to write these on whiteboards.

Carpet time.

Main activity – whole class

Give children a variety of number problems, phrased in different ways:

2 + 6	7 + 4	3 + 8	2 + 9
5 + 4	12 + 4	10 + 5	4 + 13

Ask the children to explain how they worked out the problem.

Encourage the children to put the larger number first.

Children to put up their hand when they know the answer.

Explain how they solved the problem.

Main activity – independent work

Children to complete numeracy worksheet, putting the largest number in the number sentence first. Once they have put all the larger numbers first then they can write in the answers to the number problems.

Model the extension activity. Use digit cards and squashy cards to create number problems to be answered. Circle group with digit cards, other groups with squashy cards.

Children to finish the worksheet as directed. If completed then move onto the extension activity as instructed.

Circle group to work with teacher

NTA to rotate around other groups to offer support and guidance.

Extension

Circle group – to put digit cards face down, choose two cards, write the number sentence and work it out using counting bricks.

Square, rectangle and triangle groups to use squashy cards to make a number sentence, and to work out answer mentally.

Plenary

Ask the children to explain/define 'addition'.

- Talk about addition being combining sets, to make a total and steps along a number track.
- Ask the children to explain how an addition sum can be done. Does it have to be in the order it is written? 2 + 6 or 6 + 2 can the children predict the answer to the second question?
- Ask the children how they can make a problem easier. Encourage the children to talk about having the larger number first.

Children to respond to directed questions.

Assessment
Criteria

- Do the children understand that addition can be done in any order?
- Do the children know that it is easier to count on from the larger number to find the total?

Mode:
Observations

Resources and vocabulary

Whiteboards
Worksheets
Digit cards
Squashy cards

Vocabulary
More, add, sum, total, altogether, equals, sentence

Planning Using the Curriculum Guidance for the Foundation Stage

For those working with the youngest children, planning ought to be informed by an understanding of the ways in which these pupils learn. Young children develop and grow rapidly. They learn well in situations and circumstances that are real and relevant to their lives, and through activities that are varied and interesting. While they will follow recognized patterns of development during this period, individuals vary considerably. Development may not necessarily be a smooth and continual process; it may even be susceptible to regression. Children arrive in nursery and reception classes from a wide variety of backgrounds, with a broad range of experiences, and at different stages of development. Their experiences in 3–5 settings constitute a key stage in their learning and development. As a result planning in nursery and reception settings seeks to build upon previous (home) experiences and learning, and recognizes that young children's needs and interests will grow and develop over time. Pupils are offered opportunities to explore significant events in their lives and are encouraged to engage in self-expression and discovery. Early years practitioners also capitalize on the valuable lessons to be learned through the wider curriculum such as conventions relating to health and safety, playing sensibly in the playground, behaviour both in the nursery/school and on outside visits, and involvement in events and productions such as festivals, concerts and celebrations.

Nursery and reception provision is less compartmentalized and more holistic in comparison to primary settings. While teacher accountability and national documentation may require teachers to think about and plan the curriculum in terms of specific areas of learning, young children do not automatically make the same distinctions. The under-fives' curriculum provides a coherent framework for addressing the various discrete areas of learning while at the same time offering teachers and children opportunities to make links between these areas. For example, visiting the local shops with children can offer starting points and opportunities for learning in Communication, language and literacy, Mathematical development, and Personal, social and emotional development. As a result, curriculum divisions may be less clearly delineated from the children's perspective. This does not mean that early years provision is undifferentiated, amorphous and chaotic, but that practitioners recognize the potential for learning across a number of areas of learning within any one session and therefore there is likely to be a distinction between curriculum conception (i.e. the planning), in which the different areas of learning are clearly mapped out, and curriculum delivery (Alexander *et al.*, 1992) whereby young children do not necessarily see themselves as *doing creative work* or *doing mathematics work*.

Young children are inquisitive and many everyday occurrences capture their imagination and provoke demands for explanations. Nursery/reception programmes attempt to make this natural desire to find out and a natural ability to soak up information work for pupils by providing a curriculum with opportunities for enquiry and first-hand experience. Planning includes opportunities for children to handle a range of tools and materials, to observe, listen, investigate, question, experiment and draw conclusions. This enquiry element is supported by teachers who help the children to make links between previous experiences and current discoveries and who establish an environment in which pupils feel safe, secure and confident. In addition, practitioners need to ensure a balance between teacher-initiated tasks (i.e. where the teacher is guiding the children's learning) and child-initiated activities (i.e. those activities selected by a child on the basis of their personal interests and abilities).

Eg Foundation Stage planning

Medium-term planning – reception

Theme: Plants/growth   Spring term – 2nd half

	What do we want the children to learn?		How will we enable this learning to take place?	How will we know who has learned what?	What next?
	Learning intentions (based on stepping stones/ELGs	Vocabulary	Activities/routines	Assessment	Notes on how assessments will inform future plans
Personal, social and emotional development	• Take turns • Show caring for living things • Select and use resources independently	'Please can I have a turn?'	Garden centre role-play – roles: customer/assistant Plant seeds Care for seedlings	Note which children take on roles	
Communication, language and literacy Objectives from the literacy framework	• Listen and respond to stories • Take part in role-play • Write for different purposes • Use sequence words • Hear/say phoneme 'g', 's', 't' • Recognise letters 'g', 's', 't'	first, then, after that	Jasper's Beanstalk – Titch: Pat Hutchins Songs: Oats, Peas, Beans and Barley grow Action rhyme: Growing flowers Customers/assistants in garden centre Make labels and notices for garden centre Show others how to prepare cress for planting Find objects beginning with sounds Sort letters and objects Group objects	Note use of language in role Collect example of labels created	

Mathematical development	• Use number names	Numbers 1–10	Count plant pots, bulbs and seeds	List children who know and can use numbers to 5
Objectives from the mathematics framework	• Count objects	More than	Organize different sizes of plant pots	
	• Recognize numerals	Less than		List children who know 5–10 and above
	• Use vocabulary to compare size	Bigger, smaller, more		
Knowledge and understanding of the world	• Identify features of plants	Stem, leaf, leaves, root	Sketches/paintings of plants	Can describe plant or painting using appropriate vocabulary
	• Show awareness of change	Grow/n Longer, taller More, fewer	Plant seeds in garden and inside Sow cress	
	• Recognize everyday use of ICT	scan, till	Use till, computer and price scanner in role-play area	
Physical development	• Explore malleable materials	Spade, fork, trowel, dig, plant	Outside area – earth/water	Record children who dig/can hold spade and control
	• Handle tools with care		Planting seeds and seedlings	
Creative development	• Explore colour and texture	Rough, smooth	Collect and compare leaves Collage	Use of different textures

(Burnett and Myers, 2004)

A key issue for practitioners in the Foundation Stage is the need to ensure that planning includes opportunities for play, both teacher initiated and child initiated, and for dialogue with peers and adults. In part the early years practitioner has to act as a stage manager when planning (Jones and Reynolds, 1992 in DECS, 1996) as the learning environment can have a significant impact upon young children's progress and development. An environment that stimulates the children, that is accessible to them, and which contains high quality resources is more likely to support and encourage learning. The props and resources available to the children should include as broad a range of equipment as possible. In some cases the resources may be freely available to the children, in others they may require adults to mediate and assist in accessing and/or operating them. These deliberations on the part of teachers will also need to incorporate appropriate play provision for children's diverse needs including those children with special educational needs (see pp. 189–99).

The example below shows medium-term nursery planning for an imaginative play area in which the stage managing dimension to the teacher's role is clearly visible.

'The Office'

Resources
- Photocopier
- Computer and printer
- Telephone
- Dictaphone / tape recorder
- Calculator
- OHP
- Notice board
- Calendar
- Diaries
- Mark-making materials (pens, pencils, paper)
- Envelopes
- Clock
- ID tags/badges

Roles (Children)
- Office clerk
- School secretary
- Customer relations
- Manager

Roles (Teacher/adults)
- Customer
- Worker
- 'Boss'

Key questions
- Who are you writing to?
- Can I make an appointment?
- What time/day can I come?
- How does it work?

Opportunities for learning
- Acting out office worker roles
- Become familiar with office technology
- Operating technology (switching on and off, using a keyboard, printing out)
- Writing for a purpose
- Encountering new language/vocabulary

Learning objectives
- Personal/social development – sharing and taking turns
- Communication, language and literacy – talking with peers and adults; writing for a purpose
- Knowledge and understanding of the world – operating equipment; performing simple functions; recognizing everyday uses of ICT

Story lines
- Answering the phone/making appointments
- Writing letters
- Organizing presents for Father Christmas

(O'Hara, 2004)

Short-term planning/Weekly – Nursery

Planning Sheet – week beginning: 28 April 2003

Personal, social and emotional	Communication, language and literacy	Mathematics
1. Work as part of a group or class, taking turns and sharing fairly, understanding that there needs to be agreed behaviour.	1. Listen with enjoyment and respond to stories, songs, rhymes and poems. 2. Sustain attentive listening, responding to what they have heard.	1. Use developing mathematical ideas and methods to solve practical problems. 2. Begin to use vocabulary involved with addition and subtraction.

Vehicles for learning:	Activity with parents	Carpet time	Mark-making	Mathematics	ICT
Mon	Name cards	Read *Oh Dear!* Introduce some farm animals	Labels for the tea room	Money game	KidPix
Tues	Can you share a book with your child?	In my shopping bag . . .	List of things you can buy at a shop	Money game Shopping game	KidPix
Weds	Number cards	Read *Don't Forget the Bacon* Play shopping game in a circle	Letter formation cards	Money game Shopping game	Leaps and Bounds
Thurs	Name cards Older children to write the alphabet	Number recognition game with This Old Man	Mark-making numbers and sequences	This Old Man Money Game 1p, 2p, 5p	Leaps and Bounds This Old Man Song Tape
Fri	Can you share a book with your child?	Read *Noisy Farm* Money recognition	Salt in spot tray	This Old Man Number books, jigsaws and tape	Leaps and Bounds This Old Man song tape

Knowledge and understanding	Creative	Physical
1. Select tools and techniques they need to shape, and assemble and join materials. 2. Use ICT to support their learning.	1. Use their imagination in art and design, music, dance, imaginative and role-play activities.	1. Handle tools, objects, construction and materials safely and with increasing control.

Construction	Small-world	Role-play	Creative	Sand/Water	Games/Dance
Make different sized animal homes using stickle bricks	Farm animals on spot tray	The Three Little Pigs' house	Farm jigsaws	Threading beads	Wet sand with small moulds
Make different sized animal homes using Duplo bricks	Farm animals on spot tray	The Three Little Pigs' house	Painting pigs	Wet sand with small moulds **Outdoor area**	Hall time – responding to instructions
Duplo bricks	Farm animals on spot tray **Outdoor area**	The Three Little Pigs' house	Painting mixing different colours **Outdoor area**	Wet sand and sieves	Circle games
	Farm animals on spot tray	The Three Little Pigs' house	Painting mixing different colours Jigsaws	Dry sand and sieves	Bats, balls, hoops and ropes **Outdoor area**
Box modelling	Space Station	The Three Little Pigs' house	Jigsaws Free drawings	Dry sand and sieves **Outdoor area**	

Short-term planning/session/Lesson – nursery

Nursery Session Planner

Date: 6 May 2003

Learning Objective(s)/Early Learning Goal:
K&U p. 92 – Use ICT to support their learning.

Assessment Can the children • draw using the mouse? • use menu/icons to select colours, shapes and effects?	**Activity** To use a simple computer program (KidPix) with a range of tools to enable the children to draw pictures of favourite farm animals
Context (group size, in/outdoor, role-play area, etc.) Pairs/individuals in the computer area	**Resources** Both nursery computers, KidPix program, farm visit photographs, farm animal pictures and small-world play figures
Language mouse, double click, drag, click, animal names, shape names	**Differentiation** By outcome

Introduction
Model how to use the KidPix tools to draw a recognizable pig. Encourage the children to think about what shapes the pig is made up of and what colour to fill the pig in with

Development of activity (what the children will be doing) Using the mouse and a selection of tools to draw their favourite farm animal	**Teaching points (what you will do and say to support learning)** Model the activity. Talk about how to control the mouse and how to change colour, etc.

Opportunities to recap/share/ reinforce children's learning Children to print off their work to share with the other children and their parents	**Involvement of parents/carers** Mrs . . . . (parent) to work with pairs on the computers	**Links to other areas of learning** Creative development

Planning to address the different areas of learning in the Curriculum Guidance for the Foundation Stage

Personal, social and emotional development

Your planning should include opportunities for children to

- become more self-confident; to express themselves and articulate their interests, preferences, thoughts and ideas;
- share their experiences with their peers and adults, identifying and recognizing their achievements and strengths, including perseverance and self-control;
- demonstrate concern for others (e.g. helping to clean up, or looking after someone in the playground);
- share resources with others;
- become more self-reliant (e.g. by encouraging them to learn their address and telephone number, to become increasingly proficient in dressing themselves after PE, and to make decisions about their work, such as when and where to seek help and support); and
- become more responsible (e.g. by observing conventions and routines in the nursery/classroom such as following basic safety rules).

Communication, language and literacy

Your planning should include opportunities for children to develop their speaking and listening skills through
- listening and responding to stories and rhymes;
- showing their understanding of stories by predicting outcomes;
- responding appropriately to questions;
- repeating words;
- naming letter characters and sounds;
- following simple directions; and
- describing personal experiences and retelling familiar stories.

Your planning should include opportunities for children to develop their reading and writing skills through
- identifying signs and labels;
- learning names;
- imitating writing;
- using gestures and tone of voice to communicate meaning more effectively;
- showing awareness of the conventions of written material (e.g. left to right, spaces between words, upper- and lower-case letters);
- identifying key features of books (e.g. title, pictures);
- using key features to understand and tell stories;
- contributing words and sentences to a narrative scribed by the teacher; and
- writing simple messages (e.g. printing letters in the alphabet, writing their own and familiar names, and simple words such as 'dog' and 'cat').

Mathematical development

Your planning should include opportunities for children to increase their mathematical understanding through
- demonstrating their understanding of whole numbers;
- measuring (e.g. comparing length, weight, mass, capacity and awareness of time);
- identifying characteristics of simple two- and three-dimensional shapes;
- recognizing and using patterns;
- collecting, showing and understanding simple data; and
- seeking clarification, help and equipment when needed.

Knowledge and understanding of the world

Your planning should include opportunities for children to
- show curiosity and enthusiasm for investigating and exploring;
- develop their concepts of place and time;
- demonstrate awareness and concern for living things and the environment;
- learn about the properties of familiar materials;
- take some responsibility for planning and organizing their work with support; and
- become familiar with technology (including ICT).

Physical development

Your planning should include opportunities for children to
- practise personal hygiene;
- show awareness of safe and unsafe situations and resources (e.g. sharp scissors, large apparatus);

- participate in regular physical activity including dance and movement;
- use a wide range of large and small apparatus to develop gross and fine motor control (e.g. bicycles, climbing frames, barrels, balls, crayons, paint brushes, scissors); and
- improve their balance, agility and spatial awareness (e.g. running and jumping, using scooters and other riding toys, using climbing frames).

Creative development

Your planning should include opportunities for children to
- express their thoughts and feelings using a wide range of media;
- experiment with and investigate tools, techniques and materials;
- perform (e.g. using puppet theatres, making music, dancing);
- learn songs and rhymes;
- enact and re-enact stories in the structured play area;
- respond appropriately to the tempo and mood of music (e.g. fast, slow, scary, happy); and
- learn about the visual arts (e.g. colour, shape and size).

Monitoring, Assessing, Recording and Reporting

All teachers need to be proficient at monitoring and assessing children's learning, as well as recording and reporting on their progress. The results of assessment are an integral and indispensable part of the teaching and learning process. Teachers have always made judgements about their pupils and have used those judgements in structuring their future teaching. However, the introduction of the National Curriculum and the Curriculum Guidance for the Foundation Stage, coupled with the increasing pressures associated with monitoring and public accountability, has greatly increased the amount of time and rigour being applied to this aspect of the teacher's role.

Monitoring and Assessing Children

By the end of this section you should

- know about using different kinds of assessment for different purposes;
- know about alternative forms and methods of assessing children;
- know about using assessment to improve teaching.

Why assess?

The primary purposes of assessment are: first, to improve the quality of teaching and learning; and second, to enable schools and nurseries to report on children's progress and provide summative information on their achievements. Assessment benefits all those involved in the education of young children, including the teachers and other professionals, the children themselves and their parents.

For teachers, assessment provides a better understanding of childre
learning. It offers a way to ensure progression and greater continuity for pupils as
the results of assessment provide more reliable information upon which to plan
the next step of a teaching programme. It is a process which provides information
on individual pupil experience and achievement across the curriculum, providing
a way of investigating and identifying progress in terms of what a child knows,
understands and can do. The results of assessment also provide teachers with a
more valid base for evaluating the curriculum, helping them to monitor and raise
standards (Hunter-Carsch, 2002). Assessment is helpful to children by enhancing
their motivation and confidence through the promotion of accurate and
constructive feedback from the teacher in the form of short-term learning targets
and the identification of future learning needs. It is also helpful for parents and
others, including future teachers and the wider community, who wish to evaluate
the effectiveness of a nursery/school through teachers' reports (both verbal and
written) or SATs results. Assessment, for example, can provide information on
pupil attainment to date that can be used to make the transition within and
between schools more streamlined.

Forms of assessment

Assessing children involves more than simply looking at the work they produce.
Teachers need to employ their observation and questioning skills in order to
ascertain what children know, what they can do and where they need to go next.
Assessment takes various forms and it is important to realize that the boundaries
between these different forms are permeable; considerable overlap is possible. It
can be difficult, for example, to determine whether assessment is summative or
formative in nature as different teachers may wish to use the same information
for different purposes.

Formal and informal assessment

Informal assessment is an activity in which teachers are constantly involved. This
type of assessment provides a very wide-ranging evidence base, considered over
an extended period of time. It makes an invaluable contribution to formative
assessment and acts as the basis for a considerable amount of good quality and
immediate feedback to pupils in the form of a smile, a frown, spoken comments
on the amount of effort being made, or written comments on pieces of work.
Informal assessment is such a normal part of classroom life that it can be overlooked and is sometimes undervalued; it may occur as a result of routine
discussions and observations. Children's answers to teachers' questions are
evaluated by those teachers, who then make judgements about the children's level
of understanding. Informal assessment can also occur as a result of looking at the
concrete outcomes of activities. Similarly, children's comments and behaviour may

reveal unplanned for, and unanticipated, evidence causing a teacher to assess the situation and take action.

Formal assessment, meanwhile, takes place when teachers have planned for it, at times that have been identified and where the results will be formally recorded. While informal assessment constitutes an integral part of work with young children, a natural part of the minute-by-minute interactions in the nursery or classroom, Edgington (1998) points out that informal/unplanned assessments tend to centre on those things which *draw themselves to the practitioner's attention*. While important, they do not necessarily offer a more rounded picture; they may, for example, fail to pick up the events that take place quietly (Edgington, 1998, p. 127). While it is not possible to observe everything that goes on in the nursery/classroom, making use of more planned, targeted and focused assessments may well serve to complement the informal, unplanned and ongoing kind as well as sharpening a practitioner's skills in this area generally (Edgington, 1998, p. 128). Formal assessments may, for example, challenge adult assumptions about children and their capabilities because they offer information that might otherwise be missed.

Range of formal and informal assessment

Eg

Informal assessment – unplanned observation

John and Ruth had been paired to work on a design and technology activity. It became clear to the teacher from their expressions that John was feeling self-conscious about working with a girl and that Ruth was well aware of his attitude. Although the learning objectives were centred around the subject, the teacher had an ongoing commitment to encourage children to work constructively together. She responded immediately to her informal assessment of the situation by intervening quickly to offer encouragement and support to both children and to help them to organize themselves to tackle the activity in such a way that both children had real roles in the task.

Informal assessment – examining work produced

Miss Lee was moving around her class of Year 1/2s who were engaged in number work activities as part of their regular numeracy hour. She noticed that two or three children were making the same mistake. She intervened to help the children to tackle the problem individually and made a note to pursue the matter with this group in a subsequent lesson.

Formal assessment – Sc4 Physical Processes

Mrs Jones had been conducting formal assessments of her children's scientific skills, knowledge and understanding during the week. The focus was on forces and in particular, floating and sinking. She had arranged for non-teaching support and/or parents to be in the classroom while she assessed the children in groups. The children were testing objects in the water tank and discussing their observations and ideas with Mrs Jones who was noting down any evidence of attainment against a checklist. She asked the children to predict which objects would float and which ones would sink. Wayne suggested that the apple would float. Mrs Jones asked him to explain why he thought this was the case. 'Because it was floating this morning, miss.'

Criterion-referenced and norm-referenced assessment

Assessment that is criterion-referenced seeks to assess pupils' [...] against a set of standards or competences, normally utilizing incre[...] demanding descriptions to judge and report on attainment. Such [...] helpful for teachers in sharing the purpose of the activity with children. The National Curriculum level descriptions and Foundation Stage stepping stones are examples of criterion-referencing; the Professional Standards for the Award of Qualified Teacher Status are another. Norm-referenced assessment involves making comparisons between the achievements of different children, for example *Child A finds letter formation harder than his classmates*, or *Child B is a better painter than Child C.*

It may seem that criterion-referenced assessment offers teachers a fairer, less subjective approach to assessment as it utilizes universally applied measures of attainment. Unfortunately, producing criteria or descriptions that are universally understood and unambiguous is not as easy as it might sound. Furthermore, large numbers of criteria can result in an atomized view of the curriculum making it hard on occasion to see the bigger picture. Most teachers, therefore, will draw on both criterion-referenced and norm-referenced strategies when making assessments of young children.

Summative assessment

Some assessments will be summative in nature and result in statements about what a child has achieved at a particular point in time, for example on transition from the nursery to the reception class, or at the end of Key Stage 1. A summative assessment constitutes a record of the overall achievement of a pupil in a systematic way and can be used to answer the following questions:

- How well do children understand certain ideas/concepts?
- Can the children apply this understanding in other contexts?
- What level of attainment have the children reached?
- Are the children ready to move on to the next level?

Eg   *Summative assessment sheet*

Name:
Date of birth:
Admission date:

English

AT1: Speaking and listening Comments	Rec.	Y1	Y2
Level 1			
Talks about matters of immediate interest			
Listens to others			
Responds appropriately			

	Rec.	Y1	Y2
Conveys simple meaning to range of listeners			
Speaks audibly			
Extends ideas and accounts by providing some detail			
Conveys/remembers a simple message			

Level 2	Rec.	Y1	Y2
Shows confidence when talking and listening			
Listens carefully			
Responds with increasing appropriateness to what others say			
Develops and explains ideas			
Speaks clearly and uses a growing vocabulary			
Includes relevant detail for needs of listener			
Conveys/remembers a more complex message			
Is aware of a more formal vocabulary and tone of voice			

Level 3	Rec.	Y1	Y2
Talks and listens confidently in different contexts			
Shows careful listening through relevant comment and questions			
Communicates and explores ideas in discussions, shows understanding of main points			
Adapts what they say to needs of listener varying use of vocabulary and level of detail			
Is aware of standard English and when it is used			

Summative assessments have an importance that extends beyond the nursery/classroom in which they were made by providing information that is of use and interest to the whole school, the child's next school (in the case of transition), parents and others. One example of summative assessment is the use of SATs that children take at the end of Key Stage 1. Schools can combine information from local and national SATs results with details of their own results to identify future targets for pupil achievement in the school. Although its primary purpose is not to inform the next step, the knowledge gained from summative assessment can be used in this way by subsequent teachers. An example of summative assessment being used formatively would be the use of reception teacher assessments (Foundation Stage Profile) by subsequent Year 1 teachers to inform their planning and preparation at the beginning of the year.

Summative assessment

Pupil name: Shaida   **School Year: 2003–4 (Reception)**

Language and literacy

Shaida always listens attentively and makes good contributions in class discussions. She loves reading and can read a range of texts independently. She is beginning to use a variety of strategies to tackle unfamiliar words and shows understanding of the main points of the book. Shaida is being encouraged to write at greater length and to extend her ideas. She can structure a simple story or account, and spell simple words correctly. Her handwriting is legible and she is working towards the more consistent use of upper- and lower-case letters.

Mathematics

Shaida has a good grasp of early number concepts in addition and subtraction to 20, and is developing mental recall of these facts. She has completed measurement activities involving length, weight and capacity and can use non-standard units. She can sort and classify objects and name and describe the properties of simple two-dimensional shapes. She can continue and make repeating patterns involving shape and colour with two changes.

Other areas of experience

In classroom tasks, Shaida has made observations, talked about her findings and made recordings of these in words and pictures. She can recognize similarities and differences in living things and objects, and demonstrates a good general knowledge. She draws, paints, cuts and makes with care and has plenty of ideas for her work. She shows good coordination when moving on the floor and apparatus during PE lessons. She likes to sing and can play percussion instruments.

Personal, social and emotional development

Shaida has made excellent progress in all curriculum areas, most notably in English and mathematics. She settles quickly to tasks, works hard and takes part in all areas of school life with growing confidence and a happy disposition. She is helpful and reliable and an asset to the class. I am sure that Shaida will continue to build on this super start. She is a pleasure to teach.
Number of attendances out of total number possible 300: 312
Number of unauthorized absences 0

This report may be discussed with . . . . on . . . .

at . . . .

Summative assessments have their uses as a measure of performance for children, their teachers and others. However, there can be limitations to some of these measurements. In the case of SATs, for example, they cannot hope to measure more than a small part of a child's overall capability. A further limitation of summative assessment is its limited use in assisting teachers who are seeking to identify and respond to the learning needs of their pupils during the course of the

ear. To do this teachers need to engage in ongoing formative and diagnostic
ssessment.

ormative/diagnostic assessment

Assessment ought to take place on a regular basis, not just intermittently. It should
be ongoing throughout the school year not just at the end of term, year or Key Stage.
It is a continual process which needs to be matched by a continual recording process.
Formative assessment is used to inform the next stage in a child's learning. Its
purpose is to recognize the achievements of a pupil so that these might be discussed
and the appropriate next steps taken. Diagnostic assessment occurs when teachers
seek to scrutinize and classify learning difficulties so that appropriate guidance can
be given and intervention can take place. A problem for teachers of young children is
the small amount of time that they often get to spend with any one individual pupil
and this can make diagnosis difficult. Formative assessment therefore is about where
the child has progressed to; diagnostic assessment looks at why a child is not
progressing. Both inform the next step in terms of what the children should be
learning and how to teach it. Formative (diagnostic) assessment can be used to
answer the following questions:

- What do the children know/not know about a topic/subject?
- What do they know/not know about specific ideas/skills/procedures?
- Are any aspects of the topic causing problems for children?
- Can the children apply learning in new situations?
- Do the children hold any misconceptions?
- Is the pace and level of teaching set at appropriate levels?

Assessing spelling skills

Subject: English   Date: 18.12.98

Class: 2   Year Group: 1

Work: Above Average ☐
          Average   ☐
          Below Average ✔

Focus: Word level work – onset and rime

Diagnostic Assessment: cannot always hear rime –
she was unable to write the cvc riming words even
with the pictures to help.

Assessing a little bit at a time on a regular basis using systematic observation (watching, listening and talking to, the children) is one method of assessing formatively/diagnostically. Teachers and schools also retain samples of pupils' work and/or photographs as a source of concrete evidence to support formative/diagnostic judgements based on these observations. It is, however, easy to allow the focus of assessment to be on the outcomes of a lesson rather than the process. It is easier to make judgements about the accuracy of a piece of writing than it is to assess how it was produced, but for effective diagnosis teachers need to have some idea of both. Failure to diagnose difficulties accurately means that effective matching of tasks and differentiation is harder to do. Teachers, therefore, review work with children to gain insight into processes as well as the products and use neutral or open-ended questions to get quality responses when making formative/diagnostic assessments of children. Children can be asked to report on their progress and what they have done so far. Similarly, they can be questioned about how they completed an activity or accomplished a task.

Evaluative assessment

Assessment can be used to evaluate and influence policies and planning in a school/nursery on a wider scale than merely the planning of follow-up lessons or topics by individual teachers. Such assessment is evaluative in nature. Evaluative assessment is used to determine the extent to which the goals of the teaching programme are appropriate for the pupils and how effective the teaching programme is in achieving these goals. Evaluation involves making a judgement of some kind; this judgement is based on the information obtained through assessment. Assessment provides a more valid base than the use of impression. The results of assessment, therefore, can be helpful in keeping track of the breadth and balance of the curriculum and in ensuring progression and continuity in children's learning as they move through the school from nursery and reception, to Key Stage 1 and on to Year 3.

Eg *An evaluative assessment of reading materials*

Mrs Wilson was appointed to the post of English coordinator in a primary school. Part of her responsibilities included monitoring and overseeing the loan of reading books to pupils for homework tasks. Parents were asked to help their children and the school by indicating in a report book what the children had read, how they had coped and what they thought of the stories. When Mrs Wilson reviewed the comments from parents she realized that they were strongly negative concerning the age, quality and content of the reading material. When Mrs Wilson spoke to children about the books available she discovered a reluctance to get involved in reading at home because the books were old, tatty and 'boring'. Mrs Wilson presented her assessment of the situation to her colleagues and the headteacher, who in turn discussed the matter with the governing body. The governors decided to make funds available for the school to buy new books for homework tasks and to release Mrs Wilson for two afternoons to organize the resources and loans system.

Methods of assessment

When planning to assess children, teachers need to consider what they want to assess; how they will know if the children have achieved the learning objectives; and how they will collect evidence to support their judgements.

Eg

Evaluation of assessment

- 'Do I want the pupils to demonstrate certain skills or am I trying to assess knowledge and understanding?'
- 'What will the children have to do or say to demonstrate attainment?'
- 'What mode or method will I use to assess the children?'

Assessment methods/modes could include

- classroom observations (watching children's actions, listening to their conversation, listening to presentations such as reading out their stories, or question and answer sessions);
- making judgements based on outcomes (models, pieces of writing, drawings, paintings, number work); and
- making judgements against previous outcomes (benchmarking).

Observation

While there will be times when children produce concrete evidence of their awareness and understanding, many of the judgements made by practitioners about young children's learning and development will be based on observations. Such observation is integral to work with young children and is essential for their continual assessment (Hobart and Frankel, 1999). Observations can be both informal, such as watching children interacting, and formal, such as structured observation to ascertain learning against a particular element of the National Curriculum Programmes of Study. Observations may involve the whole class, small groups or individuals. These observations, such as an overheard conversation between children, or being presented with a striking piece of art work, provide a means by which children's knowledge, skills and dispositions can be checked and explored and can help to define more clearly any individual contributions to a group task.

Although the term observation suggests passivity on the part of the teacher, the reality is usually far more active and involves more than just sitting and watching. Practitioners often have to check their observations through careful questioning, discussion and further observations. Discussing activities with children as part of classroom observation is a very useful device for locating evidence of a child's success, diagnosing learning difficulties, monitoring progress over a period of time, and developing some insight into the ways in which a particular child learns and works. As Sharman *et al.* (1995, p. 2) state, an observation is akin to a *camera shot*; while it does not lie, it can distort. A child's initial response to questioning is not necessarily an accurate or reliable guide to knowledge and competence (SCAA, 1997); similarly, actions and behaviour can be misinterpreted. Consequently, practitioners need to base their judgements and assessments about children's capabilities on more than one such snapshot.

Assessing children through observation requires good classroom organization and management, particularly where teachers wish to assess a small group of individuals in situations where non-teaching support is limited or non-existent. Assessing through observation requires attention and concentration, and teachers, therefore, need to consider not only the child or children being assessed, but also the rest of the children in the class.

The 'assessed' and the 'rest'

- How involved will you become in the activity itself? Too much involvement could make collecting the evidence difficult. Sitting too close to the children can make disengagement and note-taking almost impossible. Simultaneously teaching, listening, and making notes is not easy.
- How many children will you assess at any one time, and against how many learning objectives? It can be difficult to collect evidence for large numbers of pupils through observation and discussion. Likewise, trying to assess children against large numbers of learning objectives can become unmanageable. It is important to have a clear and uncomplicated set of objectives.
- Are the children aware of the purposes for both the task and the assessment? Explaining what you are going to be observing gives them the chance to show if they know or can do it.
- Frequent interruptions will play havoc with your attempts to conduct assessments in the nursery/classroom. Yet young children are much more dependent upon their teachers than their older counterparts. It is important, therefore, to make maximum use of any non-teaching support in the classroom and to plan low-intervention tasks for children where such support is limited or unavailable.
- Assessment through observation or discussion does not necessarily mean that the teacher has to be with the children being assessed at all times. Planning which considers the balance between independent activity and teacher participation or group discussion may be a useful approach to take. For example, when assessing a group of children teachers could visit the group at regular intervals of time throughout an activity, they could visit the group at fixed points in the programme of activities, or they could work down a list of the children. Whichever option is chosen, it is important to ensure that there will be sufficient time to gather the necessary information without ignoring the needs of the rest of the class.

Observations should also be made on a broad front reflecting the breadth of the 3–8 curricula; not just Communication, language and literacy/English and Mathematical development/mathematics but also the rest of the Foundation Stage areas of learning or National Curriculum subjects. Below are some examples of indicators that teachers might look for when assessing children's progress and learning using observation as the method. The list should in no way be seen as comprehensive. Trainee and newly qualified teachers should refer to the further sources of information at the end of this chapter to extend their knowledge and understanding in this area further.

Indicators of achievement to watch for

Possible indicators of achievement in Personal, social and emotional development; personal, social and health education (PSHE) and citizenship

The child can
- express feelings;
- communicate appropriately in social situations;
- initiate conversations with peers and adults;
- work cooperatively with peers;
- persevere when faced with a challenge; and
- cope effectively with changes in routines or staffing.

Possible indicators of achievement in Communication, language and literacy/English

The child can
- ask and answer questions;
- seek information;
- participate in discussions and imaginary play;
- respond appropriately to a speaker;
- demonstrate listening behaviour;
- recall experiences/retell stories;
- model (pretend) reading; select books;
- understand that text has meaning;
- recognize familiar signs, letters, words; and
- engage in reading and writing.

Possible indicators of achievement in Mathematical development/mathematics

The child can
- form recognizable numbers and shapes;
- understand that mathematical symbols represent number and shape;
- understand and apply concepts such as behind, above, below, large, small;
- use number in everyday contexts;
- count and order;
- estimate and approximate; and
- measure and make judgements.

Possible indicators of achievement in Knowledge and understanding of the world, science, design and technology, geography, history and information and communications technology (ICT)

The child can
- use five senses and ask questions about the world;
- suggest solutions to problems;
- demonstrate an awareness of cause and effect;

- predict consequences;
- make comparisons and identify similarities and differences;
- distinguish between living and non-living things;
- identify significant places in the locality (shops, mosque, post office) and beyond;
- demonstrate an understanding of past, present and future involving people, places and events;
- make things using a range tools and materials safely and effectively; and
- incorporate ICT into play situations and use ICT to support their learning across the curriculum.

Possible indicators of achievement in Physical development and physical education (PE)

The child can
- move safely about the learning environment;
- participate in physical activities;
- use equipment safely and in a variety of ways;
- initiate own challenges;
- demonstrate hand–eye coordination and gross motor skills;
- demonstrate fine motor skills (manipulating scissors, pencils, construction materials);
- describe ways of keeping healthy; and
- describe ways of keeping safe.

Possible indicators of achievement in Creative development and art and music

The child can
- use a range of responses in imaginary play;
- select materials for creative activities;
- participate in movement activities involving music;
- respond appropriately to different music (fast, slow, cheerful, sad);
- experiment with different art media; and
- demonstrate awareness and appreciation of aesthetics, colour, shape and pattern.

Assessing outcomes

The concrete results of an activity can be a useful guide to learning, and small collections of children's work can illustrate their attainment very effectively. Such portfolios can provide a way of displaying a range of work, not simply written or number work but also project, ICT and creative work. Concrete outcomes assessed in conjunction with teacher–pupil discussions can be very helpful in enabling children to become more involved and take an active part in the process of assessment. This approach can help children to gain some insight into their own progress, strengths and weaknesses. It can also provide a useful starting point for setting targets for future learning.

170

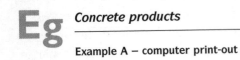

and he went to the Shop with his birchtday mowny to buy Some thing. He looked out all the Jays he chose a Little cat. just like him.

Many activities in 3–8 settings, however, will not result in concrete outcomes, for example much of the work that takes place in nurseries or PE. In addition, concrete products alone may prove insufficient and inconclusive as evidence of attainment. Many factors could influence the final outcome and lead teachers to misjudge children's learning. For example, where the collaborative setting actually belies the individual nature of the assessments being made, teachers will need to devise strategies for discerning individual contributions and comprehension. It can be difficult to identify the features of a piece of work which indicate achievement and it may be necessary to support judgements made on the basis of outcomes with reference to either observations of the process or discussions of the work with the child. Look at the two examples below of concrete products produced by nursery pupils. Using the Curriculum Guidance for the Foundation Stage what assessment would you make of these children's abilities based solely on the work below?

Eg *Concrete products*

Example A – computer print-out

DFGHJKLL;POYREW2W21ZRYUJK,MNBVC14789–632ACDKG

Example B – nursery drawing

Now read the commentary below on the two pieces of work. How does this information alter your assessments of the children concerned?

Assessments of concrete products

Commentary on Example A

Child E types at random using the computer keyboard and prints out her writing (opposite).

She points at the screen and says to a nearby adult, 'That's my name!'

Adult: 'Oh, have you written your name? Can you read it to me?'

E: 'Helen!'

(O'Hara, 2004)

Commentary on Example B

The nursery teacher asked Child F to tell her about the drawing. In the subsequent discussion the child explained that the picture represented her daily journey from home to school (a 'map'?) and gave details on who she travelled with, which route she took and what things she passed on the way, for example cars. Child F was also able to talk to the teacher about her experience of other modes of transport including an aircraft.

Benchmarking

When considering methods of assessing attainment through outcomes, teachers can also consider benchmarking. Benchmarking requires the teacher or the school to collect exemplar material (i.e. samples of children's work) as a way of indicating the quality of work that should be expected at different levels from particular groups. Benchmarking not only acts as an aid to teachers in trying to determine the level of a particular piece of work, it can also provide pupils with insights into standards and expectations and can act as a spur to greater effort and higher achievement. The School Examination and Assessment Council (SEAC) publication *Children's Work Assessed* (1991) is one example of an attempt to introduce benchmarking on a national scale for Key Stage 1 pupils in the core curriculum areas of the National Curriculum. The School Curriculum and Assessment Authority's (SCAA) *Looking at Children's Learning* (1997) is a more recent attempt to provide similar guidance for pupils in the Foundation Stage.

The contribution of parents and other adults to assessment

Attempts to gain information on children's needs and abilities upon entry to nursery/school settings can be enhanced by the involvement of parents and other adults in the process of assessment. In reception classes, where staffing levels are often lower than those in nursery, good organization and planning are essential if a parental contribution is to be obtained in a timescale of use to the practitioner. Initial assessments involving parents in the nursery/classroom may necessitate provision for the care of younger siblings while discussions take place. Parents need to be reassured that the information they are supplying is for positive reasons and will not be used to discriminate against their child. Parents also need to know that in instances where special educational needs (SEN) are identified some of the information they give may also be passed on to other professionals involved in the education and welfare of young children.

Eg
An early assessment sheet completed jointly by parents and the nursery teacher

Name:

Date of birth:

Admission date:

Asks questions e.g. Why? Who? When? Where? What? ☐

Independence/decision-making skills ☐

Expresses needs and wants, using speech and gestures ☐

Comments and directs, e.g. 'Come on', 'I like' ☐

Uses language in play ☐

Joins in conversations/interchanges with three or more turns ☐

Listens to and enjoys books, songs and poems ☐

Book skills ☐

Understands that print carries meaning ☐

Reads own 'writing' ☐

Can recognize own name ☐

Knows letter sounds ☐

Scribbling ☐ Writing ☐
Letter shapes ☐ Key words ☐

Colour identification

red ☐ blue ☐ yellow ☐
green ☐ orange ☐ purple ☐
black ☐ brown ☐ pink ☐
white ☐

Shape identification

square ☐ circle ☐ triangle ☐
rectangle ☐ oval ☐ star ☐

Matching

by colour ☐ by shape ☐
by type ☐ by more than one attribute ☐

Sorting

by colour ☐ by shape ☐
by type ☐ by more than one attribute ☐

Counting 1–5 ☐ 5–10 ☐
more than 10 ☐

Number symbol/ quantity ☐

Conservation of number ☐

Ordering ☐

Follows pattern and sequence ☐

Time ☐

Can order

by size ☐ big/little ☐
short/tall ☐ heavy/light ☐
full/empty ☐

Reports previous experiences ☐

Identifies and describes similarities and differences ☐

Reasoning skills ☐

Ability to predict ☐

Play

Solitary ☐ Parallel ☐ Cooperative ☐
Exploratory ☐ Self-pretend ☐
Sequence pretend ☐

Fine motor skills e.g. threading, small construction, pencil, brush, glue spreader, scissors ☐

Gross motor skills

coordination ☐ balancing ☐
climbing ☐ riding ☐
catching ☐ kicking ☐
throwing ☐

In addition to the contribution that parents and carers can make to assessment, non-teaching colleagues (nursery nurses, non-teaching assistants and child-care assistants (CCAs)) can also play an invaluable role in monitoring and reporting on young children's achievements and progress with the help of clipboards, post-it notes and observation notebooks. The teacher cannot be everywhere at once and the involvement of the whole team under the guidance of the teacher makes the task of focusing on groups and individuals much more manageable in terms of creating time and opportunities to observe and talk with the children. Furthermore, given the importance of establishing a team approach to the teaching of young children, assessment that excludes all but the teacher from making judgements about children's learning is likely to undermine the team.

Some principles of assessment

- Try to make assessment an integral part of teaching and learning in the nursery/classroom.
- Be clear about why you are assessing children. Enabling them to progress should have a high priority in these deliberations.
- Make sure the assessment allows pupils to demonstrate the appropriate skills, knowledge and/or attitudes.
- Assessment should not be limited to academic attainment alone. It should also provide information on progress in a child's development as an effective learner, including physical, social and emotional development.
- Share the results of assessment with pupils and parents in order to improve confidence and motivation.
- Remember that parents, carers and non-teaching colleagues can make a valuable contribution to assessment.
- Assess in ways that are ongoing (formative/diagnostic) as well as summative.
- Assess using a variety of methods and in a variety of contexts depending on the needs and capabilities of the children and the nature of what is being assessed. This diversity will
  - help to minimize possible bias in assessment;
  - provide a more balanced picture of children's capabilities;
  - help to allow for the age and level of pupils;
  - take into account children whose first language is not English;
  - be more sensitive to the sometimes different interests of boys and girls; and
  - acknowledge the fact that the context in which assessment takes place can have a significant impact upon children's performance.

Recording and Responding to the Results of Assessment

By the end of this section you should

- know about different ways of recording children's progress systematically;
- know about marking and monitoring children's work, and providing constructive oral and written feedback;
- know about some of the more common misconceptions that children can hold and errors that they can make;
- know about the statutory assessment and reporting requirements and know how to prepare and present informative reports to parents;
- know about SATs and the Foundation Stage Profile.

Recording

Recording young children's learning and experiences is an inevitable concomitant of assessment and evaluation. All schools and nurseries have to keep up-to-date records of children's progress and achievements. Since the introduction of the National Curriculum the scale of recording and reporting has greatly increased, sometimes in response to the demand for accountability rather than in recognition of the role it plays in the teaching and learning process. There is a great deal of guidance available to 3–8 teachers on recording systems but no universally imposed one. Although this approach has been beneficial in allowing for flexibility, it has also led some nurseries and schools to overestimate what is needed. Many 3–8 teachers spend considerable amounts of time trying to meet the requirements of unnecessarily complicated systems whose creation owes more to worries over their increasing accountability rather than to the need to inform teachers, pupils and others about children's progress.

Eg *Purposes of record keeping*

- To inform future teaching, enabling teachers to develop and evaluate their teaching programmes;
- To ensure that the school/nursery has an accurate and up-to-date profile of individual children's learning;
- To provide the basis for reporting to parents and carers about the children's achievements and development;
- To inform future teachers about a child's progress, needs, interests and capabilities, facilitating transition within and between schools;
- To help teachers in monitoring pupil progress over time, revealing patterns or problems and underpinning summative statements;
- To inform discussions with children on target-setting; and
- To provide evidence for a review of nursery/school policies and practices.

Recording children's progress often involves the collection of children's work as evidence to support statements about attainment. This can be problematic for teachers working with the youngest children where much of their learning and development does not always result in a concrete product and could well be demonstrated outside the confines of the nursery/classroom, for example during a breaktime, while on a visit or in an assembly. Primary pupils, however, are more likely to produce a wide range of concrete evidence on which teachers can base their judgements, including drawings or sketches, computer print-outs, digital photographs, written work, graphs and charts, junk models, clay work, diagrams, paintings, diaries, plans and posters.

When collecting and collating samples of work to act as, or support, records of pupil attainment the evidence collected ought to arise from a broad range of activities. A wide range of evidence increases the chances of making accurate judgements concerning the whole child and not simply about a narrow range of subject-specific skills and knowledge. A narrow range of learning approaches, therefore, will lead to a more impoverished evidence base. That said, teachers recording and collecting everything the children say or do is simply not practicable – excessive amounts of evidence are unwieldy and teaching would grind to a halt. Good records are a compromise between what is informative and what is manageable. Teachers should, therefore, provide sufficient evidence to back their judgements. A minimum amount of useful evidence should be the aim and 3–8 teachers will need to decide what to collect and how long to retain it. Where evidence is being collected over an extended period of time, some individual pieces of evidence are likely to be superseded by subsequent examples, so the evidence base needs to be reviewed from time to time.

Finally, practitioners need to make use of the information being provided in pupil records. This may seem an obvious, not to say banal, statement as it is clear that children ought not to be repeating things at the same level in subsequent classes. However, it is the case that some teachers like to form their own impressions of pupils and feel that others' records and evidence of past performance will colour their judgement. Yet subjective judgement is not eliminated by not looking at records and first impressions are no more reliable than any other impression. In addition, past performance ought to be the starting point for future teaching and learning. If teachers are not going to use the previous teacher's records it undermines the whole basis for keeping them.

Types of record

In part, some of the records kept by schools and nurseries will be formed by planning documents; these will provide information on the timing and content of topics that the children have experienced. Schemes of work and lesson/session plans are a form of record, albeit of future intentions. Such whole-school/nursery planning greatly reduces the need for individual teachers to spend time recording coverage of the curriculum. A session/lesson plan that has been modified or adjusted in the light of experience in order to address better the learning needs of the children also forms a concrete record of how assessment has been used to inform future teaching.

Ticklists/tick charts enable teachers to monitor those activities and elements of the curriculum that the children have experienced or completed. However, although they are relatively quick to use, a tick means only that a child has done something; it does not necessarily indicate the level of performance or achievement. Ticklists/tick charts have an additional problem in that they can become very long and unwieldy. They can be made more informative and have the capacity to record not just what has been covered but also the degree of success or achievement by using more than one symbol or by including a comments box.

Eg *Wordlist*

	read	spell		read	spell		read	spell		read	spell
I			like			for			go		
going			a			come			big		
dad			went			she			can		
up			and			he			you		
they			am			day			my		
all			was			see			look		
on			is			are			away		
cat			the			mum			get		
of			it			we			at		
said			this			play			to		
dog			no			in			me		
yes											

All teachers keep written records of some kind and often use notebooks, clipboards or post-it notes to jot down incidents and observations. It is impossible for any teacher to remember the details of observations and outcomes for any length of time; indeed, it is possible to forget the detail of a child's remark by the end of a busy day, let alone a term. However, it is neither possible nor desirable to note down everything and teachers need to exercise their professional judgement as to what is useful to record and what is needless paperwork. Some written comments may be placed directly onto children's work and thus form part of teachers' constructive feedback to pupils on their progress and attainment (see below).

27/11/2003
Andrew was unsettled on arrival today – suggested he sit/watch activity. Developed conversation about Andrew's pet – resulted in Andrew agreeing to draw his dog. Able to draw with a purpose, record his observations and recount a story. Andrew enthusiastic in recounting the event but spoken language very difficult to understand. Andrew patient in retelling when not understood but is not picking up on accurate language being modelled for him.

Post-it notes

> Irfan contributed well during the discussion and had plenty of interesting ideas

> John experienced some difficulty in handling the scissors in order to cut accurately

Many schools and nurseries compile portfolios or Primary Records of Achievement and Experience (PRAE). Examples of pupils' work, selected by the teacher, show children's achievements to date and can include information across the curriculum, not just on core subjects. Compiling portfolios of work can be time-consuming for teachers and there is a danger of duplication, especially where the children's workbooks contain much of this evidence already. However, collections of work of this sort provide concrete evidence in support of the judgements and assessments that teachers are making. Just as importantly, they enable teachers to go back in time. Reviewing children's previous work contained in a portfolio can be an illuminating activity for teachers and can provide graphic evidence of both progress and regression.

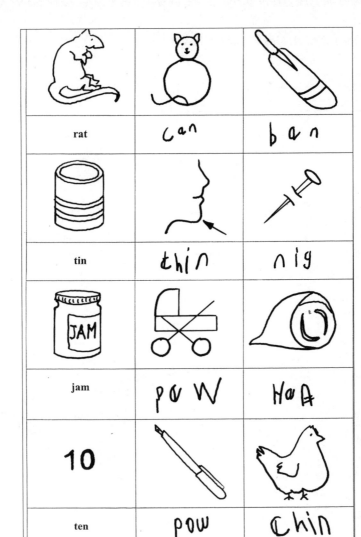

rat	c a n	b a n
tin	thin	n i g
jam	p v W	Ha A
10		
ten	pow	chin

Primary Records of Achievement and Experience offer a more child-centred approach to the use of portfolios for monitoring achievement in so far as the child selects the examples/evidence for inclusion in the portfolio, in discussion with the teacher. This approach is useful as a way of encouraging children to take greater responsibility for their own learning and to get involved in self-assessment. Furthermore, such records will not be restricted to achievement in school, but can also include successes beyond this context. However, as with other portfolios, compiling records of achievement and experience can be a time-consuming process not least because the samples need to be reviewed and updated with the children each term. It is a good idea to dispose of or send home outdated examples of children's achievements in the interests of accuracy and manageability.

Eg   *Record of Achievement and Experience*

Reception

I like to . . .

I don't like to . . .

I know these colours

red
blue
yellow
purple
green
orange

I can draw this picture

I can . . .

build with bricks
go to the toilet on my own
ride a bike
do a jigsaw
say a nursery rhyme
play with my friend
sing songs
put on my own coat and shoes
count to 5

My favourite story is

My favourite song is

I can write my own name

Some principles of recording

Records should
- show individual progress and achievements, and indicate areas for improvement;
- be accessible for all those using them, including colleagues, parents and other adults with a right to the information and, in the case of PRAE, the pupils themselves;
- be ongoing and cumulative in nature, based on regular assessment in the form of systematic observations, discussions, directed tasks and tests;
- be linked to evidence which supports the judgements recorded;
- be kept up to date and be manageable for teachers, allowing information to be included and retrieved quickly and easily;
- be used by future teachers.

Reporting to children, marking, giving constructive feedback and responding to misconceptions and errors

Discussions between teachers and pupils, including constructive feedback on their progress, take place every minute of every day in most nurseries and schools. By utilizing their communication skills effectively teachers can do much to provide accurate, helpful and motivating feedback. It is not just a matter of what is communicated but also how. Teachers need to be aware of the non-verbal messages they give to children as well as the oral and written feedback that they provide. Their body language, facial expressions and gestures can all be used to reinforce and emphasize the messages they give to children about their achievements and what they need to focus on in the future. Much of this feedback is informal in the sense that it constitutes part of the normal exchanges between children and adults. However, it is possible to institute more formal approaches by dedicating time to joint target-setting and self-appraisal/assessment with the children and even young children can get involved less formally in self-reporting.

Marking is an important, although time-consuming, aspect of providing constructive feedback and sends an important message to children about the importance of what they are doing; it also helps teachers to monitor what the children have done and to assess where they need to go next. Marking as children are working helps teachers to notice learning needs and to set targets in an ongoing fashion. However, in a classroom where there may be as many as 30 pupils it is unreasonable to expect the teacher to be marking everywhere at once; if they attempt to do all their marking in this way they may not leave themselves with any time to discuss pupils' attainment. Furthermore, as children get older and are able to cover increasing quantities of work, the task of marking as the lesson proceeds becomes increasingly challenging.

182

13.7.99

It was Jaspers birthday an he went to the shop he lookdt at the toys. He got a little cat just like him. ✓

could read his own writing, and spell cvc words.

Well done You can work more quickly

In some instances (where there are clear right and wrong answers) children can be encouraged to do some of their own marking. While there is always a danger that some children may adjust their answers to obtain perfect scores, their peers will normally alert the teacher to what is going on. In situations where judgements are more subjective, teachers will need to adopt an approach that is manageable, by marking and assessing sufficient work during the lesson to ensure that encouragement and direction are possible, without trying to do everything and be everywhere at once. In such situations teachers need to make certain that they vary their focus to ensure that all the children experience this ongoing feedback on a regular basis even though they may not all receive it at the same time.

When responding to pupil mistakes and misconceptions, trainee and newly qualified 3–8 teachers need to appreciate that a child's mistake or misconception may actually constitute partial understanding that can, and will, become more complete as they mature and gain in experience. It is not possible in the space available to deal with the whole curriculum or to go into minute detail as to how errors and misconceptions can be overcome and pupils' ideas and understanding enhanced. This section will, therefore, restrict itself to some general remarks on the subjects of English, mathematics and science. Readers are advised to refer to the texts in the section on Further Sources of Information for more detailed treatment of mistakes and misconceptions in relation to particular subjects.

In English, mistakes often arise from an incomplete understanding of grammatical rules, for example 'I weren't!' or 'Miss, we done it'. Children may also experience problems over letter formation and spelling, make errors in reading and have difficulties with punctuation.

In mathematics, children may experience difficulties associated with counting on, have misunderstandings over place value, or be unclear over the order of subtraction. The use of the phrase 'take away' when referring to subtraction is acceptable when young children can physically take away items such as sweets, bricks or marbles; however, they will also need a more extensive repertoire of terms including 'from' and 'subtract'. Some difficulties in mathematics can arise from the fact that there may be numerous ways of asking children to do the same thing.

Eg Difficulties from plurality in language

- 'find the sum of 1 and 5'
- 'add 5 to 1'
- 'add 1 and 5'
- 'what number is 5 more than 1?'

In science, some pupil ideas and misconceptions can arise from the fact that, although the children are familiar with a particular word, they have only ever heard its everyday usage and are unaware that it also has a much more precise meaning. The concept of energy is one example. Children also experience difficulties as a result of the counter-intuitive nature of some scientific ideas, for example explaining the forces acting on a ball after it has been thrown. The number of variables coupled with limited life experiences can also lead to misconceptions and incomplete understanding, for example *'plants aren't living things'*, how can they be, they do not move, breathe or eat, after all.

Eg The following scientific ideas were encountered by 3–8 student teachers during an infant teaching practice

- Strawberries are classified as animals.
- Big things sink, little things float.
- Big things are heavy, little things are light.
- We see things because light shines out of our eyes.
- Plants need to be put in a greenhouse, in the sun, in order to germinate and grow.
- Heavy objects fall faster than light objects because they are heavier.
- Seeds contain miniature plants.
- A material is a fabric.

Having identified pupil ideas, errors and misconceptions, and having made some judgements concerning possible causes, teachers are then faced with the question of what to do about them. Young children can develop certain ideas, make errors and hold misconceptions for a variety of reasons. It is certainly the case that the language used can be at the root of some problems. In some cases teachers may be using vocabulary that is inappropriately advanced or strange to pupils. In other cases, children may confuse similar-sounding words. However, not all errors arise from language difficulties and some problems can also occur when children draw incomplete conclusions from their first-hand experiences and observations.

Eg The teacher is more than just a provider of first-hand experiences

A group of reception children had been exploring whether a range of objects would float or sink when immersed in the water tray. Their teacher joined them and asked them to suggest how they could tell whether an object would be a floater or a sinker. The children replied that 'red things sink and the other colours float'. When the teacher looked at the objects tested she realized that in this particular instance that was indeed the case.

✔ Reporting to pupils: marking, offering constructive feedback and responding to misconceptions

- Find something positive to say or write. (A hundred ways to say 'Well Done' can be located at www.practicalparent.org.uk/handyhints)
- Identify something for the child to work at (target-setting).
- Try to use your feedback to help the children improve and develop. Set targets with the children at the start of an activity (e.g. 'Today I want you to remember to use capital letters at the start of a sentence').
- Where children are self-marking, conduct spot checks from time to time to inhibit cheating and to ensure opportunities for feedback to children on their performance. Offer praise and recognition for honesty and keep reinforcing the message that only honest self-marking is of any value.
- Praise effort and achievement at the end of the lesson or day by telling the rest of the class when a child has tried especially hard or been particularly successful.
- Allow for the age and maturity of the child. What might constitute an error for an 8-year-old might be a reasonable level of understanding for a reception child.
- Respond in supportive and helpful ways that promote progress and do not belittle and demotivate pupils. Children can learn a lot from mistakes if they are handled in a sensitive way and are accompanied by regular experiences of success.
- Some sensitive correction can be instructive for children and may even be motivating as they feel more skilled and knowledgeable as a result. Picking up on every little error and correcting incessantly, however, is likely to make children less confident and less willing to take risks and *have a go*.
- Introduce activities and experiences that result in challenges to children's current understanding (causing disequilibrium) to encourage them to modify their ideas.
- Do not make the intellectual jump required of pupils so large that they are unable to link contrary experiences with their existing ideas.
- Remember that experience alone guarantees nothing. Be aware that some children may incorporate contrary experience into their existing schemas rather than alter the schema. Teachers need to intervene to help children develop their skills, knowledge and understanding (scaffolding). Using focused questions and making time to discuss children's experiences and ideas are useful ways of doing this.

Reporting to parents

In nurseries and infant schools where there is a high level of day-to-day contact between teachers and parents a great deal of informal and ongoing reporting is already taking place. In addition, every parent whose child is of statutory school age is entitled to an annual written report on their child's performance and achievement during the year. Annual reports have to contain brief particulars on the child's achievements in the form of a series of short statements outlining successes and areas of weakness. The report should also contain information on a pupil's general educational progress which might include remarks on behaviour and attitude as well as academic attainment.

Eg   *Annual report to parents*

Pupil name: Stephen   **School Year: 2003–4 (Year 2)**

English

Stephen always listens attentively in class discussions, and he confidently makes thoughtful and interesting contributions. He continues to enjoy reading and can read a wide range of simple texts independently. He is developing the ability to use a range of strategies to read new words, and shows that he understands what he has read through oral questioning and comprehension exercises. He is always keen to write and puts real effort into his work. Stephen can develop his ideas for stories and accounts, and is working hard to use capital letters and full stops consistently, and to use descriptive language. He spells many words with regular spelling patterns correctly and is learning irregular words.

Mathematics

Stephen can use addition and subtraction when solving problems involving up to 20-plus objects. He has begun to understand the place value of each digit in a number and can use this to order numbers to 100. He has mental recall of number bonds to 20, and is developing this with higher numbers. He is working on early multiplication through continuous addition and counting-on activities. He can use non-standard and some standard units to measure and order objects. Stephen has made data collections and recorded these in simple charts.

Science

He has completed science tasks about sound and light, forces, and plants. He can describe and name the simple features of objects, living things and events, and recognize similarities and differences. He can offer suggestions about how to find things out, has made predictions and tested his ideas. He asks and answers questions related to a task with interest. Stephen has made individual and group recordings of his work in a variety of ways including simple tables. He has an excellent general knowledge and is always eager to find out more.

Design and technology

When designing and making Stephen can select from a range of materials and techniques and explain his choices. He has developed his skills in cutting, joining and assembling. He has made pictures and models to show his designs and can discuss his ideas and suggest improvements.

Information and communications technology

Stephen can recognize a range of ICT equipment and has learned to control and operate different devices. He has used the computer to communicate in pictures and text and learned more about using the keyboard and the mouse.

History

Stephen can recognize changes in his own and others' lives and use related vocabulary to describe the passing of time. He has used objects, books and photographs to find out more about the past, and can sequence objects and events into simple chronological order.

Geography

He has made observations and recordings about the features of the local environment – the types and uses of buildings and land, and the people and their roles. He has talked about attractive and unattractive features and made simple plans and routes.

Art

Stephen has worked practically and imaginatively with materials, tools and techniques to create pieces of art work. He is developing his use of colour, pattern and texture, and takes care in observational work.

Music

He has learned songs and rhymes, and is an excellent singer who confidently performs on his own. He has learned to name and play simple percussion instruments, and to explore and select sounds to express ideas.

Physical Education

Stephen is well coordinated and moves confidently on the floor and apparatus during PE lessons. He has developed and refined his skills in using small apparatus, and works enthusiastically in games.

Religious Education

Stephen has listened to Bible stories and learned about the life of Jesus and the work of the church. He always shows care and concern for others, and has a responsible and reliable attitude.

General comments

Stephen approaches all his work with enthusiasm and a desire to do well. He has made very good progress in his work across all areas of the curriculum. He is a happy, friendly member of the class who has been a pleasure to teach. Thank you for your home support which, coupled with Stephen's hard work, will ensure his continuing success.

Number of attendances out of total number possible 302: 312

Number of unauthorized absences 0

This report may be discussed with . . . . on . . . .

at . . . .

Reporting on the Foundation Stage Profile

Following a consultation exercise in 2001 concerning Baseline Assessment for reception pupils a national system of assessment within the Foundation Stage was developed and introduced in 2002–2003 (QCA, 2002). The new scheme is referred to as the Foundation Stage Profile (FSP). Completion of the profile takes place at the end of the Foundation Stage (usually during the second half of the Summer term in reception) and is followed by reporting to parents before the end of the school year. Foundation Stage Profile assessments seek to identify the strengths and learning needs of individual children, to enable future teachers to plan appropriate teaching and learning activities to meet these needs and to inform discussions with parents and future teachers on progress and performance. The Foundation Stage Profile aims to provide

- both a summative record of pupil attainment and a formative and diagnostic tool for future Year 1 teachers;
- information that is useful to a school as a whole in helping it to plan and manage its provision in terms of curriculum and resources; and
- a benchmark against which a school and inspection teams can make judgements on the extent of pupils' progress by the end of Key Stage 1.

The FSP applies throughout the maintained sector and includes statements covering all six areas of learning contained in the Curriculum Guidance for the Foundation Stage in an effort to reflect properly the breadth of learning in which children have been engaged. This does, however, have implications in terms of manageability as the FSP is largely based on teachers' observations of children's performance in everyday classroom activities. Manageability is a key issue as many reception classes have more than one intake during a year and include rising-five pupils (children who will reach the age of 5 in the coming term). Recording and conducting FSP assessments in such a changing environment therefore is heavily influenced by

- the perceived benefit to the teacher;
- the extent of the paperwork involved;
- the numbers, ages and full-time/part-time status of the children; and
- the amount and quality of non-teaching classroom support available.

The introduction of the FSP caused concern among some practitioners who feared downward pressure and the establishment of a culture of overassessment characterized by excessive use of tick boxes. These concerns and others were exacerbated by the manner in which the FSP was introduced whereby reception practitioners had little time to familiarize themselves with the documentation and intended procedures before having to complete the profile at the end of the year. However, the FSP does not involve testing and should be based on ongoing observations over an extended period of time, in a wide range of contexts, not simply at the end of the reception year. It also gives parity of esteem to all areas of the Foundation Stage curriculum and provides for input from parents and carers and other early years practitioners (e.g. non-teaching colleagues). At the time of writing it remains to be seen whether the FSP becomes a boon or a burden to children and their teachers. Trainee and newly qualified teachers wishing to look at the documentation that reception teachers have to complete, plus the guidance notes to support this process, can locate the information on the Qualification and Curriculum Authority website (www.qca.org.uk/ca/foundation/profiles).

Reporting on Standard Attainment Tests (SATs)

All Year 2 pupils must undertake SATs during their final term of Key Stage 1, during which time they will be assessed against level descriptions contained in the National Curriculum Attainment Targets (ATs). The final overall results of these tasks on a school level will be made public, but only teachers, parents and pupils see the detailed results for individual children. Schools are expected to report annually to parents on the SATs results, and teacher assessments (based on the same level descriptions) are reported alongside the test results. For many people formal assessments, particularly public examinations or tasks such as SATs, are seen as being more objective than the judgements and critical appraisal made by individual teachers. However, the concept of objectivity is something of an illusion in that the mere fact that an assessment is universal does not eliminate bias. The manageability of assessment is crucial, and the need for it often results in compromises over validity, reliability and objectivity. The SATs may be valid in that they assess what they say they are assessing, and they may be reliable in that they offer consistency of results over different activities and times, but that is not the same as saying that they are objective and hence should be given primacy over teacher assessments. Prior to 2003 where discrepancies occurred between a teacher's judgements about a child's achievements as a result of teacher assessment and what the child achieved in the SAT, the test result was preferred. However, this may change in future years with increasing weight given to teacher assessments for Key Stage 1 pupils.

In many ways SATs are a product of the tensions inherent in a system which is seeking to measure children's performance to support the teaching and learning process while at the same time measuring that performance as a way of ensuring teacher accountability. In a climate featuring high levels of teacher accountability, assessments such as the SATs can skew the curriculum and the teacher's efforts away from a broad and balanced education and towards passing the test, sometimes undermining the professionals' capacity to determine children's wider achievement and potential in the process. Standard Attainment Tests and tests are inherently reductionist. They can offer useful comparisons, but across a relatively narrow front.

Some principles of reporting and accountability

When reporting on pupil attainment
- begin your comments by referring to positive factors and ensure any subsequent criticism is constructive in nature;
- make reference to children's achievements in relation to the Early Learning Goals or National Curriculum level descriptions;
- include some description of children's achievements in relation to the wider curriculum;
- suggest areas and ways in which children can improve on their attainment to date;
- maintain a professional commitment to confidentiality;
- value the contribution made by pupils, parents and non-teaching colleagues in assessment and recording; and
- use methods that are manageable and understandable for all involved.

Catering for Individual Pupil Needs and Abilities

By the end of this section you should

- understand how to match learning objectives and content to the needs and abilities of pupils;
- be aware of the importance of challenging children and having appropriate expectations for children's learning;
- understand the need to build on prior attainment, and to share the content and purposes of lessons and activities with the children;
- be familiar with ways in which teaching and learning can be adapted and modified in response to some of the special educational needs that might be encountered in mainstream settings.

Differentiation

Children vary: from each other, from day to day, from year to year, in their abilities, in their behaviour, and in their attitudes. Young children can learn in different ways, at different speeds, can experience a variety of different learning difficulties, and can reach very different levels of attainment. Most teachers would acknowledge that diversity exists in their classes and they respond to individual pupil needs and abilities by employing organizational strategies such as ability grouping, by adjusting the curriculum for different children when planning and teaching, and by tailoring expectations according to the pupils' needs and abilities. Differentiation, therefore, is an important element in effective teaching and learning in order to *maximize the motivation, progress and achievement of each student* (Stradling and Saunders, 1993). Howard Gardner (2003) and other psychologists, for example, have suggested that people possess a range of intelligences and that some may be much more highly developed than others. Awareness of these intelligences could be helpful for teachers when considering how tasks could be devised to allow children to capitalize on their strengths to support learning across the curriculum.

Gardner's original multiple intelligences

- **Linguistic**: the ability to use words (orally or in writing) effectively;
- **Mathematical (logical)**: the ability to use reason and numbers effectively;
- **Visual (spatial)**: the ability to visualize the world around you accurately, to represent things visually and to manipulate images mentally;
- **Musical**: the ability to identify clearly, change and express music;
- **Bodily (kinaesthetic)**: the ability to use your body and/or hands to express ideas and make or change objects;
- **Interpersonal**: the ability to be sensitive to the emotions and thoughts of other people;
- **Intrapersonal**: the ability to be reflective and understand one's own strengths and weaknesses.

Differentiating – matching tasks to children's abilities – is not a new idea for 3–8 teachers. Long before the introduction of the National Curriculum or Early Learning Goals, authors concerned with good nursery and primary practice were referring to the need for teachers to think about the children's abilities, previous experience, interests, knowledge and skills, as well as paying attention to the subject matter and the range of teaching styles and methods. Differentiation should result in the provision of tasks which will enable all children to

- consolidate their existing understanding;
- practise their existing skills;
- build on such understanding and skills;
- encounter and master new ideas and enlarge their knowledge of a subject; and
- engage in creative and imaginative thinking and action.

(Alexander *et al.*, 1992)

A key factor to consider when differentiating is that ability is not necessarily fixed. A pupil's ability may well alter over time as a result of maturation and could depend on the context or the subject matter. The notion that children have habitual levels of achievement is supported by common sense and anecdotal evidence rather than by hard facts (SCAA, 1994). It is entirely possible that achievement is domain specific rather than universal, and is unstable rather than fixed (SCAA, 1994, p. 26). In addition, the domains in question may not be different subjects, such as English and art, but could quite easily be between different aspects of the same subject such as writing and reading (e.g. children who can read words that they cannot yet spell).

Universal ability. A child's ability is the same across the whole curriculum.
Fixed ability. A child's ability relative to his/her peers will not alter over time.
Domain specific ability. A child performs better in some areas of the curriculum than in others.
Unstable ability. A child's ability can improve and regress.

Given that ability may be domain specific and unstable, those working in 3–8 settings need to start from the premise that every child is good at something, and success in one area can breed success and increased confidence in other areas. In conjunction with this article of faith teachers need to retain a degree of flexibility and deploy a range of different strategies, including differentiation by outcome, by support and by task.

191

Differentiation by outcome involves a group or class of pupils undertaking the same task while working at their own level. While this will always be a useful option, it should not be used as an excuse for not considering differentiation at all, or, in other words, differentiation by *accident*. When teachers differentiate by outcome they recognize the implications. First, activities and materials must be equally accessible to all children and ought not to be dependent upon knowledge and skills which only some of the children have. Second, there should be a range of possible answers and outcomes. Ultimately, if a task is to be truly defined as differentiated by outcome it needs to offer all children involved the chance to make progress.

Differentiation by support refers to a variation in the level of teacher intervention provided and in the level of autonomy offered to children during activities. Although the difficulties involved in differentiating should not be underestimated, much of what is already common practice in nurseries and classrooms can make a contribution to the task. Most teachers already adapt, alter and adjust the demands placed on children during teaching and learning in order to support or extend particular individuals or groups. This can have implications for the organization and management of lessons and activities, as it is often the case that the dialogue and interaction between teachers and individual children is less than it could be, and is often concentrated at the start and conclusion of sessions.

Differentiation by task may take a number of forms, including

- children covering the same content but at different levels;
- children covering the same content but with different activities;
- children covering the same content, activity and level, but being taught using different approaches.

When differentiating by task teachers need to remember that children have an entitlement to certain skills and knowledge within the National Curriculum and Early

Learning Goals. In order to ensure that differentiation by task and the entitlement curriculum are compatible, a distinction needs to be drawn between the purpose of an activity and the way in which that purpose is addressed. For example, if teachers wish children to learn to *count reliably up to 20 objects* (QCA, 1999, p. 62) then there are many ways in which they can set about achieving this.

It is sometimes hard to say with any certainty where one form of differentiation ends and another begins, particularly as different approaches could be employed at different points within the same lesson or activity. A task may be identified as differentiated by outcome on the surface, yet within that the teacher may use a range of different techniques (including challenges, questions and procedures) for different individuals and groups.

The example below outlines a design and technology activity for a class of Year 2 infants following a visit to the local playground. The teacher's primary purpose was to teach the pupils to *measure, mark out, cut* and *shape a range of materials* (QCA, 1999, p. 92). The columns show how the same task could be differentiated either by outcome or by task/support.

Eg *A design and technology class activity*

Differentiation by outcome

- When *clarifying the task* the children talked about their visit to the site and were then told that they would be designing a piece of apparatus. The teacher discussed the features of playground apparatus with the children and they decided that all the products should be fun to use and safe.

- The children were then asked to *design* their apparatus in pairs using pencil and paper.

- When *making* their playground models the teacher put out a limited selection of tools and materials (including hacksaws, bench hooks, square section softwood, cardboard, PVA adhesive, string and scissors) to which all the children had access.

Differentiation by task

- When *clarifying the task*, following the visit, some children were asked to respond to the broad question 'What would make an exciting piece of playground equipment?' Others were asked to respond to much more specific queries such as 'What should our climbing frame be like?' The teacher assisted and guided one group of children closely as they began to identify criteria and specifications arising from the answers to the second question. The first group was expected to operate more independently and to make a written list in pairs.

- Some of the children *designed* their models verbally and by handling the materials at their disposal to show their intentions. Most of the class drew their designs. Three very able children were asked to review different designs in catalogues and to produce two alternative designs of their own and then to select the best.

- When *making*, different children were provided with different materials and equipment. For the majority of the class this meant scissors, paper, card, softwood and hacksaws. One pair, which was proceeding rapidly and effectively, was offered additional tools and materials with which to produce their final model. One pair was asked to construct their climbing frame using a commercially produced construction kit.

- When *evaluating* their models the children all used the original criteria of fun and safety.

- When engaged in critical reflection and *evaluation* of their work some children used a worksheet, while a small group who had difficulty with writing discussed their views with the teacher acting as scribe. The teacher employed different types of questions with different children including procedural questions such as 'How are you going to do that?', questions about outcomes such as 'Have you done what you set out to do?' and questions about understanding such as 'How does it work?' and 'How could you make it work better?'

The ability to differentiate tasks for children, based on judgements about their needs and abilities, plays an important role in helping children to achieve in any subject or area of learning. However, the realities of nursery and primary class-rooms make these things *aspirations* rather than *absolutes* (Alexander *et al.*, 1992, p. 28). Differentiation is a demanding task for teachers, one that is made even more difficult in situations where teachers experience a lack of access to support from other adults (e.g. curriculum coordinators, child-care assistants (CCAs), non-teaching assistants (NTAs) and parents), where resources are limited or not available and where class sizes are large and the available space is insufficient. Eliciting children's ideas and using knowledge of their strengths, weaknesses and previous experiences to inform planning and teaching cannot be expected to result in 30 or more separate lesson plans. Not only would such an approach be unmanageable, it would also ignore the fact that while there are many individual differences between children, there are also similarities and common needs. These similarities can make differentiation more manageable, as matching tasks to pupils may involve consideration of groups and classes as well as individuals. Appreciating the differences between children in this more general fashion can be helpful to trainee and newly qualified teachers as a starting point when beginning to decide on which approach to differentiation may work, in which context and with which children.

Differentiation checklist

- Monitor your teaching materials to ensure that they support, extend and allow for achievement by all children.
- Alter the amount, range and complexity of information given.
- Adjust the degree of independence and responsibility for organizing and running tasks and activities. Structure a task tightly for some children while allowing others more room to plan, organize and manage themselves.
- Identify those children likely to struggle and plan ways of assisting them to cope with the demands of the lesson or session.
- Identify those children likely to find the task easy and plan ways of making the task more demanding to ensure they are suitably challenged.
- Use a wide range of recording methods.

- Recognize the successes of all pupils and challenge them to extend their knowledge and skills.
- Organize the nursery/classroom to support groupwork and collaborative learning as well as class and individual teaching.
- Monitor children's experiences, target your time and attention towards certain children at certain points, and alter the intensity of teacher intervention between levels that could be described as high, medium or low.
- Undertake formative assessment and enter into dialogue with pupils as a way of setting new targets and identifying learning difficulties.
- Make effective use of other adults and support staff in the classroom, including parents, NTAs and visitors.

Teaching and Inclusion

It has been estimated that as many as one in five children will have some form of SEN at some point during their school lives and the reader is advised to refer to sections in the other chapters on the range of needs that might be encountered in nurseries and schools and the underlying rationale behind the policy of inclusion.

Teachers of young children play an important part in identifying, and providing appropriate educational experiences for, children with SEN. Developing inclusive provision may involve consultation and collaboration with external agencies and others to discuss and plan learning programmes aimed at meeting children's specific needs (see Chapter 2). Where a teacher has suspicions or knows that a child has a SEN advice and guidance ought to be sought from those with relevant expertise and experience such as parents, the school's special educational needs coordinator (SENCO) and/or local support services as any strategies employed will need to fit with the school's SEN policy and procedures. The teacher's role in responding to SEN includes providing support and an environment to enable children to have equal access to the curriculum, and providing appropriate learning experiences, including social ones.

Efforts to support children with SEN can be greatly aided by positive relationships with parents and carers. Parental involvement can be highly effective in assisting children to overcome cognitive, linguistic, behavioural or emotional difficulties. Parents and carers should be included and involved in the decision-making concerning their child and be encouraged to contribute and support their child's development in partnership with the nursery/school (Paige-Smith, 2002). Where such involvement is encouraged, parents are more likely to have a positive attitude towards the process and their child. Where such involvement is not encouraged, parents may feel threatened or criticized, and reluctant either to accept that a need exists or to support the efforts of professionals to help their child achieve their full potential.

Involving parents and carers

- Listen to what parents have to say.
- Include parents and carers at an early stage.
- Demonstrate an understanding of, and respect for, the feelings of parents and carers.
- Make every effort to maintain good channels of communication so that children's progress can be reported.

The remainder of this section considers some of the strategies that student and newly qualified teachers may wish to employ to help children with SEN to achieve. The remarks are organized under the headings of physical disabilities, learning and behavioural difficulties and gifted and talented pupils. These categories are a considerable oversimplification and the reader is urged to seek additional information on specific needs by accessing some of the references in the Further Sources of Information sections at the end of this chapter and Chapter 1.

Including children with physical disabilities

Handling objects and accessing out-of-nursery/school sites may present difficulties for some pupils with physical disabilities. For example, teachers need to anticipate likely triggers for asthma attacks, or the need for diabetic pupils to keep their blood sugar levels stable. Places where children can sit, rest or be quiet are a good idea. Non-teaching support staff need to be properly briefed about supporting the children's health and education; for example, an adult working with an epileptic pupil who experiences an absence attack may need to repeat or check on information and instructions given. Some children with physical disabilities may need additional time or alternative ways to complete activities such as written work, and making the most of educational technology (video, ICT, concept keyboard) is one possible response to this. Resources may need to be carefully chosen to ensure participation by all including those pupils who may experience difficulties with gross or fine motor skills. The stability of equipment can be improved (e.g. using Velcro), as can ease of handling/control (e.g. attaching handles or increasing the size of resources) and accessibility of resources (e.g. attaching strings/cords for movement or retrieval). Where necessary, provide physical assistance. In some cases, teachers may need to look for alternative learning objectives even though all the children are engaged in the same activity. Providing alternative activities ought to be a last resort, when it is the only way to meet a child's needs.

Eg | *Adapting/altering learning objectives to support inclusion*

- Class objective: matching shapes and recognizing similarities (QCA, 2000, p. 80).
- Objective for pupil with mobility difficulties: reaching, grasping, releasing.

Supporting the learning of a visually impaired child

- Make sure that the child is close enough to see; or allow the child to use other senses (touch, smell, hearing) to investigate the world around him/her.
- Allow additional time for the completion of certain tasks.
- Use alternative recording methods.
- Make sure that the lighting where the child is working is not too dim.
- Make sure the child can use aids such as glasses or magnifiers.

Supporting the learning of a hearing impaired child

- Provide visual clues to support oral work.
- Rephrase/emphasize spoken language (e.g. key words or phrases).
- Reduce background noise levels.
- Face the child when talking and articulate words clearly.
- Check that instructions/information are understood.
- Use hearing aid technology (e.g. induction coils and microphones).

Including children with learning and behavioural difficulties

Pupils with learning difficulties are more likely to work best and stay on-task longer in situations where routines are clearly understood, where they are able to exercise some control over their work with support, and where work is set at an appropriate level. Teachers may have to build a series of shorter activities into lessons/sessions. Similarly, taking care to avoid overly long strings of instructions is useful. Autistic pupils, for example, may respond better to statements, instructions and directions rather than asking questions and demanding choices. Teacher-centred or high pupil autonomy approaches (e.g. 'chalk and talk', dictation, note taking from books, or unstructured/free writing) are the least effective teaching methods to employ. Children with learning difficulties will need plenty of opportunity for reinforcement and repetition, and using and applying similar vocabulary and ideas in different contexts. Teachers may need to keep referring to previous work and experience to help children make sense of what is going on.

- Be ready to simplify and rephrase instructions. Use shorter, less complex sentences that draw on concrete first-hand experience.
- Provide verbal and visual cues and prompts as well as written information. Use concrete materials, demonstrations and examples. Utilize a range of non-text based teaching methods, for example drama and socio-dramatic play, visits, guest speakers or story telling.
- Differentiate tasks to enable children to engage in them at different levels of comprehension and/or capability.
- Provide numerous opportunities to practise skills.
- Model language and skills.
- Recognize the distinction between communication and comprehension; the latter may be sophisticated even though the former proves challenging.
- Use assistive technologies and/or augmentative communication systems including ICT to facilitate pupils' ability to communicate and demonstrate comprehension.
- Adapt written material by simplifying/translating texts into language that is easier for the children to understand. Précis longer texts into single paragraphs or short sentences.
- Read with or for a child and/or act as a scribe.
- Mark pages in reference books to enable children to find the information they want more easily.
- Use key words, work sheets or writing frames to help children structure their written work, organize information and express themselves, rather than asking them to 'write about it'.
- Work around, rather than shoot down, incorrect or partial answers. Foster discussion among children to develop partial into more complete answers.

Children with emotional and behavioural difficulties (EBD) or Attention-Deficit (Hyperactivity) Disorder (AD(H)D) may struggle to concentrate and focus on a task for the same length of time as their peers. It is often assumed that children with behavioural problems are seeking attention and that they obtain satisfaction from that attention. However, children with EBD or AD(H)D may not be enjoying their behaviour any more than their teachers. Unwanted behaviour, such as aggression, may result from frustration and alienation or may be because the child has never learned or been taught strategies for resolving conflict and confrontation. Some of the difficulties that these pupils present may, therefore, be susceptible to some modification and improvement over time by examining and altering the setting in which the children's behaviour manifests itself. Looking at when and where disruption occurs is the first step in this process.

Potential stress points in emotional and behavioural difficulties

Children with EBD may become difficult for a teacher to manage
- during particular sorts of lessons (such as sessions in which there is little structure and direction);
- at particular times of the day;
- when particular methods of classroom organization are chosen;
- when the teacher is doing certain things; or
- when the child is asked to do certain things.

198

The situation may be exacerbated when
- teachers respond in certain ways; or
- when other children do certain things.

Trying to keep the child productively engaged and on-task is the aim, and liaison with non-teaching support staff on the best ways of providing extra support in group settings can be helpful. Appropriate pacing of lessons too can make a big difference to children with EBD.

Supporting the work of pupils with emotional and behavioural difficulties

- Structure lessons to avoid 'dead time' and a lack of supervision.
- Establish expectations, conventions and routines that reduce the need for constant teacher instruction at key points during the day such as transition times.
- Develop your ability to anticipate events. Classroom layouts that create blindspots are likely to exacerbate disruption and task avoidance.
- There may be ways in which the child can be assisted in modifying his/her behaviour and developing new strategies for coping with school. Teach children to verbalize anger, for example by asking for equipment/resources to be returned or for pupils to express their feelings, then praise and reward them for doing it.
- Monitor pupil progress, provide positive feedback and include children with EBD in setting simple goals and targets that can be achieved within a short period.
- Offer an easy task to do, stay with the pupil while the task is completed and make sure positive feedback is given. Success in one area can transfer to other areas.
- Find out what children with EBD or AD(H)D see as a reward, and ensure that they are rewarded when they show determination and perseverance.
- Be prepared to step in quickly once you have spotted the build-up of disruptive behaviour. It is sometimes possible to head off, divert or defuse an imminent outburst using questions, offering a change of task, a change of location or a simple housekeeping chore that those pupils enjoy and which confers responsibility on them for which they can receive praise and recognition.

Including gifted and talented pupils

It is essential to maintain the interest and motivation of gifted and talented pupils by presenting curriculum content in clear and exciting ways. If the special needs of gifted and talented pupils are not addressed it risks the onset of underachievement, boredom and even disruptive behaviour. Although able to complete teacher set tasks quickly these pupils may benefit from opportunities to have additional time and from being asked to study in much greater depth than their peers. Teachers should not hesitate to use more challenging vocabulary and language, as well as offering them greater variety and autonomy in tasks. Research skills can be a particularly productive area in which gifted and talented children can be challenged, and is one that fits well with their characteristic thirst for knowledge (see Chapter 2). Providing gifted and talented children with opportunities to use and apply ideas and skills in a range of different contexts puts them in the position of having to make deductions, develop and test hypotheses, and take their research into new areas. Children can also be encouraged to share their learning and skills with their peers as a way of raising the knowledge and understanding of the whole class.

Supporting the work of gifted and talented pupils

- Provide extension work and enrichment activities with greater depth and variety (some of which may be extra-curricular).
- Challenge pupils to think at a higher level, for example querying assumptions.
- Give them the chance to solve demanding problems.
- Provide opportunities for autonomous and independent learning such as project work.
- Find a way to enable them to work at their own pace and cover the normal curriculum more quickly, combined with opportunities to engage in sustained work without timetable interruptions.
- Make sure that giftedness does not become exclusiveness; gifted and talented children need experience of working with non-gifted/talented peers.
- Do not make the assumption that because a child is exceptionally able teacher intervention is unnecessary. Thoughtful teacher intervention, inspiration, challenge and constructive criticism are vital in avoiding underachievement.

Classroom Organization and Management

AUDIT

By the end of this section you should

- understand how to make effective use of teaching time in whole-class and group situations;
- know about ways of creating safe and stimulating environments (indoors and outdoors) to support teaching and learning;
- know how to plan for learning beyond the nursery/school through homework tasks and visits;
- know about a range of teaching methods which will help to support children's learning by sustaining the momentum of pupils' work and keeping pupils engaged.

Organizing the Children

This section is based on the premise that strategies such as class teaching and groupwork are not inherently good or bad but are simply options open to teachers who have to make choices about the best way to organize and manage a particular lesson or session. Teachers should group children on the basis of fitness for purpose rather than on the basis of dogmatic adherence to established practices.

Young children have always experienced some form of class teaching whether at morning registration, at story time, in PE or in dance and movement. As a method of organizing children for learning, it has become increasingly common in infant schools, particularly with the advent of literacy and numeracy hours. Alexander *et al.* (1992) made a strong case for seeing class teaching as an essential part of the teacher's repertoire, placing the onus on him/her to be an organizer, giver of information, leader and the focus of attention.

Benefits and disadvantages associated with class teaching

Benefits	Disadvantages
• higher-order questioning	• too much teacher talk
• more detailed explanations	• an absence of active learning by children
• higher levels of pupil performance	• individual differences ignored

(Alexander *et al.*, 1992)

When working with a large number of young children, trainee and newly qualified teachers need to bear in mind the age and maturity of these learners. Teachers who keep young pupils sitting passively for too long are asking for trouble. So, too, are teachers who do not check that their instructions have been understood before setting the children to work. The following suggestions are intended to assist trainee and newly qualified teachers to organize children and manage class situations.

Managing a whole class

• Ensure that the necessary resources are set out or readily available.
• Think about the language and vocabulary that you will use.
• Obtain and maintain the children's attention. Waiting for silence can be done actively through effective use of the voice and non-verbal communication. Having something interesting to show can be highly effective as a technique for getting little eyes, ears and minds all pointed in the right direction. A teacher whose whole body says 'Look at me! This is going to be really interesting' is more likely to gain the children's attention, and gaining this attention is crucial if you are to create a window of opportunity.

- Do not squander the chance to start the lesson well. A prompt start, followed by an appropriate, yet business-like, pace will help to set the tone for the lesson and avoid the creation of 'dead time'.
- Pacing and timing are crucial. Some children may be left floundering if the pace is too rapid. Others may lose their concentration and enthusiasm if the pace is too languid; they may start fiddling or interrupting. You can lose the initiative and spend unnecessary amounts of time trying to regain their attention.
- Give some thought to transition times within a lesson, for example moving from a whole-class situation into groups or back again. Use strategies such as checking on instructions and staggered movement times to reduce disruption. For example, 'Let's see who's sitting up nicely and is ready to start'.
- Finishing class lessons in an organized fashion is every bit as important as starting them well. It is part of the learning process, providing opportunities for review and reflection and giving you a chance to ascertain the extent of the children's experiences and learning.
- Being overtaken by time is often a problem for trainee and newly qualified teachers when teaching the whole class. Allow time for plenary sessions and putting things away. Learning to put things away properly is a long-term process with young children, and requires determination and consistency on the teacher's part. Encourage children to take some responsibility for tidying up and looking after their learning environment; a shared classroom ethos in which the children have had an opportunity to decide that 'In our class we always . . .' will help.

A significant amount of teaching with the 3–8 age range takes place using groupwork. In some cases, an apparently collaborative and groupwork setting belies the fact that children are actually engaged in a task as individuals. In other instances, groupwork involves true collaboration with small numbers of children working collectively on the same task (Alexander *et al.*, 1992). It is also worth noting that in early years settings, such as nurseries, the membership of groups can be unstable and short-lived as young children are able to opt into and out of group tasks, albeit usually with adult support and direction.

Benefits and disadvantages of groupwork

Benefits	Disadvantages
<ul><li>encourages pupil–pupil interaction</li><li>promotes communication and cooperation</li><li>encourages children to take more responsibility for their own learning, setting the pace, asking questions and developing answers</li><li>promotes participation, high involvement and commitment</li></ul>	<ul><li>can be quite slow</li><li>the positive social dynamics of groupwork are not automatic and can require input from the teacher</li><li>can be difficult to manage several groups simultaneously</li></ul>

Eg *Some groupwork options*

- Grouping for learning (on the basis of ability or needs) can be a very effective and efficient way of teaching. However, if the groups are permanent two problems can arise. First, children pick up unspoken messages about their ranking and status in the classroom; they soon know that the Red group is the *top group*, for example. For those children who see themselves as less able this can have an adverse effect on their self-esteem and motivation. Second, teachers themselves can be affected in that their expectations can be coloured by their own groupings, leading to under- and over-estimating ability.
- Some teachers will seek to group children by age/maturity. This is frequently the case in vertically grouped classes (e.g. Y1 and Y2 together) that often appear where school numbers dictate.
- Grouping by friendship can be a powerful motivator for children but there are dangers. Single sex groups may appear where you would prefer mixed sex groups. There can be children that no one wants to work with (e.g. *the last child on the bench* in PE); and *like with like* can fail to challenge and stimulate, can stifle the introduction of new ideas and can become exclusive or elitist.
- Grouping by interest/enthusiasm is a fourth possibility. Although not really practical as a permanent arrangement it can be very powerful for short-term projects.

Children need to be in a position to work effectively as a group. The self-discipline and social skills required for greater concentration, perseverance and effective groupwork take time to develop. Encouraging children to articulate their feelings about themselves can be a good starting point when trying to promote these skills. Readiness for groupwork can also be underpinned by providing common experiences for all the pupils involved, such as a class visit. Teachers of young children can look for indicators to help them assess the extent to which their children are improving and increasing their groupworking capabilities and readiness.

Eg *Groupwork indicators*

Children

- can play cooperatively, work collaboratively, share and take turns;
- have developed positive relationships with others in the classroom, demonstrated by a willingness and an ability to initiate verbal and non-verbal interactions with adults and peers;
- are able and willing to participate in discussions;
- can identify the effects of their behaviour on others with help;
- are able to observe and adhere to rules and conventions such as accepting and respecting differences;
- are developing an ability to cope with change;
- are developing strategies for coping with frustration, for example having another go or trying different approaches; and
- are displaying an increasing confidence to try things out independently.

The suggestions below may be helpful to trainee and newly qualified teachers when planning and managing groupwork sessions.

Managing young children's learning in groups

- Ensure that everyone knows the purpose of the task.
- Think about roles in groups. Who is going to do what? Are there real roles for all?
- Offer the group guidance on procedures at the start, and remind them about class conventions and timescales.
- Do not play a numbers game. A group is not defined by the number 4 or 6. The larger the group, the easier it is for some young children to find themselves on the margins of an activity. The size of the group also interferes with procedure. It can take pupils all their time just to decide what they want to do and then there is no time left to do it.
- Allow for variety and flexibility when grouping children; this is determined to some extent by the purposes or objectives of the activity and the fact that relationships change over time.
- Remember that younger children's need for security can be undermined by constantly chopping and changing groups.
- Capitalize on the similarities between pupils in order to make children feel more secure in groups.
- Capitalize on the differences between pupils in order to encourage creativity and excitement. Groups based on diversity can benefit from the challenges and tensions created by differences, but you must ensure that these challenges are tackled in a positive and supportive fashion.
- Provide opportunities for reflection about groupwork. For children to become better at groupwork they need to be given the chance to think about how they worked together. Praise and recognition reinforce desirable behaviour.
- Where will you be and what will you be doing while groupwork is taking place? When will adult interventions be needed? Have you made effective use of other adult support?
- Do not attempt to chair multiple groups simultaneously yourself. Use a classroom map to predict potential clashes and avoid trying to be everywhere at once. Make sure that there are some sessions when groups engaged in structured play and practical and creative activities also receive higher levels of teacher attention.

Eg Using a classroom map to plan for groupwork

- **Red**: high intervention. Needs you most/all of the time.
- **Orange/amber**: medium intervention. Needs you some of the time, for example starting the group off and monitoring from a distance.
- **Green**: low intervention. Needs occasional visits and checks.

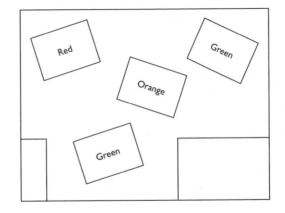

Organizing the Learning Environment: Indoors

Within classrooms, many teachers operate a mixed economy with their equipment and resources. Some resources will be assigned to individual classes or teachers, some will be available to teams of staff (e.g. the nursery team or the Y2 classes), others may be held centrally for use by the whole school; some are teacher-controlled, others are open-access. The issue of access will often be shaped by concerns about health and safety, and classroom management. At the same time the physical environment should be welcoming and designed with younger children in mind. Safety gates and doors in nursery settings and scaled-down furniture in Key Stage 1 classes are two examples.

Creating a safe learning environment

Does the nursery/school have
- safety glass or plastic covering for low windows and doors?
- well-lit stairways?
- slow closing internal doors?
- safety gates?
- safe floor coverings?
- fire-retardant curtains and soft furnishings?
- guards on fires or radiators?
- protected power sockets?
- closely supervised use of heavy or sharp equipment?
- fire exits clearly marked and accessible?
- non-lockable toilets?
- hygienic toilet facilities?
- rubbish points that are inaccessible to children?
- systems for recording and reporting accidents, especially head injuries?
- safe car parking?
- effective supervision of children before and after nursery/school?
- effective supervision of children in the playground?
- high standards of organization and management during off-site visits?

(Leeds City Council, 1996)

In addition to thinking about the resources, fixtures, fittings and furniture, the use of display also helps to create an attractive learning environment and plays a vital part in the process of motivating children, setting standards and communicating information to parents and other visitors about pupils' experiences and work. A good display can start children talking, thinking, asking questions and working, as well as offering a means of praising, recognizing and encouraging them. Putting children's work on display shows publicly the value that the teacher places on their efforts, and pupils' involvement in some of the decision-making about what to display, and where and how to display it can help to ensure that a display is used and referred to.

Eg ***An unusual display***

A class of Year 2/3 children made a model of a pteranadon out of bin liners (for wings) and large cardboard boxes. They painted it bright blue with red eyes the size of plates. One of the children had learned that no one could be sure what colour dinosaurs were but since it flew in the sky the pupils thought it should be blue. Their teacher decided to surprise the children by arriving especially early the next day and suspending the model from the ceiling. It took the children more than 30 minutes to notice the model hanging six feet above their heads.

Note: If young children can miss a prehistoric monster with a 10–metre wingspan, how much easier is it for them to miss a drawing or a piece of writing?

Displays should be professionally presented; a sloppy display can make good work look poor and does not do justice to the efforts of the children. Not all 3–8 teachers have artistic talents, nor is this necessary in order to produce a professional display. Trainee and newly qualified teachers may wish to make use of the checklist below when mounting displays in 3–8 settings.

Enhancing Displays

- Whose work is displayed and why? If the aim is to motivate pupils, then it ought to be the children's work, not the teacher's, that is displayed.
- Include *effort* alongside *outcome* as criteria for judging which pieces of work are put on show. If effort is not used as a criterion for selection, then some children may be consistently overlooked while others may receive disproportionate recognition.
- Make sure that displays reflect the variety and breadth of the 3–8 curricula, showing practical activities as well as written work, celebrating personal and social development as well as academic achievement, and showing the development of skills as well as the acquisition of knowledge.
- Utilize a range of methods which include two- as well as three-dimensional techniques, and hands-on interactive displays as well as static ones.
- Use your displays in your teaching.
- Change displays on a regular basis.
- Ensure that displays are professionally presented.
  - Make certain the display conforms to school/nursery conventions (e.g. single/double mounted, limited colour schemes).
  - Mounts should be cut using a guillotine to ensure they are straight and even, with square corners.
  - Margins on mounts should be of equal width or if they are unequal, this should be based on the aesthetics of the display and not the result of carelessness.
  - Provide labels with correct spellings and the children's names.
  - Handwriting on the display should conform to the nursery's/school's guidelines.
  - Avoid overcrowding; remember that the spaces between work are as important as those occupied by the work.
  - Check the height and level at which work is displayed; pieces of writing six feet up a wall will be unreadable by the children.
  - Make sure the overall impression is one of neatness and tidiness, with evidence of pride taken.

Organizing the Learning Environment: Outdoors

An important resource and additional learning environment is the space outside the nursery/classroom. Edgington (2002) points out that for many children today access to outdoor spaces is less than in the past as a result of increased traffic or parental fears about child abduction, and when they do get access it is often adult organized (e.g. attendance at sports clubs) rather than roaming freely. Lack of outdoor experiences of this sort could inhibit children's risk assessment abilities making them overly nervous or reckless as they get older. At the same time the rise of television, video and computer technologies also leads to many children getting less experience of outdoor play and raises the issue of health problems arising from a lack of exercise.

Many teachers of nursery/reception children make extensive use of outdoor areas as a way of broadening their pupils' experience. These areas offer opportunities for a wide range of activities including imaginative play, construction play, traditional games (e.g. hide and seek) and physical play (e.g. running, throwing, climbing). Many primary teachers, too, take advantage of opportunities to use outdoor areas, for example collecting minibeasts in the school garden or teaching PE on the school field. While much of this work can be done inside the nursery/school, the outdoor area provides an alternative arena for learning, one that may suit some children better and one that may also compensate for changes in lifestyles.

Well-resourced outdoor areas consist of spaces on a number of levels, containing a variety of soft and hard surfaces. In addition, there will be a mixture of open and secluded areas to allow for both boisterous play and more reflective activities.

Eg *Resources for the outdoor area*

- **Climbing area**. Stepping stones/tyres, climbing frame, planks, tunnels/barrels, A-frames.
- **Open space for running and riding**. Use parking spaces, road markings and signs to reduce collisions.
- **Playground markings**. Snakes, hopscotch, 'follow the footsteps', wall targets/goal mouths.
- **Small equipment**. Balls, bats, bean bags, hoops, coits, skipping ropes, bins, buckets and nets.
- **Quiet area**. Blankets/mats, chairs and tables, umbrellas/parasols, writing/drawing materials, books, easels, paints, tape recorder, radio.
- **Hiding places**. Natural (e.g. dens under bushes) and manufactured (e.g. tents, blankets over 'A' frames, 'Wendy House' or large cardboard boxes).
- **Role-play materials**. Dressing-up clothes, props.
- **Wild/garden area**. Logs, mulched surface, soil, sand, flower pots, plants, magnifiers, binoculars, cameras, streamers, wind socks/chimes, mirrors.
- **Large-scale construction kits**.
- **Sand, water and small-world play area**. Sand pit, water trough, buckets and spades, containers, pipes, tubes, funnels, dolls, figures, cars, programmable vehicles.
- **Wet weather clothing**. Hats, Wellington boots, waterproof jackets.

(Edgington, 2002)

Not only must nurseries and schools provide appropriate outdoor spaces, teachers also need to make effective use of them. Just because children are working in the outdoor area does not mean that planning, teaching and assessment cease to be necessary. This means treating the outdoor area as if it were an extension of the classroom. While the opportunities for using the outdoor area to support children's Physical development are obvious, this space should also contribute to learning across the curriculum. Teachers, therefore, may wish to complement the balls, bikes and climbing frame with seating areas and benches or tables to facilitate play and work in other areas of learning.

Eg *Opportunities for learning across the curriculum in the outdoor area*

• Personal, social and emotional development • RE • PSHE and citizenship	Developing positive relations with others (suggesting ideas, sharing, taking turns, negotiation). Developing self-confidence, independence, responsibility, and risk assessment skills. Experiencing a sense of achievement.
• Communication, language and literacy • English	Developing speaking and listening skills. Reading and writing/mark-making in quiet areas.
• Mathematical development • Mathematics	Counting activities. Number recognition (e.g. number the tricycles and bicycles). Measuring distance, time and volume.
• Knowledge and understanding of the world • Science • Design and technology • ICT • Geography • History	Investigating plants, animals and the natural environment – introduce bird tables and feeders into the garden area, plant and grow seeds, carry out weather work (e.g. experiencing the wind, rain, sun or snow). Explore the properties of materials (e.g. wet and dry) and forces (e.g. floating and sinking, building structures). Exploring the built environment. Taking digital photographs.
• Physical development • PE	Developing physical strength and skills including coordination and control through the use of a wide range of equipment and resources.
• Creative development • Art • Music	Listening to sounds in the environment (natural and man-made). Playing musical instruments. Observational drawings and paintings.

- Managing the space and resources involves outdoor as well as indoor provision.
- Remember that the learning environment needs to facilitate an inclusive approach to teaching and learning. Factors to consider might include lighting, noise levels, visual/auditory input, layout, accessibility and adapting equipment.
- In the case of shared resources and loans, advance action may well be needed in order to ensure access to them at the right moment, for example, booking library loans.
- Label storage areas and containers with words and pictures. Encourage children to refer to the labels.
- When arranging and organizing resources used on a daily basis consider ease of access and rules.
- Encourage pupils to make choices, to select equipment and materials, to take responsibility for keeping things tidy, and to develop their own resource management skills. Teachers and children can help caretakers and cleaners by ensuring that the nursery/classroom is properly tidied up at the end of the day.
- Do not put potentially hazardous tools and materials (such as hot glue guns) in open access. Ensure that children understand the importance of safety and restrict use of some resources to adults only, or situations where strict supervision is available. Make sure that any chemicals (such as cleaning fluids) and medicines are securely locked away, and find out who the trained first aider on the staff team is.
- Remember that teachers and other responsible adults are the most valuable resource available. High adult–child ratios help to make the most effective use of materials and equipment. They help to foster a sense of security, and are important in reinforcing learning in young children. Adults are also very important as role models for children.
- Use furniture to mark out and define areas, including quiet areas, but bear in mind the need to be able to observe and monitor children.
- Plan and establish a mixture of clearly defined areas and general purpose spaces. There should be sufficient and varied space for a range of activities. Include a wide range of interesting objects, materials and equipment to create a stimulating environment. Use bright, colourful, interesting and interactive displays in the nursery/classroom.
- Some activities will be noisy and messy, others quiet and orderly. Different activities can be separated by time as well as by space. Try to keep indoor messy activities near the sink.

Out-of-School Learning Environments: Home and Homework

Homework refers to any work that children are asked to do outside lesson time, either on their own or with parents and carers. Children will not normally encounter formal homework tasks prior to Key Stage 1. Homework tasks can offer schools a way of developing further their partnership arrangements with parents and carers by involving them actively in their children's learning. They can provide opportunities for children to talk about what they are learning to an interested adult and to practise key skills in a supportive environment. Such tasks can, for example, be helpful in supporting individual children's consolidation,

208

reinforcement and understanding of literacy and numeracy skills. This said, if pupils have been working hard all day homework tasks need to be set carefully so as not to overburden them. Children with SEN should not automatically be excluded from homework. They may benefit from special tasks separate from those given to their peers; however, it is also important that they do as much in common with other children as possible. Homework for pupils with SEN will need to have a very clear focus, be varied (not just written assignments) and where appropriate will need to be linked to their Individual Education Plan (IEP) targets.

Eg *Homework tasks at Key Stage 1*

- Playing simple word/number games.
- Learning spellings (once a week).
- Learning number facts (once a week).
- Reading together (daily). All children should either read to their parents/carers or be read to. Fluent readers need to read on their own for at least ten minutes each day.

Both parents and teachers have a part to play in making homework policies an effective device for raising standards of achievement. It is the job of the teacher and the school to plan and resource homework activities. The role of parents and carers, meanwhile, is equally crucial. Regular dialogue can and should take place between teachers and parents (e.g. through reading record diaries); teachers can use feedback on a weekly basis as a means of informing their own assessments. In addition, parents' attitudes will have a significant impact on children's efforts and achievements. Schools need to liaise with parents to ensure that the latter realize just what a pivotal role they play in:

- ensuring that the child has a reasonably peaceful place in which they can do their homework with support;
- making it clear to the child that time spent completing homework is valuable and worthwhile time spent together; and
- encouraging and giving lots of praise to the child when he/she is completing homework.

Out-of-School Learning Environments: Educational Visits

Trips and visits can be a wonderful stimulus for teaching and learning across the curriculum. Using the local environment makes a contribution to the intellectual and practical development of pupils as individuals and as informed members of society. Educationally, outside visits offer real opportunities for community interaction and for linking nursery and school experiences with the wider world, enabling young children to become more aware of the diversity of people, places and objects. There are, however, major implications in terms of health and safety; educational visits will also test a teacher's relationships, control and organization. Teachers who fail to encourage their children to exhibit responsible behaviour in the nursery/classroom can hardly expect them suddenly to exhibit it on the local bus. Outside the school gates, pupils are beyond their normal closed environment and consequently, they are not so easily observed, not as easily held accountable and are subjected to wider influences. In this looser context it is not as easy for teachers to exercise control, and lack of control carries with it potential risks to the health and safety of children.

Eg

Know your pupils

A student teacher arranged a visit to the local canal, situated approximately three-quarters of a mile from the school. There were 30 Year 1/2 pupils in the class, one of whom suffered from arthritis. The student teacher had not fully appreciated the child's condition. Half-way to the canal it became clear that the child was experiencing some discomfort and that if the walk continued this discomfort could become more serious. The student teacher gave the child a piggyback ride all the way there and all the way back rather than abort the visit for the whole class. Not surprisingly this was not an ideal solution. Other children wondered why they could not have a ride too and, by the time they returned to the school, the student teacher was also unwell.

Preparation can greatly increase the chances of a safe and successful visit. Local walks can give young children useful training in crossing roads, public behaviour and staying with designated adults. Such walks provide teachers with good opportunities for making it clear to the children that in the outside world the standards of behaviour expected are even more rigorous than those in school/nursery. Ensuring good behaviour is not just a method of preserving the teacher's sanity; it is a prerequisite for safety and learning. Teachers of young children should always conduct a risk assessment prior to a class visit. It is important to bear in mind the need to give consideration to likelihood as well as severity, and to be prepared to deal with any accidents should they occur.

Eg

Risk assessment of reception/Year 1 visit to the local park

Risk	Severity	Likelihood	Action
Small brook running through the park, danger of pupils falling in	Water very shallow – low	Medium to high	Pack spare clothes, allocate specific children to specific adults for better supervision and brief adult helpers about the risk.
Dogs off the lead	Potentially high	Medium to high	Talk to children prior to the visit about not approaching strange dogs; suggest strategies such as ignoring animals and staying with adults. Alert adult helpers.

A well-organized and executed visit can inspire and enthuse young children and the momentum can last for quite some time. A poorly organized and riotous visit endangers pupils and could rebound on the nursery/school, and hence on the teacher in charge. Trainee and newly qualified teachers are advised to consult the DfES good practice guide *Health and Safety of Pupils on Educational Visits* (DfES, 2001a) for further information on the responsibilities, planning, supervision, preparation, liaison and emergency procedures involved in taking children beyond the nursery/school gates.

Considerations before taking young children on walks and visits

The children
- Do any of the children have a medical condition such as epilepsy or asthma which needs to be taken into account?
- Do any of them suffer from travel sickness and if so, do their parents give them medication prior to journeys?
- Have the children been told where they are going, with whom, why and what's expected?
- How will they remember and/or record their experiences?

The parents/adult helpers
- No child can be taken out of nursery/school without the parents' permission. Letters, therefore, need to be sent to parents informing them of the details of the visit such as appropriate clothing, date, time and cost.
- Accompanying parents should be briefed as to what is being asked of them. Which children are they to accompany? What should they wear? Why are the pupils going, and what are the (learning) purposes of the visit?
- Make sure that there are enough adults to supervise the children adequately (3 : 1 in nursery and 6 : 1 with infants are the optimum ratios).

The route
- On local visits it is advisable to check the route. What are the safest crossing points? Are there any toilets *en route* just in case?
- Are you familiar with details such as bus times, stopping places and alternative buses in the event of a non-arrival? In some areas it is necessary to ring the bus company beforehand to inform them of the trip; failure to do so could mean drivers refusing to take the party on board.

The occasional emergency
- Careful and responsible supervision, combined with good preparation, will do much to reduce the risk of emergencies. However, some cotton wool and a flask of clean water for cuts and grazes can be very useful.
- Sick bags are essential if using road transport.
- Spare clothes are a good idea if travelling anywhere near water.

The site
- Where will the children eat, sit, keep dry, go to the toilet?
- Are there any particular hazards to avoid?
- What are the procedures in the event of an emergency, for example a fire alarm?
- Wherever possible, teachers should check the site before setting out with the children. This may be done in person or, in the case of more distant locations, by telephone. Even if the teacher has been to the site in previous years, things change.

A student teacher arranged a whole day visit to a zoo in the next county for two reception classes. The school hired two coaches, parents were recruited and the headteacher decided to accompany the party. The children were prepared for the visit and, in particular, for the reptile house which was the main focus of the trip. When the coaches arrived at the zoo they were informed that the reptile house was closed that day and that, had the student teacher contacted the zoo beforehand about the visit, they could have informed her of this fact.

Effective Teaching Methods

As a trainee or newly qualified teacher, it is important to learn about and acquire a range of effective teaching strategies as soon as possible. Without the ability to do this, the learning opportunities planned for the children may never be realized. This section concentrates on some of the key skills 3–8 teachers need to acquire in order to support children's learning by sustaining the momentum of pupils' work and keeping them engaged. It will touch upon one important aspect which is often at the forefront of trainees' and NQTs' minds – discipline and control, and the reader is advised to refer back to Chapter 1 for further information on this topic. However, although good discipline is a prerequisite for successful teaching, it is not a sufficient condition on its own and it must be underpinned by positive professional teaching methods.

Awareness and mobility

Teachers of young children need to maintain a high degree of vigilance at all times. This awareness, sometimes referred to as 'with-it-ness', is a crucial skill for anyone attempting to ensure high-quality teaching and effective class management with 3–8 pupils. It takes time to develop a fully fledged appreciation of young children; however, it is possible to acquire and master the skills associated with awareness by making a conscious effort in the early stages of training and teaching. Retaining a degree of mobility in the classroom greatly increases a teacher's awareness; the mere presence or proximity of an adult can have a calming and controlling effect. Simply being there can do much to help young pupils stay on-task. At the same time, moving around can also help to avoid long queues of children requesting the teacher's attention. Finally, awareness and mobility are prerequisite skills for identifying and consolidating learning.

Expect the unexpected

An NQT had just finished a very well-organized and structured PE lesson with a Year 1/2 class. The children were getting changed at one end of the hall and the teacher moved away from them for a short time to return some balls to a box. On the teacher's return, Suzanne approached her to say that she could not find her leotard. Everyone helped to look for it, corners were explored, kit bags were emptied, apparatus boxes were opened. Every possible place where a leotard might have been mislaid was investigated. There appeared to be no sign of it. Meanwhile, the class was becoming unsettled and disruptive. The next class was queuing to come into the hall, and their well-established teacher was looking disapprovingly through the glass. A horrible suspicion began to dawn on the NQT. 'Suzanne, just lift your T-shirt up one moment will you please?' She did, and the mystery was solved: she was still wearing the leotard!

213

Maintaining your awareness

- Make a point of scanning the immediate teaching area at intervals.
- Remember to check to the sides and rear.
- Demonstrate a degree of prescience by trying to anticipate events.
- Make a conscious effort to listen to the noise in the classroom; there is a qualitative difference between a busy hum and the sound of children who are off-task.

Communication

The ability to communicate effectively and appropriately with young children is another essential teaching skill. Clear and concise instructions play a valuable part in effective classroom organization and management, while exposition (discussing, explaining and outlining things verbally) is one way in which a teacher can inspire and motivate children (Waterhouse, 1983). That said, by their very nature, discussions of this sort are likely to involve a few departures. Teachers need to be ready to deal sensitively but efficiently with unexpected contributions, taking on board children's comments while avoiding being sidetracked.

Gentle steering of a discussion

A class of Year 1 children were listening and responding to questions about a story that their teacher was reading. The teacher asked the children what they thought was about to happen. Ellen put up her hand and the teacher said, 'Yes, Ellen. What do you think will happen?' Ellen responded 'I went to my Gran's on Saturday.' The teacher replied, 'Did you? That's very interesting, do you think you could tell us a bit more about it when we've finished our story? Thank you. Now then, can anyone tell us what they think is going to happen next?'

Teachers of young children use their communication skills in the nursery/ classroom to:

- generate interest and curiosity;
- review and consolidate previous learning;
- share the programme and purposes of a session/lesson;
- offer encouragement and support; and
- organize the children and maintain good order.

Eg *Preparing the ground*

Mrs Clark asked all her Year 1s to stop what they were doing and look at her. After a minute or so, during which time she asked one or two individuals by name to look her way, she then informed the children that in five minutes they would have to start clearing away ready to go to assembly. She asked the children to start to finish off the piece of work that they were doing, and checked with one or two 'key' individuals that they had understood what they had to do. When Mrs Clark stopped the children again five minutes later and asked them to start clearing up, the transition went very smoothly – the children were prepared for the task.

 Improving your communication skills with children

- Exposition, including any questioning and discussion, ought to be thought about beforehand. A list of key questions, useful vocabulary and explanations can be helpful.
- Use a wide range of questioning techniques including open-ended and closed, procedural (e.g. 'What are they trying to do?'), and organizational (e.g. 'How are they going to do something?').
- Use question and answer times to make judgements about children's understanding and learning needs, and to pick up on any ideas or misconceptions.
- When discussing things with young children or asking questions, be prepared to show a little patience while they marshal their thoughts.
- Use praise and recognition to foster participation.
- Be inclusive. Avoid addressing the front and centre of the group or class while ignoring pupils at the back and sides.
- Promote respect for others. Follow rules, such as 'hands up' and 'await your turn'.
- Make sure that instructions are clear and concise and that before giving them you have the children's attention.
- Do not string multiple instructions together. Young children may not be able to remember them all.
- Check that your instructions have been understood.

Monitoring the controlling the learning process

While planning and preparation are prerequisites for effective 3–8 education, teachers still have to make their plans work. They have to control the learning process, ensuring that the timing and pacing of activities is appropriate, that transitions between tasks are managed smoothly and that children's progress is monitored and consolidated in an ongoing fashion.

Monitoring and consolidating learning

- Have a clear focus for the activity or lesson and share this with the children.
- Think about any checking and monitoring that needs to take place during a lesson/session. Retaining a degree of mobility will help you to do at least some of this checking and monitoring as you go along. Ongoing monitoring has two advantages. First, it enables you to consolidate learning and assist children with problems and difficulties at a point of need while simultaneously reducing your work at breaktime and at the end of the day. Second, it shows pupils that you are interested in and value their work; this can be a powerful source of motivation for children.
- Have a clearly identified location where work is to be placed, such as a finished work box. This makes it easier to locate the material for checking or marking and stops a lot of time-consuming queries from children.
- Base your standards and expectations on your knowledge of the children's abilities and include attention to the process of learning as well as to the outcomes of that process. The ever-increasing accountability of teachers places pressure on them to prioritize the finished product, but the commitment shown by the children, their willingness to concentrate and persevere, and their ability to cooperate and work constructively and positively with their peers ought to be equally worthy of comment and feedback.
- If engaged on a teaching practice with unfamiliar pupils or working with your first class, look back at previous work from time to time. It can be a useful way of identifying pupils whose work seems to be deteriorating rather than progressing.
- When errors or misconceptions arise, deal with them in a sensitive and humane fashion.

Establishing conventions and routines

Establishing and maintaining simple conventions and routines within the nursery/classroom underpins a teacher's efforts to achieve good class management. Not only are ground rules important from the point of view of health and safety, young children also feel much more secure in an environment where certain boundaries are clearly understood (Cowley, 2001). Establishing such conventions can require a major effort at the beginning of a year or term. However, it is an investment that will more than repay the teacher as the year progresses.

Eg *Promoting good behaviour and independence through classroom conventions*

'In our class we share things and look after things.'
'In our class we look after one another.'
'In our class we are kind to one another.'
'In our class we put things back where they came from.'
'In our class we don't shout.'
'In our class we don't run.'

Classroom conventions need to be appropriate for the age and maturity of the children and it is a good idea to keep these conventions simple and few in number so that they are manageable and understandable for the children. Using praise and recognition for displays of honesty, fairness and respect can help positively to reinforce desired behaviours. Teachers need to be consistent about classroom conventions through firm, although gentle, insistence and where minor infractions do occur, to handle the situation in a calm, firm and fair manner. It is important to remember that obedience is a means to an end, not an end in itself. Although conventions underpin good behaviour in the nursery/classroom, so, too, does experience of freedom, exercising responsibility and making choices. It is through being able to exercise their decision-making skills that children can begin to grow up into responsible, independent and self-disciplined adults. Such abilities cannot be acquired simply through being told; they need to be fostered by first-hand experience.

Matching conventions to situations

Instances where conventions may apply
- Lunchtime.
- Putting things away.
- Not taking things that do not belong to you.
- Not running across roads, hitting or biting.
- Movement as a class (e.g. to PE, assembly, or out to play).
- Movement by individuals within the class (e.g. Does it have a purpose? Does it limit the freedom of others?).
- Noise levels (e.g. not shouting out but raising hands, listening while others speak, using normal voices when speaking individually to one another).
- Handling equipment and materials sensibly (e.g. lifting, not dragging, chairs).

Instances where free choice and decision-making might be promoted
- Choosing games and toys.
- Choosing which friends to work with.
- Choosing which activity to go to.
- Developing role-play scenarios.
- Selecting equipment.

Children can be included in the decisions on what form classroom conventions will take as a way of encouraging them to take ownership of, and responsibility for, the rules and routines that are eventually agreed upon. Discussing conventions in terms of personal responsibility, consequences and feelings can help children to appreciate their importance and to understand *right* and *wrong* behaviours. Like learning purposes, such expectations need to be communicated to children and reinforced at every opportunity.

Teachers expect children to
- walk, not run, around the classroom;
- seek permission before leaving the room or area;
- listen to others;
- converse in normal voices without shouting;
- take care when handling tools and materials;
- show care and consideration for their peers irrespective of race, gender, ability or class; and
- show care for the learning environment.

FURTHER SOURCES OF INFORMATION

Planning

Drake, J. (2001) *Planning Children's Play and Learning in the Foundation Stage*. London: David Fulton.

Moyles, J. (2002) 'What shall we do today? Planning for learning – children and teachers!', in Moyles, J. and Robinson, G. (eds), *Beginning Teaching: Beginning Learning in Primary Education*, 2nd edn. Buckingham: Open University Press.

QCA (1999) *The National Curriculum: Handbook for Primary Teachers in England Key Stages 1 and 2*. London: QCA.

QCA (2000) *Curriculum Guidance for the Foundation Stage*. London: QCA.

Rodger, R. (1999) *Planning an Appropriate Curriculum for the Under Fives*. London: David Fulton.

SCAA (1995) *Planning the Curriculum at Key Stages 1 and 2*. London: SCAA.

Smidt, S. (2002) *A Guide to Early Years Practice*, 2nd edn. London: Routledge/Falmer.

Monitoring, Assessing, Recording and Reporting

Ackers, J. (1994) '"Why involve me?" Encouraging children and their parents to participate in the assessment process', in Abbott, L. and Rodger, R. (eds), *Quality Education in the Early Years*. Buckingham: Open University Press.

Hobart, C. and Frankel, J. (1999) *A Practical Guide to Child Observation and Assessment*, 2nd edn. London: Stanley Thornes.

Hunter-Carsch, M. (2002) 'Keeping track: assessing, monitoring and recording children's progress and achievement', in Moyles, J. and Robinson, G. (eds), *Beginning Teaching: Beginning Learning in Primary Education*. Buckingham: Open University Press.

QCA (1999) *Keeping Track: Effective Ways of Recording Pupil Achievement to Help Raise Standards*. London: QCA.

Sharman, C., Cross, W. and Vennis, D. (1995) *Observing Children: A Practical Guide*. London: Cassell.

Catering for Individual Pupil Needs and Abilities

Daniels, H., Visser, J., Cole, T. and Reybekill, N. (1999) Emotional and Behavioural difficulties in Mainstream Schools, DfEE Research Brief No. 90. London: HMSO.

DfES (2001) *Special Educational Needs Code of Practice*. London: DfES.

Hart, S. (1996) *Beyond Special Needs*. London: Chapman.

Naylor, S. and Keogh, B. (1995) 'Making differentiation manageable', *School Science Review*, **77** December, 106–10.

Paige-Smith, A. (2002) 'Parent partnership and inclusion in the early years', in Miller, L., Drury, R. and Campbell, R. (eds), *Exploring Early Years Education and Care*. London: David Fulton.

Roffey, S. (1999) *Special Needs in the Early Years: Collaboration, Communication and Coordination*. London: David Fulton.

Sharman, C., Cross, W. and Vennis, D. (1999) *Observing Children: A Practical Guide*, 2nd edn. London: Cassell.

Stradling, B. and Saunders, L. (1993) 'Differentiation in practice: responding to the needs of all pupils', *Educational Research*, **35** (2) Summer, 127–37.

Classroom Organization and Management

Beard, J. and Lloyd, C. (1995) *Managing Classroom Collaboration*. London: Cassell.

Bilton, H. (1998) *Outdoor Play in the Early Years: Management and Innovation*. London: David Fulton.

Cole, M. and Hill, D. (eds) (1997) *Promoting Equality in Primary Schools*. London: Cassell.

Cowley, S. (2001) *Getting the Buggers to Behave*. London: Continuum.

Edgington, M. (1998) *The Nursery Teacher in Action: Teaching 3, 4 and 5-Year Olds*, 2nd edn. London: Paul Chapman.

Pollard, A. (1997) *Reflective Teaching in the Primary School*, 3rd edn. London: Cassell.

Smith, C. J. and Laslett, R. (1993) *Effective Classroom Management: A Teacher's Guide*, 2nd edn. London: Routledge.

Wragg, E. C. (1993) *Class Management*. London: Routledge.

References

Abbott, L. (1994) 'The search for quality in the early years', in Abbott, L. and Rodger, R. (eds), *Quality Education in the Early Years*. Buckingham: Open University Press.

Adams, J. (1994) '"She'll have a go at anything": Towards an equal opportunities policy', in Abbott, L. and Rodger, R. (eds), *Quality Education in the Early Years*. Buckingham: Open University Press.

Alexander, R., Rose, J. and Woodhead, C. (1992) *Curriculum Organisation and Classroom Practice in Primary Schools: A Discussion Paper*. London: DES.

Athey, C. (1990) *Extending Thought in Young Children: A Parent–Teacher Partnership*. London: Chapman.

Barratt-Pugh, C. (1994) 'We only speak English here, don't we? Supporting language development in a multilingual context', in Abbott, L. and Rodger, R. (eds), *Quality Education in the Early Years*. Buckingham: Open University Press.

Bengtsson, J. (1995) 'What is reflection? On reflection in the teaching profession and teacher education', *Teachers and Teaching: Theory and Practice*, **1** (1) March, 23–32.

Bonnett, M. (1994) *Children's Thinking Promoting Understanding in Primary Schools*. London and New York: Cassell.

Bruce, T. (1997) *Early Childhood Education*, 2nd edn. London: Hodder and Stoughton.

Burnett, C. and Myers, J. (2004) *Teaching English 3–11: The Essential Guide*. London: Continuum.

Campbell, J. and Little, V. (eds) (1989) *Humanities in the Primary School*. London: The Falmer Press.

Caruso Davis, B. and Shade, D. D. (1994) 'Integrate, Don't Isolate! – Computers in the Early Childhood Curriculum', ERIC/EECE Publications Digests, www.ericeece.org

Cooper, B. and Brna, P. (2002) 'Hidden Curriculum, Hidden Feelings: Emotions, Relationships and Learning with ICT and the Whole Child', Conference Paper, British Educational Research Association.

Cowley, S. (2001) *Getting the Buggers to Behave*. London: Continuum.

Craft, A. (1999) 'Creative development in the early years: some implications of policy for practice', *The Curriculum Journal*, **10** (1), 135–50.

Curry, M. and Bromfield, C. (1995) *Personal and Social Education for Primary Schools through Circle Time*. Tamworth: Nasen.

Davies, D. (1997) 'The relationship between science and technology in the primary curriculum: alternative perspectives', *The Journal of Design and Technology Education*, **2** (2) Summer, 101–11.

Davies, D. and Howe, A. (2003) *Teaching Science, Design and Technology in the Early Years*. London: David Fulton.

Department for Education and Children's Services South Australia (DECS) (1996) *Curriculum Framework for Early Childhood Settings: Foundation Areas of Learning*. Adelaide: DECS.

DES (1992) *The Education of Children under Five*. London: HMSO.

DFE (1994) *Circular 9/94: The Education of Children with Emotional and Behavioural Difficulties*. London: HMSO.

DFE (1995) *Key Stages 1 and 2 of the National Curriculum*. London: HMSO.

DfEE (1995) *Circular 10/95: Protecting Children from Abuse: The Role of the Education Service.* London: HMSO.

DfEE (1997) '"Starting with Quality": The 1990 Report of the Committee of Inquiry into the Quality of the Educational Experience offered to 3- and 4-year-olds', chaired by Mrs Angela Rumbold CBE, MP. Reprinted 1997.

DfEE (1998a) *Circular 10/98: The Use of Force to Control or Restrain Pupils.* London: DfEE.

DfEE (1998b) *The National Literacy Strategy.* London: DfEE.

DfEE (1999) *The National Numeracy Strategy.* London: DfEE.

DfES (2001a) *Health and Safety of Pupils on Educational Visits.* London: DfES.

DfES (2001b) *Special Educational Needs Code of Practice.* London: DfES.

DfES (2003a) *Aiming High: Raising the Achievement of Ethnic Minority Pupils.* London: DfES.

DfES (2003b) 'Historic Agreement to Reform School Workforce – Clarke', www.dfes.gov.uk/pns

Drake, J. (2001) *Planning Children's Play and Learning in the Foundation Stage.* London: David Fulton.

Edgington, M. (1998) *The Nursery Teacher in Action: Teaching 3, 4 and 5-year olds*, 2nd edn. London: Paul Chapman.

Edgington, M. (2002) *The Great Outdoors: Developing Children's Learning through Outdoor Provision.* London: The British Association for Early Childhood Education.

Edwards, A. and Knight, P. (1994) *Effective Early Years Education: Teaching Young Children.* Buckingham: Open University Press.

Ellis, J. (1986) 'Equal Opportunities and Computer Education in the Primary School'. Equal Opportunities Commission/Microelectronics Education Support Unit.

Farmery, C. (2002) *Teaching Science 3–11: The Essential Guide.* London: Continuum.

Fleer, M. (2000) 'Working technologically: investigations into how young children design and make during technology education', *International Journal of Technology and Design Education*, **10**, 43–59.

Gardner, H. (2003) 'Multiple Intelligences after Twenty Years'. Paper presented at the American Educational Research Association, Chicago, Illinois, 21 April 2003.

Hobart, C. and Frankel, J. (1999) *A Practical Guide to Child Observation and Assessment*, 2nd edn. London: Stanley Thornes.

Hughes, M. (1986) *Children and Number.* Oxford: Blackwell.

Hunter-Carsch, M. (2002) 'Keeping track: assessing, monitoring and recording children's progress and achievement', in Moyles, J. and Robinson, G. (eds), *Beginning Teaching: Beginning Learning in Primary Education.* Buckingham: Open University Press.

Hyson, M. C. (1994) *The Emotional Development of Young Children: Building an Emotion Centered Curriculum.* New York: Teachers College Press.

Isaacs, S. (1951) *Social Development in Young Children*, abr. edn. London: Routledge Kegan Paul.

Kay, J. (1999) *Protecting Children: A Practical Guide.* London: Cassell.

Keenan, T. (2002) *An Introduction to Child Development.* London: Sage.

Kerawalla, L. and Crook, C. (2002) 'Children's computer use at home and at school: context and continuity', *British Educational Research Journal*, **28** (6), 751–71.

Leeds City Council (1996) 'Let's Get it Right', Leeds City Council, Under Eights Service.

Macintyre, C. (2001) *Enhancing Learning through Play: A Developmental Perspective for Early Years Settings.* London: David Fulton.

MacNaughton, G., (1997) 'Who's got the power? Rethinking gender equity strategies in early childhood', *International Journal of Early Years Education*, **5** (1).

Miller, L., Drury, R. and Campbell, R. (eds) (2002) *Exploring Early Years Education and Care.* London: David Fulton.

Moyles, J., Adams, S. and Musgrove, A. (2002) 'SPEEL: Study of Pedagogical Effectiveness in Early Learning', DfES Research Brief No. RB363, www.dfes.gov.uk/research/

Moyles, J. and Robinson, G. (2002) *Beginning Teaching: Beginning Learning in Primary Education*, 2nd edn. Buckingham: Open University Press.

Myer, C. (2002) *Not Just Pictures: Children Developing Creativity through Art*. London: The British Association for Early Childhood Education.

National Curriculum Council (1990) *The Whole Curriculum*. York: NCC.

National Union of Teachers (1998) *1265 And All That*. London: NUT.

National Union of Teachers (2002) *Conditions of Service: Notes*. London: NUT.

Ofsted (2003) *Handbook for Inspecting Nursery and Primary Schools*. London: Ofsted.

Ofsted/DfE (1994) 'Exceptionally able children: October 1993 Report of conferences'. London: Ofsted.

O'Hara, L. and O'Hara, M. (2001) *Teaching History 3–11: The Essential Guide*. London: Continuum.

O'Hara, M. (2004) *ICT in the Early Years*. London: Continuum.

Owen, D. and Ryan, A. (2001) *Teaching Geography 3–11: The Essential Guide*. London: Continuum.

Paige-Smith, A. (2002) 'Parent partnership and inclusion in the early years', in Miller, L., Drury, R. and Campbell, R. (eds), *Exploring Early Years Education and Care*. London: David Fulton.

Pierce, P. L. (1994) 'Technology Integration into Early Childhood Curricula: Where We've Been, Where We Are, Where We Should Go', ERIC/EECE Publications Digests, www.ericeece.org

Pike, G. and Selby, D. (1988) *Human Rights: An Activity File*. University of York, Centre for Global Education.

Prentice, R. (2000) 'Creativity: a reaffirmation of its place in early childhood education', *The Curriculum Journal*, **11** (2), 145–58.

QCA (1998a) 'Early Years Conference Report', www.qca.org

QCA (1998b) *Maintaining Breadth and Balance at Key Stages 1 and 2*. London: QCA.

QCA (1999) *The National Curriculum: Handbook for Primary Teachers in England Key Stages 1 and 2*. London: QCA.

QCA (2000) *Curriculum guidance for the Foundation Stage*. London: QCA.

QCA (2002) 'The Foundation Stage Profile', www.qca.org.uk/ca/foundation

Robertson, J. (1989) *Effective Classroom Control*. London: Hodder and Stoughton.

Roffey, S. (2001) *Special Needs in the Early Years: Collaboration, Communication and Coordination*, 2nd edn. London: David Fulton.

Roffey, S. and O'Reirdan, T. (2001) *Young Children and Classroom Behaviour: Needs, Perspectives and Strategies*. London: David Fulton.

Sayeed, Z. and Guerin, E. (2000) *Early Years Play: A Happy Medium for Assessment and Intervention*. London: David Fulton.

SCAA (1994) *Evaluation of the Implementation of Science in the National Curriculum at Key Stages 1, 2 and 3. Vol. 3: Differentiation*. London: SCAA.

SCAA (1995) *Planning the Curriculum at Key Stages 1 and 2*. London: SCAA.

SCAA (1996) *Nursery Education: Desirable Outcomes for Children's Learning on Entering Compulsory Education*. London: DfEE/SCAA.

SCAA (1997) *Looking at Children's Learning*. London: SCAA.

School Examination and Assessment Council (1991) *Children's Work Assessed: Key Stage 1*. London: HMSO.

Select Committee on Education and Employment (2000) 'Memorandum from the Qualifications and Curriculum Authority (EY 83)', www.publications.parliament.uk/

Sharman, C., Cross, W. and Vennis, D. (1995) *Observing Children: A Practical Guide*. London: Cassell.

Sharp, J., Potter, J., Allen, J. and Loveless, A. (2002) *Primary ICT: Knowledge, Understanding and Practice*. Exeter: Learning Matters.

Siraj-Blatchford, I., Sylva, K., Muttock, S., Gilden, R. and Bell, D. (2002) 'Researching Effective Pedagogy in the Early Years', DfES Research Brief No. 356, www.dfes.gov.uk/research/

Siraj-Blatchford, J. and Siraj-Blatchford, I. (2002) 'Guidance for Practitioners on Appropriate Technology Education in Early Childhood', www.ioe.ac.uk/cdl/DATEC

Sowden, S., Stea, D., Blades, M., Spencer, C. and Blaut, J. M. (1995) 'Mapping abilities of four year old children in York, England', *Journal of Geography*, May/June, 107–11.

Stradling, B. and Saunders, L. (1993) 'Differentiation in practice: responding to the needs of all pupils', *Educational Research*, **35** (2) Summer, 127–37.

Teacher Training Agency (2002) *Qualifying to Teach: Handbook of Guidance*. London: TTA.

Teacher Training Agency (2003) *Into Induction 2003: An Introduction for Trainee Teachers to the Induction Period for Newly Qualified Teachers*. London: TTA.

Turner-Bisset, R. (2002) 'The essence of history in the early years', in Miller, L., Drury, R. and Campbell, R. (eds), *Exploring Early Years Education and Care*. London: David Fulton

Waterhouse, P. (1983) *Managing the Learning Process*. New York: McGraw-Hill.

Westwood, P. (1997) *Commonsense methods for children with special needs*, 3rd edn. London: Routledge

Wood, D. (1998) *How children think and learn*, 2nd edn. Oxford, Blackwell

Wragg, E. C. (1993) *Class Management*. London: Routledge.

222

Index